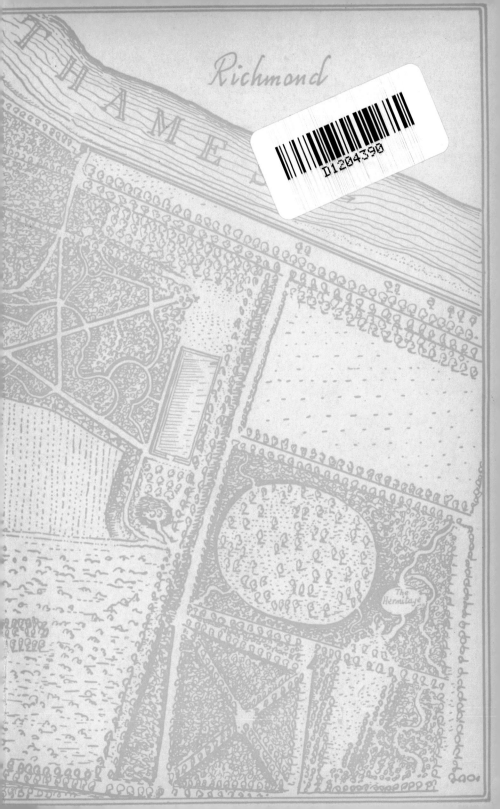

Richmond

THAMES

The Hermitage

CAROLINE
OF
ANSBACH

QUEEN CAROLINE

(*By* JOHN MICHAEL RYSBRACK)

CAROLINE

OF

ANSBACH

GEORGE THE SECOND'S QUEEN

By

R. L. ARKELL

OXFORD UNIVERSITY PRESS

LONDON   NEW YORK   TORONTO

1939

OXFORD UNIVERSITY PRESS
AMEN HOUSE, E.C.4
London Edinburgh Glasgow New York
Toronto Melbourne Capetown Bombay
Calcutta Madras
HUMPHREY MILFORD
PUBLISHER TO THE UNIVERSITY

PRINTED IN GREAT BRITAIN

PREFACE

THE first two Georges were merely tolerated as alternatives to a Popish king, who might have been preferred to them upon slight provocation. But Queen Caroline, by her acumen and geniality, ensured the dynasty's rooting itself in England, where it has long since been held in affectionate esteem. For this service she has a claim upon our memory. But because notoriety often outlives merit, 'Queen Caroline' to most people connotes George IV's wife, who was never crowned as his consort. Her divorce and the clamour she made at his coronation have exercised a hold upon the public mind quite undeserved by such a mediocre character. If this book makes her illustrious predecessor, Caroline of Ansbach, better appreciated it will not have been written in vain.

No biographer of the Queen can evade the quarrel between Prince Frederick and his parents. I hope I have disproved the contentions sometimes advanced that the Prince's parents hated him from the day of his birth and deliberately abandoned him at Hanover in 1714. For the rest, I believe Mr. R. Sedgwick, in his penetrating introduction to Lord Hervey's *Memoirs*, has probed correctly the causes of the quarrel and has shown it to have been almost inevitable in the political circumstances. It smirched the reputation of all the principal actors and becomes a bore to any student of the period.

Nearly forty years have passed since W. H. Wilkins

published the only biography of the Queen, which purported to be a study of her times as well as her life. My canvas is smaller than Wilkins's: a portrait, not a conversation piece. The archives at Hanover have proved a treasure hoard too little used by English students. They yielded the manuscript upon which is based the narrative of Caroline's courtship by the Archduke Charles of Austria. The same manuscript contains the stiff epistolary exercises in wooing which are now, apparently, the only extant letters from George II to Caroline. In Berlin-Dahlem, the papers of the Prussian representatives at the Court of St. James's provide a spicy commentary upon their Majesties (to be used with caution), written for the delectation of King Frederick William I, their unloving cousin. Lord Hervey's *Memoirs* remain the chief source for Court life during Queen Caroline's 'reign'. An exhaustive dissection has lately confirmed their value, apart from prejudices so glaring as to be easily discounted.

I have translated the extracts from George II's courting letters to Queen Caroline and the Queen's letters to Princess Anne from their original French. The New Style dating, as employed on the Continent, is followed in the first three chapters; from the beginning of Chapter IV onwards, corresponding with Caroline's arrival in England, I change to the Old Style, as used in England until 1759.

I have been privileged to make use of the Royal archives at Windsor, where Mr. O. F. Morshead has given me every facility, and the Royal Dutch archives at The Hague. I am indebted to H.M. Office of Works for permission to search through certain departmental records; to the authorities of the Prussian State Archives at Berlin and Hanover, and of the Haus-, Hof- und Staatsarchiv in Vienna. I owe especial gratitude to Dr. G. Schnath and Dr. R. Drögereit in Hanover and to Dr. Susanne Hampe of Berlin. Professor V. T. Harlow has helped me by his kindly criticism of the first chapter. Mr. E. Croft Murray has kindly allowed me to have photographed his copy of J. Rocque's map of Richmond Gardens. Dr. Schnath, the author, and Messrs. Koehler of Berlin, the publishers, have kindly allowed me to reproduce the pictures of George II and Queen Caroline about the time of their marriage, from his *Briefwechsel der Kurfürstin Sophie von Hannover*. Finally most thanks are due to my husband for bearing with the book in manuscript and proof, making invaluable suggestions, and watching over the punctuation. Any errors are of course my own responsibility.

R. L. ARKELL.

CUMNOR,
March 1939.

CONTENTS

CONTENTS

ILLUSTRATIONS

ILLUSTRATIONS

CHRONOLOGICAL GUIDE TO QUEEN CAROLINE'S LIFE

	Private Affairs	Political Events
1683	Caroline born at Ansbach, March 1st.	
1686	Her father dies.	
1696	Her mother dies.	
1701		Grand Alliance formed against France. Act of Settlement.
1702		Accession of Queen Anne.
1704	Caroline wooed by the Archduke Charles of Austria.	
1705	Caroline marries George Augustus of Hanover, Sept.	
1707	Frederick Louis (Prince of Wales) born, Jan.	Regency Act.
1708	Caroline has small-pox, July. George Augustus distinguishes himself at Oudenarde.	
1709	Princess Anne born.	
1711	Princess Amelia born.	
1713	Princess Caroline born	Treaty of Utrecht.
1714	Electress Sophia dies, June. Caroline arrives in England, October.	Accession of King Frederick William I, of Prussia. Accession of King George I.
1715		Death of Louis XIV. Jacobite rebellion in Scotland.
1716	George Augustus Regent, July-Jan. 1717	Septennial Act.
1717	Royal quarrel over christening of Prince George William, who died Feb. 1718	Whig Schism. Triple Alliance.
1718	George Augustus and Caroline acquire Leicester House and Richmond Lodge.	Quadruple Alliance.
1719	George I in Hanover, May-November.	Peerage Bill defeated.
1720	Royal reconciliation. George I in Hanover, June-Nov.	South Sea Bubble.
1721	William, Duke of Cumberland, born	Walpole in power.
1722	Princesses Amelia and Caroline successfully inoculated against small-pox.	
1723	Princess Mary born. George I in Hanover, June-Nov.	
1724	Princess Louisa born.	
1727		Accession of King George II.
1728	Frederick Louis, Prince of Wales, arrives in England.	Anglo-Spanish war.
1729	Queen Caroline's first Regency, May-Sept.	Congress of Soissons.
1731		Treaty of Seville. Second Treaty of Vienna; England recognizes Pragmatic Sanction.
1732	Queen Caroline's second Regency, June-Sept.	Excise Bill. Polish Succession war.
1733		General Election.
1734	Princess Anne marries William, Prince of Orange, March. Lady Suffolk retires from Court, Nov.	
1735	Queen Caroline's third Regency, May-Oct. King enchanted with Madame Walmoden	Porteous Riots in Edinburgh. Preliminaries of Vienna end Polish Succession war.
1736	Prince of Wales's marriage, April.	
1737	Queen Caroline's fourth Regency, May-Jan. 1737. Royal quarrel over birth of Prince of Wales's eldest child, Augusta, July. Queen Caroline taken ill, Nov. 9th. Queen Caroline dies at St. James's, Nov. 20th.	Parliamentary debates over Prince of Wales's allowance, Feb.

PART I

1683 - 1727

I

'SHE SCORN'D AN EMPIRE'

LATE in the seventeenth century Ansbach was the capital of a state smaller than Devon, encompassed by the rich Bavarian uplands. Turreted walls guarded its two Gothic churches and cluster of half-timbered houses with their high-pitched roofs pierced by windows like slots in a dovecote. A Renaissance castle, encircled by a moat, dominated the town. It was a sedate building of four plain stories, tapering upwards to a riot of intricate curved gables. Adjoining it was the Hofgarten, a prim essay in parterres, with orange groves and shady plantations of palms. There was an armoury, a hospital, a law court, and an opera house; there were stables and lodges for hunting and shooting; in fact, all the appurtenances essential to the residence of a prince.[1]

Ansbach was ruled by a line of Hohenzollern margraves and formed a particle of that confusing mosaic, the Holy Roman Empire, a collective name for some 300 virtually independent territories and free towns. Its history began with the foundation of a Benedictine monastery in the eighth century, and six hundred years elapsed before its first connexion with the Hohenzollerns. In 1415 the contemporary ruler acquired the North German electorate of Brandenburg as a reward for loyal services to his Emperor, and migrated to Berlin. Ansbach became a consolation

3

prize for younger sons, who were often subjected to the dictation of their grander relatives.

While most German princes neglected their obligations and exceeded their revenues in aping the splendour of Louis XIV, their subjects remained politically impotent and economically frustrated. But the Margrave John Frederick, who ruled Ansbach from 1667–86, eschewed such frivolity, and devoted his talent for organization to the good of his State. An unimaginative portrait of him, aged about 30, hangs in the picture gallery at the palace. It shows a solid young man wearing a brown wig, and gives no hint of his cultured tastes or his enterprise in reviving local crafts. He invited foreigners skilled in weaving cloth, and in making belts, spurs, and bronzeware to settle in Ansbach, and he ordered his officials to dress in textiles produced locally. When he died his projects were thriving and his people prosperous once more after the ravages of the Thirty Years War.[2]

Under his intelligent patronage Ansbach enjoyed good opera and orchestral music, while he himself spent his spare time in writing romantic novels. His family life was a pattern of homely virtue. Two boys and a girl were born of his first marriage. Nothing else is known of this marriage, except that it was brief, for when he was 28 he took as his second wife Eleanor Erdmuth Luise of Saxe-Eisenach. She was a blonde, blue-eyed vision of loveliness, whom poets called the most beautiful princess in Germany.

On March 1st, 1683, she gave birth to a daughter who was christened Wilhelmine Caroline and was known always by her second name. Subsequent events were to prove that Ansbach's most illustrious child had been born,

CAROLINE'S BIRTHPLACE, THE OLD SCHLOSS AT ANSBACH
Burnt down in 1710

(Part of an engraving by WENZEL HOLLAR*)*

but she did not long enjoy a happy childhood there. A brother arrived when Caroline was two years old. The next year her father, aged only 32, died of small-pox, which killed thousands, until Caroline herself, many years later, encouraged the experiments for inoculating against it. The little family at Ansbach was separated soon afterwards, for the widow took her own children, Caroline and William Frederick, to live at her old home in Eisenach on the outskirts of the Thuringian forest.

From a tender age small princesses were encouraged to cultivate the virtues considered to fit them to acquire a husband. Caroline, as a poor and fatherless child, must early have realized that her only prospect for a career was to marry some princeling whose rank equalled the Margrave's. Then, occupied with breeding and mild diversions, she could lose herself in the pleasant obscurity of a petty court. If she failed in the competition for a husband and became a surplus daughter, she could dedicate herself to religion and enter a convent or a priory as one of the superiors, but again there was keen competition for the best places. Whether it was these depressing alternatives that spurred her on to greater achievements is unknown. At any rate there is a gap in her history until she is revealed as a beautiful and intelligent young lady, whose independence created a sensation. By examining her background and acquaintances, it is possible to learn something of how her character was shaped.

For two years her environment was highly abnormal. In 1692 her mother was hustled into a marriage of policy with the Elector John George IV of Saxony, whose infatuation for his mistress made the union a mockery.[3] The poor wife was so preoccupied by marital problems that she had no time to spare for her children. Sharp nine-year-old Caroline tired of perpetual freedom. To play truant from lessons was good fun, but never to have any lessons or settled occupations soon became boring. So this young edition of her mother, with blue eyes and fair curls, struggled alone to make a pen obey her orders, and to wrest sense from a printed page. Her sturdy determination for learning showed her to be a true daughter of John Frederick. It had other less excellent results. She persevered until she conquered. But the spidery handwriting and appalling phonetic spelling, though a triumph for the self-taught child, remained a permanent handicap. Years later, when she was esteemed a cultured woman, sentences untrammelled by punctuation or correct division of words flowed from her pen.

Her mother's sordid second marriage was brought to an end on April 7th, 1694, when John George died of smallpox, caught nursing his mistress. Freedom came to the widow too late. While the new Saxon Elector, Augustus the Strong, began his notorious rule, she lingered two years in the dower house assigned her outside Dresden, and then, spent by misfortune, she died.

Though Caroline and her brother were a tragic pair to be orphans at 13 and 11, it was some compensation that they were thereby removed from the Saxon court. The new Elector was amassing illegitimate offspring too fast to concern himself with small relations. The orphans first went back to Ansbach, where their younger stepbrother had become Margrave. He was loath to play the part of their father before he was 20, and readily agreed when

Caroline's guardian, the Elector of Brandenburg, suggested that since he and his wife had no daughter, only a precious son aged 8, Caroline might live with them. The Elector wrote assuring Caroline of his protection:

I will never fail as your guardian, to espouse your interests, and to care for you as a loving father, and pray your Highness to have me in the same confidence as your mother always had, which I shall perpetually endeavour to deserve.[4]

Caroline remembered being taken to visit him just before her mother's remarriage, and expecting so important a person to look the part, had been disappointed to find him a short, pale man with hunched shoulders. Unlike a true Prussian, he loathed militarism, but he cherished the insignificant man's passion for social success, and in 1701 he achieved his desire for a King's crown. He figures hereafter as the King of Prussia.

Whilst the King pursued his social ambitions in Berlin, Caroline lived with Queen Sophia Charlotte at Lützenburg, her country retreat, now long since engulfed by the capital. There the genial Queen presided over a salon which, during its brief existence, stimulated more intellectual activity than any other place in Germany. She made the ideal mentor for a promising child like Caroline. Most ladies accepted the proprieties, which condemned them to be the pampered, despised playthings of men. Child-bearing was their only function; gossip, intrigue, and cards their only alleviations from intolerable boredom. But the Queen devoted herself to rational interests, and developed in Caroline the same delight in knowledge and feeling for truth and beauty.

Caroline realized that she could never be satisfied with-

7

out the mental stimulus that she enjoyed at Lützenburg. Yet she knew that a portionless princess like herself should not make terms for happiness but humbly accept whatever fate offered. Though her mirror gave back a charming reflection, she was aware that princes preferred fat dowries or rich lands when they chose a bride. She would have felt more hopeful if she could have known her friends' thoughts. They all agreed that her personality matched her looks, and instinctively coupled her name with some pleasant adjective when they mentioned her to each other. They thought her charming, vivacious, and warm-hearted. No one met her for the first time without feeling delighted by her friendliness. The Queen praised her love of music, and Leibniz, who was often at Lützenburg, mentioned *la voix merveilleuse*. A Göttingen Professor, recalling his schooldays at Ansbach at the turn of the century, related how Caroline was followed by an admiring crowd whenever she walked through the streets.

These tributes being withheld from her, the chain of events which began in the autumn of 1703, her twenty-first year, amazed her exceedingly. Caroline was visiting Freiburg in Saxony when two urgent letters came for her. One was written by a Bishop from Vienna, who introduced himself as an old friend of her mother's. His portentous tone reminded Caroline of a fortune-teller, for he urged her:

Immediately after receiving this letter, go without the very slightest delay to the Duchess at Weissenfels, because of extremely important matters concerning your Serene Highness's greatest happiness, about which the Duchess will inform your Serene Highness.[5]

The writer of the second letter had acted as courier, and

8

requested an explanatory interview with Caroline, hinting discreetly at a 'distinguished gentleman' (not the Bishop) whom she would meet at Weissenfels. After this piquant start she went off to Weissenfels, a village among vineyards some forty miles from Leipzig, on the River Saale. Its Duke John George gratified his expensive tastes without heeding the resulting debts.[6] Presumably he took part in Caroline's affairs because he was related to her mother.

These discreet preparations heralded the astonishing news that the Emperor's second son, the Archduke Charles, was then hurrying to Weissenfels to meet Caroline. However much his subjects pestered him for privileges, they still honoured the Emperor as the living symbol of a glorious past. His title had survived from the splendid days when the Empire had been a mighty force. Contact with the Imperial family was a distinction which Caroline in highest optimism had never thought likely for some one so politically insignificant as herself. Before she properly savoured the news it became a reality.

The Archduke Charles, a gravely romantic prince of 19, was on his way to win a kingdom by his sword. Already they called him King of Spain, in recognition of his family's claims upon the country when the Spanish King Charles II died childless. But the Spaniards, with unmannerly caution, preferred the grandson of their powerful neighbour Louis XIV as their ruler. Both young men were related to the late King of Spain. William III of England had fashioned the Grand Alliance, consisting of England, Holland, and Austria, joined later by other allies, to prevent the French hegemony, which the possession of Spain and her extensive territories both in Europe and

9

overseas would ensure, if another Bourbon ruled the undivided Spanish empire. The armies of the Grand Alliance fought to place the Habsburg Archduke Charles instead of the Bourbon Philip upon the Spanish throne.

Austria, who expected her friends to do the fighting, only grudgingly sent the titular King of Spain as her single, splendid contribution to the campaign. He branched off at Leipzig for this meeting, and was allowed just five hours with Caroline.[7] Even so their host spent 'tons of gold' over his hospitable welcome to the guest. The King's aide-de-camp wrote thanking Caroline profusely for 'the generous and magnificent reception at Weissenfels . . . this most happy and very delightful meeting had filled him [the King of Spain] with the liveliest admiration'.

Thereafter he kept Caroline informed of their progress, naively emphasizing his young sovereign's perfections, which everywhere inspired such animated greetings, and must surely, he thought, impress Caroline with her own good luck. From The Hague, where the ships come to fetch them barely rode out a storm which looked like destroying the British fleet in a day and a night, the King crossed to England and made his way to Windsor. Queen Anne 'received His Majesty my most gracious King and Master with a magnificence and generosity that reflected the greatest credit on both parties'. After being feasted at Windsor he was escorted to Portugal in mid-winter to open the campaign for Spain along the Portuguese border.[8] He perforce left his family in Vienna to arrange about his marriage but they proceeded with their usual lethargy.

The spring of 1704 arrived before Caroline heard from Vienna again. Though she realized that finding a bride

for an Emperor's son must be a solemn affair, she supposed
the hardest part accomplished when he met her and, if she
could believe his aide-de-camp, liked her. Slowly she perceived that this was considered a minor point. The Imperial family were Roman Catholics and in their marriages
they could tolerate no compromise on religious questions.
Since Caroline was a Lutheran, they decided that they
must first arrange about her conversion, and then make
her a proposal of marriage.[9] Whatever risk there might be
of the marriage not taking place after she had become a
Catholic, she must accept with good grace. Obviously the
prospect was worth it. Was it so hard for a princess to
change her religion and gain a King-Archduke as a husband? The secrecy that had hedged Caroline's meeting
with him at Weissenfels safeguarded Imperial pride. If
the affair miscarried, malicious gossip would be intolerable. That the Empress's brother, the Elector Palatine,
who undertook to arrange about her conversion, contemplated no hitch, was evident from his leisurely proceedings.[10]

King Frederick of Prussia was duly informed of the
honour intended for his ward, who, it was suggested,
should meet the Elector Palatine at Weissenfels on his
return from a visit to Vienna. With some amusement
Caroline remembered that the King of Prussia had seen
'God's providence' in the matter when she privately told
him about her meeting with the King of Spain. He
now passed on the Elector's wish in revealing words:

For your part perhaps you may be able to exercise a moderating
influence, not to mention the advantages therefrom that might
accrue to our royal and princely house. I do not very well see how
your Highness can decline such an offer, since it is to be hoped that

you will be so firmly established in your religion that no one need feel anxious about your soul.

Caroline was annoyed at having this long journey foisted upon her after five months of silence from Vienna. But since her guardian repeated his persuasions, she went in June to Weissenfels, only to find herself dallying there without definite news of the Elector Palatine's arrival. The King stressed how 'very wrong' she would be to carry out her wish to leave for Lützenburg without seeing the Elector, because their meeting concerned her 'everlasting welfare'. The Elector did not leave Vienna until August, and only wrote to Caroline on the 20th, announcing his approach. But by then she had lost patience and started for Lützenburg, where she arrived three days later.[11] The Elector realized his bad tactics in letting slip this chance of personal contact. His next few letters were extremely persuasive, and he sent his Jesuit confessor, Father Orban, hurrying after Caroline to show her the errors of Lutheranism.

The Father brought a letter from the Elector bidding Caroline be 'completely persuaded that what he (Orban) will lay before your noble incomparable self . . . is the pure, undefiled, genuine, holy truth. I feel assured that your Highness will not doubt it, but will first accord him a patient hearing and then your fullest approval.' Every one looked upon her conversion as a matter of routine: polite theological skirmishes between Father Orban and the Lutheran champions for her benefit, to be followed by some private interviews when he would gracefully smooth her objections away. After a slight pause for meditation, she would announce herself converted—and marriage

would be her reward. Although Caroline never shared in
the general complacency, Orban possessed an intellect too
refined for the Lutherans, and dealt fairly with her own
scruples. So she jauntily wrote off to the Elector Palatine
that she did indeed perceive the errors of her Lutheran
beliefs.[12] The Austrian Resident in Berlin reported that she
'had already changed and was resolved to marry the King
of Spain'. She told Father Orban that she would go to
Düsseldorf to meet the Elector Palatine.

Then her decision vanished as suddenly as the sun in a
boisterous sky. Panic, doubt, and irresolution obscured
her conviction. She must thrash out the question afresh,
but how decide finally? She felt wretched as she wrestled
with Father Orban, quoting from the Bible that lay open
between them; and though he scored his points neatly he
could not infuse her with the peace that comes from faith.
Often she was in tears when she left him.[13] The Queen of
Prussia, though sympathetic, was studiously non-com-
mittal, saying Caroline must really decide for herself.
Most people, however, took the practical view that she
would be very silly to renounce such excellent prospects.
Thus the days passed without easing her misery.

One point emerged from her perplexity. She must think
things over quietly at Ansbach before making a final
decision or meeting the Elector Palatine. After the letter
she had written him and the trouble he had taken, she
could not possibly carry matters a stage further by meeting
him unless she was resolved to let her conversion stand.
She informed the King, her guardian, that she wanted to
go straight to Ansbach. Back came his reply dated
November 3rd observing that any postponement of the

meeting would harm her reputation. Really she was glad he said it, because it helped her to formulate clearly what she had so far only felt subconsciously. She could not change her religion in good conscience. Her upbringing with Queen Sophia Charlotte had instilled such a love of integrity that she could only accept conversion if convinced of its rightness. Her irresolution was ended at last.

The relief nerved her to the unpleasant task of making her decision known. The interview with her guardian passed off better than she expected. If he was irritated, he hid it well and told her 'since she had taken that resolution he thought her much in the right and that she would have been the first Princess of his family that was a Roman Catholic'.[14] The next problem was the letter to the Elector Palatine, a ticklish matter after her early optimism over conversion. Leibniz, who was a guest at Lützenburg, helped her to compose a suitably humble epistle which Father Orban took away with him.[15] Poor Father Orban: he was extremely mortified by his failure. Later they had corresponded and she had found out that his hobby was mathematics, so she made graceful amends by presenting him with a set of instruments procured for her by Leibniz.

The Austrian clique at Berlin was furious. They had 'thought themselves so sure of her' and could not 'bear the thought of having the King of Spain refused after it was publicly known the Emperor and he desired the match'.[16] On the other hand there were many to compliment her mightily 'on her refusal to change her religion for so great a match'. 'She scorn'd an Empire for Religion's sake', said Gay much later. It caused a tremendous stir. Indeed, she wondered at her own audacity. The nimbus of prestige wreathing the Emperor was almost holy. In spite of the care taken to make her no proposal of marriage, every one treated the matter as if the King of Spain had proposed and been refused. She risked antagonizing the most powerful social force in her world as well as her own guardian, who might well have thought her scruples tiresome when compared with the solid benefits her assent would have brought them both. Then her dependent position would have been most unpleasant. Happily her sincerity carried victory with it.

All the same she left Lützenburg with relief. Ansbach seemed a grateful oasis of peace after those harassing weeks, which made her ill for awhile. Kind words hastened recovery. Queen Sophia Charlotte spoke of the 'generous heart that would not swear to things it did not believe'. Through Leibniz came news that at Hanover, stronghold of Protestantism, every one applauded her decision and the neighbouring Duke Anthony Ulric of Wolfenbüttel wanted to make her the heroine in one of his romantic novels. William Frederick her brother, now Margrave, also sympathized with her, for none of the King of Spain's relatives had troubled to consult him about this matter. They had simply assumed Caroline's eager acceptance.[17] He suffered too much from Prussian dictation to regret the loss of this august connexion. Rarely could he indulge the sly pleasure of seeing important people sent about their business. Moreover, he felt delighted to have Caroline's company. They were always happy together for all their contrast in temperament, or perhaps because of it. She could see that others might think him raw and timid. Who would not be, after their weird childhood? He had not

15

had the stimulus of Lützenburg to correct his introversion. Now they were left the only survivors of their family except for the step-sister who had married and gone away while they were still children. They enjoyed managing compact little Ansbach, though the King of Prussia was free with advice and admonition. Caroline's brother was a splendid ally in the campaign over the King of Spain's suit which still confronted her.

Her refusal to be converted jolted the Elector Palatine's complacence without dispelling it. Not for a moment did he suppose that she based her refusal purely on her own conviction. Other people had influenced her; she had not been left a free choice; her coy phase would pass. He reopened the attack in letters that mingled honeyed phrases with stern words about the sinfulness of rejecting salvation. Princess von Liechtenstein (the wife of the King of Spain's aide-de-camp) put her faith in the effects of a liberal dose of pathos, by forwarding Caroline two letters that she had received from the young sovereign. One charmingly expressed his devotion to Caroline; the other, written after he heard of her defection, conveyed a pathetic impression of his disappointment. But up till the time Caroline read those letters it was considered beside the point to tell her that the young man really wanted her as his wife. Only Prince von Liechtenstein had attempted to introduce the personal element, but he, manlike, told Caroline all about the King without sending her any messages from him.

While she parried these appeals to heart and conscience, verbal persuasion was also tried. A Count came from the Elector Palatine's Court, and bethought himself of asking Queen Sophia Charlotte's influence on his behalf, but he was snubbed for his pains. The Queen knew that any decision not taken by Caroline's own free will would never let her rest happy. The august Bishop whose letter had opened the affair arrived within a month. Tearful sessions with Father Orban had taught Caroline sagacity in her handling of priests. The Bishop complained a trifle petulantly that she had permitted him no private interview with her and retaliated by accusing her of basing her refusal of Catholicism on prejudice and caprice. Early in the spring of 1705 Princess von Liechtenstein wrote to assure Caroline that her conversion would certainly be followed by marriage. They might all have spared themselves their pains. Once Caroline had made up her mind after such mental agonies, nothing could persuade her to reconsider the decision. She had put the stress and strain behind her forever and cheerfully prepared to take the consequences.

As if to shake her resolve came a tragic blow. Queen Sophia Charlotte died suddenly. An apparently slight throat complaint took a fatal turn and killed her at 36, not before she had made herself forever memorable by her stoicism. At last, she told those around her, her curiosity would be satisfied over those eternal mysteries which she had discussed with Leibniz; and she died in the spirit of scientific experiment. Caroline thought that no one else could fill her place, for the Queen had befriended her as a lonely child, treated her like a daughter and trained her mind. Utterly miserable, she wrote to Leibniz: 'Heaven, jealous of our happiness, has just taken our beloved Queen from us. The fatal blow has made me yield to excessive misery. . . . Wholeheartedly I sympathize with you, this loss is irreparable to you.' The King of Prussia renamed his wife's palace Charlottenburg in her memory. Dispirited and weary of the marriage negotiations, Caroline went with her brother to their summer home at Triesdorf.

Soon afterwards, in June 1705, two strangers from Hanover presented themselves at Triesdorf and were politely received. The younger especially, a Monsieur de Busch, radiated good spirits which cheered Caroline. He was dapper, polite, even warmly attentive as they played cards together one evening. But he and his friend were quickly called away, giving it to be understood that some travel plan had miscarried.

The strangers rode back to Hanover with all imaginable speed. For 'Monsieur de Busch' was the alias assumed by George Augustus, Electoral Prince of Hanover and future King of England. One midnight not a week before, he and Baron von Eltz, his companion in the adventure, had clattered out of that city. They had aroused curiosity by keeping their destination secret from every one save the Elector, his father.

Though George Augustus was the same age as Caroline, 22, this had been his first expedition outside the electorate. He rode south to Ansbach, spurred on to seeing Caroline by his grandmother's description of her as 'the most agreeable Princess in Germany'. And the Electress Sophia's standards were high. She had met Caroline at Lützenburg, where she used regularly to visit her daughter the Queen of Prussia. Contrary to custom, the Electoral Prince was being left 'entirely to his own choice of a wife', wisdom born of his father's disastrous marriage. Earlier this year he, like every one else, supposed Caroline would marry the King of Spain. When that seemed unlikely, rumour from Berlin had it that his boorish cousin the Prussian Crown Prince desired her.[18] What business had Frederick William with love at 17? Uncouth cub, fit company only for his preposterous grenadiers! George Augustus had not hesitated long after that. Combining enterprise with caution, he chose to pay Caroline this incognito visit of inspection. Retreat would be easy if he were not impressed.

Equipped with plausible reasons for their visit, the travellers came quickly to Ansbach, their respectability guaranteed by an introduction from the Prime Minister. The briefest acquaintance convinced the cautious wooer that Caroline so completely answered to 'the good character he had of her that he would not think of anybody else after her'.[19] Her good looks surpassed his highest hopes. Fair hair, fine features, lily-pale skin and shapely hands; such charms as would ravish any young man. His grandmother's approval was sufficient indication of her intelligence, but that aspect had not interested him so much just then. Not the least pleasure of the journey was the success of his simple ruse.

The Electoral Prince waited on his father while the town chattered with speculation. The English Envoy, Poley, pumping Baron von Eltz for clues, found him so 'prepared to avoid' the subject that he regretfully desisted. The Baron 'disappeared on a sudden and I do not question but he is gone to enter into some negotiation towards obtaining the Princess (whoever she be) whom the Prince desires', Poley wrote, but he failed in the astute attempt to discover from whence came Baron von Eltz's dispatches.

The Princess's name only emerged a few days before the Elector formally announced his son's betrothal to her and ended Poley's sport.

Baron von Eltz reappeared at Ansbach in the evening of June 22nd, charged with requesting Caroline's hand for the Electoral Prince and bearing a letter signed by the Elector which bade her accept the proposal: 'Such (an event) will place me under a great obligation to you, and give me all the more eagerness and opportunity of showing how particularly I honour your great talents and merits.'[20] The Baron proceeded with dispatch in his amiable task. He drove to Triesdorf next morning,[21] and though he was presented to the Margrave and his sister under his assumed name, he did not long keep up the pretence. Caroline interviewed him in her own room. When the discreet lady-in-waiting had left them, the Baron inquired whether the Princess was free from all other engagements; 'that being so was she inclined to his Highness, the Prince Electoral?' Had she after all suspected young 'Monsieur de Busch's' identity? She must have found him sympathetic. The Baron's question surprised her certainly, but it did not fluster her. She assured him that negotiations with the King of Spain's relatives were ended. Then, with composure which showed her maturity, she said quite simply: though she had never flattered herself that any one at Hanover thought about her, she would greatly prefer an alliance with that family to all others, and count the opportunity of forming fresh, congenial ties especially fortunate after the Queen of Prussia's death. Her acceptance naturally depended on her brother's consent, which he would doubtless give willingly.

The Baron expressed his warm appreciation of such commendable decision. Significantly they both agreed to avoid premature communication with the Prussian Court. As Caroline said, 'The King of Prussia (her guardian) took so much upon himself that her brother had cause to be circumspect.' Family ties could not prevent jealousy between Prussia and Hanover. The King would consider this mission as detestable intrusion within his own sphere of influence. Happily the court official most favourably disposed towards Prussia had just left for Berlin to attend the Queen's six months deferred funeral. Caroline promised that she would consult her brother forthwith, meanwhile she thought it safest for the Baron to retain his pseudonym in public. He thereupon returned to Ansbach delighted with the interview, of which he wrote the Elector of Hanover a full account that same day. Then had come a final, friendly letter from the Elector Palatine, still urging conversion and bidding Caroline decide quickly or else other plans for marrying the King must be considered.[22] His threat was wasted. For months now the indecision had not been in her mind. Indeed she had told the Baron that the episode was closed.

Caroline's brother readily sanctioned the marriage. George Augustus was an eligible young man who would one day inherit not only the electorate prospering under his father's thrifty management, but the English crown as well. Then proceeded with all speed the prosaic but needful business of drawing up the marriage settlements. The Baron, properly mindful of danger threatening from Berlin, gave assurances that his master disliked ceremonial preparations and 'needed nothing else but to see the

Princess in person and hoped as soon as possible to receive her'. To the Elector of Hanover he reported that the only difference of opinion arose from the Margrave wishing to give his sister more than she would accept. She took with her some £4,000, besides being already provided with 'a splendid outfit of jewels, silver vessels, clothes, and so on'.[23] In return she renounced all claims to Ansbach so long as there were male heirs.

At Hanover the news was made public on Sunday, July 26th, 'just before dinner', which gave opportunity for drinking healths and offering congratulations. Poley conversing with the Electress Sophia that evening learnt the full history of the wooing. Caroline, being consulted about her reception, 'chose to come with as little ceremony as may be'; a decision that pleased the Elector, ever averse from unnecessary show. But the bride's modesty did not prevent 'great preparations to appear with much finery at the coming of the Princess of Ansbach and the Electress in kindness and compliment to her gives new clothes to all the Ladies about her'.[24]

The Electress Sophia showed her good sense by taking no offence at being kept out of the secret of the wooing.[25] She wrote of her pleasure to her son-in-law, King Frederick in Berlin,[26] but he had lately received an official notification from Ansbach 'that all things were now concluded for the marriage' and did not find the news in the least agreeable, for precisely the reason that Caroline and Baron von Eltz had foreseen. King Frederick curtly answered his 'dearest Mama' that the marriage had obviously been planned when she and Caroline were visiting his late wife at Charlottenburg the past autumn. He let it be known that

he was 'out of humour with the House of Lüneburg for
sending so late to notify the conclusion of the marriage . . .
but he is more angry with the Court of Ansbach who are a
branch of his family and he a guardian to the Princess'.[27]
Those at Hanover did not disturb themselves over the
King's wrath. Such friction had occurred before without
permanently affecting their relations. The Electress even
ventured on a joke, suggesting that the King cherished a
sneaking fancy to marry Caroline himself since the prospect of her becoming some one else's wife made him so
angry.

Meanwhile, 'Monsieur de Busch', metamorphosed into
the Electoral Prince of Hanover, wrote his first love-letters
to Caroline. He might have copied them from a manual
on etiquette, so tamely do they read. However, living
with Caroline inspired his pen, because his later effusions
won the envy of those who were privileged to read extracts from them. His early exercises are worth quoting
for the first time as the only examples known to us outside
the pages of Hervey.

Gratified by news of her interview with Baron von
Eltz, the Electoral Prince wrote:

You have conferred so great a favour upon me in expressing
no aversion to the proposal with which Baron d'Eltz was charged,
that I can no longer refrain from showing you my gratitude for
it. . . . I found that all I had heard about your charms did not nearly
equal what I saw. After being so strongly impressed, Madam, judge
whether I should not have felt for ever wretched if you had rejected
me. I owe you every imaginable obligation for permitting the
greatest happiness that I desire in my life. I have no regret save
that my services do not merit such favour, and nothing would console me, Madam, had I not the hope of showing you by my

inviolable respect and eternal affection that I shall remain all my life:

Your very humble and very obedient and most obliged servant.[28]

A week later he told her that he longed to thank her in person for her kindness to him: 'I beseech you, Madam, not to defer your journey too long. All my quiet depends on it and I shall never believe myself completely happy until I have the honour of seeing you again, and showing you by my attachment and all the tenderness imaginable to what degree I am your very humble servant.' Directly he heard that the formalities had been settled he expressed his elation, and when he received a letter from her he replied immediately:

I cannot express in words the rapture I felt on receiving your very dear letter, which has given me such kind proofs of your goodness. This happiness grew with Baron d'Eltz's verbal assurance that you had fixed on the 24th of this month for your departure. Although the time seems infinitely distant, making me count every day and every hour until its arrival, it does not prevent my offering you most humble thanks for having no longer deferred the accomplishment of my wishes.

As the date of her departure approached and left him latterly without news of her, he wrote:

Being denied the happiness of any news of your Highness, I can no longer languish in my uncertainty over your departure. The delays which I fear may arise cause me excessive disquiet. Let me supplicate you, Madam, to postpone no longer the fulfilment of all my wishes. I desire nothing so much as to throw myself at my Princess's feet and promise her eternal devotion; you alone, Madam, can make me happy; but I shall not be entirely convinced of my happiness until I have the satisfaction of testifying to the excess of my fondness and love for you.

24

Only two months after Baron von Eltz had made her the Prince's proposal, Caroline sat beside William Frederick in their coach bound for Hanover. Memories and familiar figures of youth were their travelling companions until at last their native Franconian uplands lay behind them, and ahead the sober North German plains spread to the two seas. George Augustus was waiting for them on the borders of the electorate, eager to show Caroline that his impatience was not the sort that existed merely for its romantic properties in love letters. Together they faced the ordeal of Caroline's first meeting with the Elector, his father, who tactfully made it as informal as possible. He greeted them at a little village just south of Hanover, where Caroline awaited her wedding day, and 'extremely content with her', he accompanied his son back to the capital.[29] Caroline and William Frederick spent their last comradely evening together.

Hanover in its ceremonial decking already waited for to-morrow's bride. George Augustus exhibited the nervous impatience of a bridegroom. Would to-morrow never come? Three months ago he had drawn his mental picture of Caroline from what others told him, but when he saw her, he knew at once that his picture was insipid beside the original. And now, when dawn next crept along the cold streets and fell upon the expectant Leine Palace his waiting would be ended.

Hanover greeted the wedding-day briskly. Preparation in the Palace came to a well-timed close. In the chief courtyard soldiers wheeled gravely into place for the bride's arrival. Court officials grouped themselves behind the electoral family. The cheers grew louder; and trumpets spoke their greeting as the bridal coach reached its journey's end. The kind Electress Sophia came to the coach door and bade Caroline warm welcome. Her geniality and the young couple's good humour eased the customary stiffness of Hanoverian court functions. Every one was friendly, and wished Caroline much happiness. In the evening they gathered in the palace church to hear the words spoken which made Wilhelmine Caroline Electoral Princess of Hanover.

'I praise God that our Electoral Princess seems extremely content with him [the Prince, her husband]; they appear to be very much in love with each other. God grant that the proverb may always be true for them "the longer, the dearer",' was the Electress's wish.

II

ELECTORAL PRINCESS

GEORGE AUGUSTUS was the most attentive of husbands. Caroline was touched by his love and his pride in winning a prize denied the King of Spain. As an orphan she had not been overpetted and she knew that his childhood, too, had been bleak. She responded the more warmly to their new experience, delighted that he could scarcely let her out of his sight. 'A happier friendship than that between the Prince Electoral and his wife has never been seen. They seem to have been made for each other,' approved the old Electress Sophia.[1]

Caroline's father-in-law, the Elector, regulated her affairs with a precision that allowed no extravagance. He fixed her income at some £950 a year, and he paid her servants and retained authority over them. He left George Augustus to provide her with carriages and horses, and bade him set aside a tenth of his own allowance of £2,000 a year in case she were left a widow.[2] However, his exact provisions, being in scale with the other items on his pay roll, did not rankle.

But family relationships intruded upon the young pair's delight, for by an arrangement wholly devoid of tact, the electoral family made the Leine Palace their communal home.[3] It stood on the fringe of Hanover's medieval streets. The first Elector had improved its lay-out to suit

27

his rising fortunes. His son George Louis, the reigning Elector, followed him. He was a prudent, restrained man who could never have embarked upon such grandiose schemes, but he completed them methodically. The opera house, deemed finer than those at Vienna and Brussels, ranked as the show piece and received the liberal application of gold colourings, sculptured ornament and red velvet hangings so dear to baroque taste. Nevertheless it fostered an interest in opera. The Knights' Chamber was another room upon which the late Elector had lavished 'a particular show of splendour and art', designing it for such scenes of pomp as when his subjects came to do him homage on his elevation from Duke to Elector.

Four relatives besides the bride and bridegroom lived amidst these flamboyant delights. They were the widowed Electress Sophia, vigorous grandmother of the party, and her two sons, the Elector George Louis and Duke Ernest Augustus. The elder was a cold automaton, the other a jovial Brunswicker who revelled in food and fun and fighting. The Elector's docile eighteen-year-old daughter completed the family circle. Close proximity stressed the differences inevitable between six adults whose ages ranged from 75 to 18, and produced friction which common sense could have avoided.

Most disturbing to Caroline was the antipathy between her husband and his father, the Elector. She realized that it sprang from basic differences in temperament, which made harmony impossible, and it made her feel as if she lived by a smouldering volcano, ready to erupt without warning. Her father-in-law was the only man she could never manage. Though he approved of her marrying

GEORGE AUGUSTUS AND CAROLINE, ABOUT THE TIME OF THEIR MARRIAGE

(*Unknown Artists*)

George Augustus, he repulsed attempts at friendliness. A sweet submissiveness gained her her ends with conceited men, while an easy good humour served her well with the rest, but the Elector responded to neither approach. His dourness was a force to be reckoned with throughout their association.

Caroline knew that he, like most rulers at that time, had always found monogamy distasteful. Lanky, inoffensive Mademoiselle Schulenberg had long claimed his affections, and people murmured that his regard for his gay half-sister, Madame Kielmansegge, was not strictly fraternal. The young Countess Platen, too, certainly won his favour. However, most Courts suffered from their rulers' illicit loves. At least Hanover was never plundered and the Elector kept his decorum. Indeed it was a mystery to Caroline how these ladies thawed him.

She fancied that he really prized his electorate above any human being. Other States surpassed it in splendour but none displayed greater order or a spirit of more purposeful progress. Its agriculture prospered, and its few manufacturers throve. Rich royalties came from the Harz mines and the revenues totalled a million and a half crowns exclusive of these profits. The Elector's capability was of course the key to such prosperity. He enjoyed prestige abroad and ruled justly at home.[4]

But Caroline thought that his despotism lost its benevolent tinge in his dealings with his family. He had blighted his children's youth by depriving them of their mother. The story could hardly have been sadder. He had been forced into marrying his first cousin, Sophia Dorothea, in order to secure her inheritance of Celle for Hanover,

29

scheming for electoral status. He was suitor to the duchy rather than to the girl princess, and did not let marriage interfere with his pleasures. His spirited young wife, finding him unfaithful, had her own romance. It was discovered while her husband was absent campaigning, but the family vindicated his honour by arranging her lover's murder, euphemistically termed a disappearance. The Elector divorced unhappy Sophia Dorothea and confined her in the remote castle of Ahlden, where he had left her for twenty years and let no one save her mother visit her. In the month of Caroline's wedding, the Elector reaped her inheritance, for Duke George of Celle died and his duchy passed to Hanover.

Caroline correctly traced the enmity of father for son to this bitter episode. For George Augustus, both in looks and temperament, resembled the wife whom the Elector despised. While the Elector himself was dark, plain, and reticent, his son's hair was fair and his person so shapely as to compensate a little for his shortness. Vivacity usually enlivened the Prince's neat features; he moved quickly and talked much, accompanying his words with emphatic gestures. It was as if the Elector had long ago decided that his son would shape badly and was worth no trouble. His neglect or jealousy denied the lad a suitable training for future responsibilities. As an eager young man, George Augustus found a veto laid on travel, campaigns, or a modest share in state affairs.[5] Denied essential activities, he improved his sartorial tastes; his knowledge of intricate genealogies widened; and the Elector's contempt increased. Yet the young man's enterprise in courting Caroline as he had, and winning her affection, gave hope of good qualities which only needed to be developed.

George Augustus chafed most at being kept from the war waging to dispute French hegemony. Punctually every season a Hanoverian contingent left for Flanders or the Upper Rhine. About May the Elector and his brother packed their baggage and departed to the campaign. Sometimes the great Marlborough appeared at Hanover to concert plans beforehand, charming the ladies with his gentle courtesy. But always George Augustus was left behind. Reviewing troops at home was the only outlet for his military aspirations.[6] Back in January 1706 he had begged the command of some forces going to the war, but the same stale refusal met him, 'the Court is against it and will not give their consent to let him go into the field until he has children'.[7] Caroline hoped she could very soon help him by making him a father. With the publicity usual in these matters, every one interested was informed that she expected a baby.[8] Her guardian, King Frederick of Prussia, felicitated the Electoral Prince in token of restored good humour.[9] When the Court moved out to the summer residence at Herrenhausen in May, Caroline stayed in the Leine Palace expecting her confinement. Even to the unperceptive male eye she seemed to show the usual signs of her hopes.[10] But the summer sped by in disappointment, which was aggravated by another event.

The Prussian Crown Prince followed his father's example in seeking a bride at Hanover, and became engaged to George Augustus's sister, Sophia Dorothea the younger. Their common grandmother, the Electress Sophia, was especially delighted, and the celebrations were planned with unusual pomp to honour King Frederick. Then the Crown Prince hurried to his baptism of warfare in the Netherlands, returning two months later in exuberant spirits. George Augustus was galled past endurance. He had always loathed cousin Frederick William. To have this unmarried puppy, five years his junior, winning the race to the battle-front was unbearable. He was rude to the Electress; consistently perverse with others; and he temporarily forgot his impeccable intentions as a husband. Caroline hoped the phase would pass: 'The Electoral Princess merits great praise for being so patient over everything.'[11] Pass it did, and his anger evaporated, leaving a contrite young man who monopolized his wife to such an extent that people feared she would tire of him.[12] The connexion between his ill-humour and thwarted aspirations was apparently unsuspected.

When Caroline was not a mother by November 1706, she knew that her hopes had been premature. Probably she had been suffering from pseudo-cyesis, a condition induced by the ardent wish for children. However, only three more months of real pregnancy lay ahead of her. Her sister-in-law, Sophia Dorothea, left for Berlin, after being married by proxy at home. There passed between the new Crown Princess and the Electress Sophia a busy correspondence which often mentioned the young couple at Hanover. They felt slightly irritated with Sophia Dorothea for being their elders' favourite.[13] Even the Elector thawed when she left Hanover, letting his affection appear in surprising ways. He wrote to her regularly in a fatherly tone, exchanged gifts, and presently sent along his own physician to attend her confinements.[14] Such solicitude contrasted with his frigidity towards his son.

Each New Year brought Carnival time, when Hanover cast off its sobriety and enjoyed itself boisterously for about a month. Business stood still. Harassed envoys could obtain no interviews with privy councillors, and the most important decisions were deferred. The Elector entertained his revelling burghers at comedies and operas in the Palace theatre. On other nights they thronged the Town Hall, where they danced masked or in fancy dress, gambled freely, and ate prodigiously. The Court sometimes joined in the noisy fray. During one such festivity the previous year, Caroline was surprised to see a young man in fancy dress beckoning to her. Realizing that the stranger was her brother, arrived secretly, 'she tore off her mask in such haste that her hair came tumbling about her and every one wondered why the Electoral Princess embraced a young fellow'.[15]

On January 31st 'the court having for some time past almost despaired of the Princess Electoral's being brought to bed',[16] Caroline gave birth to a son. The event deserved celebration: anxiety was dispelled, four generations were alive together, and George Augustus was free to soldier at last. Instead, a wretched furtiveness concealed the baby's arrival, as if he had entered his mother's room in a warming-pan. The secrecy persisted over his christening, which took place in Caroline's room. The Electress Sophia then saw the child for the first time and remarked drily, 'if Duke Maximilian (her second surviving son) had as much power as the English Parliament he would declare his nephew a spurious child, for no one from here was

33   D

present (at his birth)'. The English Envoy, Mr. Howe, only heard news of the birth through one of Caroline's ladies-in-waiting, and did not see the baby until the last week in February, when he found 'the women are all admiring the largeness and strength of the child'.[17] 'The child has such merry big eyes, mouth wide open to suck and seems to be a lively little fellow,' the Electress wrote to King Frederick.[18] She added more outspokenly to Leibniz, 'I hope it will have more sense than its father.' But George Augustus was not to blame for the curious secrecy. The Elector himself had ordered a christening without 'pomp, which he cannot endure'. Or was he nervous that the Englishmen would make the Electoral Prince and Princess the centre of some demonstration? He always preferred to forget their part in the English scheme of things. George Augustus apologized to Mr. Howe for the small respect shown him as Queen Anne's representative: his father's ministers could not be persuaded to act as he would have wished.[19] He could scarcely have blamed his father's stubbornness.

Caroline considered that the English Parliament introduced discord amongst the family by passing the Act of Settlement, which named the Electress Sophia heiress to Queen Anne. Of course it enlivened life at Hanover with entertainments in honour of diplomatic missions, and it brought agreeable Englishmen to Court. Caroline engaged a plain young lady as her English instructress and read newspapers so that she enjoyed trying to talk to the visitors.[20] While the main policies of Godolphin's ministry found steady support in Hanover, Germans and Englishmen seldom agreed over comparatively minor issues, and it was obvious to Caroline that the Electress and her son contemplated their succession with opposite feelings.

At first the Electress had demurred to the Settlement, sympathizing with James II.[21] At 71, moreover, she was too old to think of any crown save a heavenly one. But once her scruples were overcome, she admitted her spirited ambition to be Queen of England if only for a day. She was proud of her Stuart blood and had spoken English since childhood; and her brother, Prince Rupert, was the dashing Cavalier of the Civil War. King William III intended asking her over to England and giving her a pension as Heiress Presumptive, but though Queen Anne paid lip-service to the Protestant Succession, she refrained from implementing his intentions. The Electress did not conceal her annoyance from her English friends, but plain speaking never altered the Queen's aversion to bringing any member of the family to England. She declared it would be like having her coffin perpetually before her. This aversion spoilt Anne's peace of mind, precluded cordiality with her electoral relations and, by causing doubt of her true intentions, encouraged intrigues for a Stuart restoration. When Parliament discussed inviting over Sophia, the ministers sought to propitiate her with honours and titles which only gave offence to all parties concerned.

The Elector, Sophia's son, felt unmoved by Queen Anne's shortcomings. The prospect of one day becoming a royal cipher in a foreign country was unattractive to him. His interests and achievements centred round Hanover, where he was master. England made an admirable countercheck to French ambition, but he could find little else in her favour. Many were the vexations resulting from the English Succession: swollen mail bags, spasmodic influxes of English visitors and envoys, official, unofficial, and shady; the necessity of following tortuous party politics in order to safeguard Hanoverian interests; and the annoying English habit of treating his son as a separate person to be courted and honoured. What he could not avoid he endured, grimly resolved to spend no unnecessary money or effort upon a prospect which pleased him so little.

Early in the summer of 1706 Caroline took part in unwilling celebrations to honour Lord Halifax, who headed an imposing embassy bringing the texts of the new Regency and Naturalization Acts. The former contained practical provisions which duly ensured the next sovereign a peaceful accession.[22] Parliament felt proud of its work, but Hanover underrated the value of the Regency Act and deemed the other unnecessary. The Electress intimated that she would like her good friend Mr. Howe to present the texts, saying privately that the pension and invitation to England would have been more practical proofs of esteem. This evoked wrath, parried by the Elector's truthful excuse, 'I am naturally an enemy to ceremonies and compliments', but they were not spared him.[23] Caroline had the pleasure of seeing Garter Herald drive in state to the Leine Palace to present her husband with the George and the Garter. Two days later his family and the courtiers watched him ceremoniously invested with his Garter robes.[24] That same day guns were fired round the town and Te Deums rose from churches to celebrate the news of Ramillies.[25] A ball marked the double rejoicings.

Lord Halifax departed home the richer by a service of gold plate, but he had not changed electoral opinion about embassies from England.

Soon after the investiture, Queen Anne created George Augustus Duke of Cambridge. Through Mr. Howe he sent the Queen his humble thanks, whilst his grandmother told her envoy in England that a pension would have been worth two more titles besides the dukedom![26] Caroline and the Prince felt nervous lest the Queen should send some one over with the patent, knowing how infuriated their elders would be.[27] A private word with Mr. Howe averted the danger. Howe reported that the electoral court would consider him slighted if he were not authorized to present the patent. Only a few weeks had passed by since the incidents over Fritz's birth, when the patent reached Hanover in March 1707, accompanied by an autograph letter from Queen Anne. Mr. Howe thought patent and letter merited a ceremonial audience. The Elector, however, declared that his son should grant no official audiences during his own lifetime. Flustered ministers debated the propriety of Elector and Prince jointly receiving Mr. Howe, whom they parried with evasions, which he reported to England.[28] Meanwhile George Augustus's sullen temper returned, and Caroline began her only phase of coolness with the Electress. Twice the young couple's conduct had been made to appear rude in omitting the proper ceremony simply because the Elector feared that they might turn the occasions to their own advantage. Mr. Howe ended by going 'to court in a private manner as I found would be most agreeable to them'. The Prince received patent and letter gratefully and 'desired me to represent that it was not his fault that the receiving of the patent was not performed in the most respectful manner'.[29]

When campaigning started that spring Caroline and George Augustus felt sure that Fritzchen's arrival signified freedom to fight. A visit from Prince Eugene and the Duke of Marlborough, come to see that the Elector accepted command of the Upper Rhine army, whipped up his keenness. He set about choosing his horses: one for the marches, one for parade, one for battle and the swiftest he could find for pursuits. 'I am afraid all this will only end in his staying at Hanover and driving out in a well-sprung carriage,' his uncle commented, and he was right.[30] Whether the Elector thought he had enough responsibility without teaching his son the principles of warfare, or simply because they were on bad terms, once more the Prince was left behind. A baffled young couple pouted in the Leine Palace while the Electress summered at Herrenhausen. Their desultory visits to her were so obviously inspired by duty that they gave no one pleasure. George Augustus kept gloomily silent, leaving Caroline to be polite for them both. The uneasy task forced her into a nervous gaiety, which the Electress labelled insincerity.[31] The relatives heard all about these rude grandchildren. Sophia Dorothea in Berlin was told confidentially that the Elector wished George Augustus shared her own sweet temperament. When Caroline caught small-pox in July, trouble seemed never ending.

At first they pretended that her blood was overheated, but she noticed that they kept Fritzchen away, and that George Augustus looked excessively worried.[32] The kindest intentions could not make him a good sick nurse. He

38

fidgeted, scolded, and fussed, staying by her all day, but she knew that affection prompted his anxiety. In the evenings he went for vigorous rides, hoping to keep well.[33] Caroline passed the critical stage, but then, speeding recovery too fast, she caught a chill and nearly died. Slowly the will to live returned, but the struggle exhausted her strength, and her relations grew alarmed at the weary languor which assailed her for some time.[34] Of course the Prince paid for his incautious devotion by catching small-pox too. The Electress Sophia, who never harboured ill-will, came to visit the convalescents, amusing them by remarking that George Augustus really did not look as if he had had the small-pox. All the same, people might perhaps wonder whether some fleas had bitten his face.[35] She privately thought Caroline very much changed in features and colouring.[36] These three became good friends again. The Electress approved of her grandson's devotion to Caroline. And he, sobered by the awful possibility of losing her, tempered his behaviour with new considerateness.

The year 1708 brought George Augustus his chance to soldier. With Fritzchen above a year old, and a small companion on the way, so Caroline thought, the excuse for caution was gone. The young campaigner completed the preparations for his schooling with Marlborough's army guarding Belgium. His father, watching the French in Alsace that year, testified to 'joy in seeing' George Augustus 'beginning the art of war under so great a captain. You will oblige me, my lord, if you will be so good as to give him advice, when he shall have occasion for it.'[37] Caroline one June evening had taken Fritzchen out to the electoral summer residence at Herrenhausen where they kept the Electress company. There, as dusk fell, she said good-bye to her husband for the first time, praying that their companionship would not be shattered by French shot or sword. Whispered promises to write often, warm hugs, tiresome tears mocked their show of bravery; and he was gone.[38] She was left watching for the courier with greater keenness than when he carried her love-letters to Ansbach three summers ago.

This first holiday at Herrenhausen recalled Charlotten-burg days to Caroline. The Electress's versatile interests created the same excitement, which stimulated Caroline after the materialism of life in the Leine Palace. Herren-hausen was Sophia's favourite setting. Three successive Venetian architects had designed it like a Palladian villa to remind her brother-in-law and her husband of the glamorous carnivals they had enjoyed in Venice.[39] To the Venetian succeeded French influence, shown by the Orangery building where Sophia had her rooms. There she gathered her porcelain collection, her books and bulky stacks of letters. There she philosophized with Leibniz and invited Handel to make music for her. She liked variety in her guests. A Swedish general brought stark tales of a Russian imprisonment; a Neapolitan officer with his stories of the Viennese court raised more mirth than the comedians. Russian princes, some polite and some uncouth, brought the glamour of their barbaric land, but the Emperor of China's learned doctor came to collect pictures of healing herbs. Englishmen arrived 'with the swallows', making the place a little England while culti-vating Queen Anne's successor.

To Sophia a few hours exercise was a daily rite which propitiated the fretful ailments that usually beset old ladies of 77. When rain forbade a garden tour, she paced the 220 feet of the Orangery's chief apartment, which served both as orangery and as reception room. Her chief delight was to supervise the vast display of garden geometry which emerged from the designs of Martin Charbonnier. Bordering the gardens on three sides lapped a canal whereon processions of Venetian gondolas glided at the appointed times. Along the banks sprouted a triple row of slim young lime-trees. Visitors flocked to be diverted in the garden theatre, which Caroline could see from her rooms in the east wing of the Orangery. The stage was raised a metre from the ground; beech hedges planted along its rectangular length formed 'so many bowers and summer houses' for the actors' dressing-rooms; 'the whole being set off with many fine statues . . . and an excellent waterwork behind'. Garden architecture decreed waterworks, so they were provided first, and the problem of supplying water at sufficient pressure pondered afterwards. As the little procession toured the grounds these summer days, they watched two domed pavilions rising at the southernmost corners; they selected sites for groups of statuary; and noted growth in new hedges and parterres. The garden theatre had only reached its twelfth birthday; the gondola house its sixth; and two years ago the orangery from Celle came to join the galaxy already so splendidly housed.

Fritzchen became Sophia's firm admirer when she presented him with some home-baked cake that had been sent her. He was a pretty little fellow but small and backward for his age. He only spoke a few words and still made no attempt to stand.[40] Later Caroline discovered that he had rickets, which accounted for his slow progress.[41]

She was happy at receiving two or three letters a week from her husband, and she spent much time in answering them.[42] He had only been gone a month when she had a bad fright. A young Prussian passed through Hanover carrying news from the Prince's sector to King Frederick in Berlin. There had been some activity, it appeared, but no courier came from the Prince despite his promise to send one if a battle took place. Two mornings later, soon after dawn, the courier arrived. He brought not only news of a glorious victory at Oudenarde, but vivid descriptions of the Electoral Prince's valour at the head of the Brunswick cavalry. Caroline needed to share the story at once. Picking up Fritz, she rushed with the courier to the Electress's bedroom, making scant apology for waking the old lady so early.[43] Proudly they discussed each point of the Prince's behaviour. In Cadogan's vanguard, he had gone into action first that day. Their picked force decimated four French battalions, and then the Hanoverian dragoons crashed gloriously into twenty squadrons of French cavalry, and in the presence of the two approaching main forces, scattered the enemy horsemen in confusion. The Prince distinguished himself in the charge, showing fine courage in a hand-to-hand encounter. When his horse was shot under him, and the officer beside him killed, he was up and on in the thick of the battle without pause.[44]

English ballads sang his bravery, English families toasted the 'young Hanover Brave'.[45] And Marlborough, the victor of the battle, congratulated the Elector on his son's courage, 'the Prince Electoral distinguished himself extremely, charging at the head of and animating by his example your Electoral Highness's troops, who played a good part in this happy victory'.[46] The Prince's popularity in England caused a political ruffle. Rumour whispered that Marlborough planned to make the electoral family beholden only to Lord Treasurer Godolphin and himself, by seeing that the Prince or his grandmother received the invitation to come to England.[47] Both Whigs and Tories feared his success in the matter. Queen Anne questioned him about the gossip, bidding him discover whether the Prince really designed visiting England, and expressing her repugnance at the idea.[48] Her aversion killed it, if ever it had existed outside the scheming brains of Tory politicians, anxious to discredit Marlborough and the Whigs by the ruse. The Tories wrongly exulted that they had destroyed Marlborough's favour at Hanover; for that Court continued to admire him who humbled the French so regularly.

Caroline contented herself with the splendid news until autumn ended the campaign and her husband surprised her one evening late in October.[49] Their supper was joyful that night. Every one hoped that the pleasant shock would hasten the baby, long overdue, but Caroline had again miscalculated her time. She soon observed that the Prince had gained manliness from his initiation into battle. A new note of responsibility banished the tantrums and sulks, and his bearing was most courteous.[50] If he rated his martial prowess high, he could scarcely be blamed, because he was treated like a hero.

43

By autumn 1709 Caroline knew that her hopes of a second baby were no longer premature. The electoral family greeted most autumns by hunting vigorously over the Lüneburg heaths.[51] Intrepid ladies followed the chase in flimsy chariots known as *calèches*. In the evening weather-beaten sportsmen formed an appreciative audience for 'Pickelhering' and his troupe playing the latest cosmopolitan comedies. This particular November found all the family at the Göhrde hunting-box, except Caroline left sentinel at Hanover.[52] She bade George Augustus go too, saying that wet-nursing was no man's job. For company she had the faithful Countess of Bückeburg, and her diminutive Fritzchen, nearly turned three, making progress now that his rickets were cured. For occupation her books. She never found time enough for all she wanted to read. George Augustus told her that she was more schoolmarm than princess, and liked her to chat with him instead of reading, but Leibniz urged her to digest this and that work, for they had been firm friends since Charlottenburg times. When she first came to Hanover, a refugee French abbé living there urged Leibniz to

cultivate her good qualities assiduously, for there you have a spirit naturally beautiful, and an intellect completely disposed to reason. In working for her you work for the world's advantage, especially if her lot calls her to grace the English throne, as there is reason to suppose.[53]

Leibniz obeyed. When he was away from Hanover he continued his metaphysical discussions by letter. His ideas for unifying all Christian beliefs aroused her interest in the history of religion and in the famous disputes of her day. She followed the quarrel raging in France between Jansenists and Jesuits, and pondered over the theories advanced by English Deists.

Her retentive memory revelled in facts, pedigrees, and biographies. Gradually she amassed that historical knowledge which later caused an English friend to write in astonishment:

She had a most incredible memory and was as learned both in ancient and modern history as the most learned men. For there was hardly a romance of ten or twenty volumes ever written of which she was not able to give as good and exact account as to all the facts as she could of any of the most remarkable incidents or celebrated heroes in the history of Greece and Rome, and she was as well versed in pedigrees that were of no more significance than Pantagruel's . . . as she was of any reigning prince then in Europe.[54]

The Electress sent Caroline the latest news from the Göhrde:[55]

. . . there are no lively pleasures here except for hunting men, we others do nothing but play [cards]. Towards suppertime yesterday the Prince Royal [of Prussia] arrived; he seems to me in good spirits and was delighted at finding your Highness in Hanover. . . . I assure you without exaggeration that I am always thinking about you, and miss you everywhere; but for this year I must neither think nor hope to see you here. Another year you will be very well lodged and will find the whole assembly of Cardinals in your ante-room, with the Pope over the mantelpiece blessing them. Signor Quirini has evoked admiration for his building as well as for his re-arrangement of the rooms;* and truly it all seems like a miracle to any one who saw the place before. When it is cold our best walk is to the stables, which are at least as beautiful as the Orangery at Herrenhausen, but they do not smell so good; and that, my dear Princess, is all the news I can send you from here: I am sure you do not doubt that my heart is completely yours and that I defy even

* Göhrde passed to the Elector on the death of his father-in-law, Duke George of Celle, and Signor Quirini was engaged to enlarge it.

your Prince to love you more than I will do all my life. I hug Fritzchen *en idée*! Sophia.

On November 2nd Caroline gave birth to a daughter, christened Anne in compliment to the English Queen, who presently consented to be godmother and sent the babe a gift by one of her special representatives going to Hanover. 'I take keen pleasure in giving, as often as I am able, proofs of the perfect friendship I bear for your husband as well as the whole electoral family,' the Queen wrote to Caroline.[56] The letter that warmed her most came from her husband.[57] Their tastes differed more than she had foreseen but they had attained a sympathetic comradeship:

My very dear wife, I have just received the good news of the birth of a daughter at which I feel all imaginable pleasure, and I am delighted to learn from Helmold's letter that you are well. I am only a little bit angry that it has caused you pain. You should know me well enough, my very dear Caroline, to believe that everything that concerns you is infinitely precious to me. This new token of your love attaches me the more deeply to you, and I assure you, dear heart, that I love the baby without having seen it. I pray you, take care of yourself, that I may have the pleasure of finding you well, and that still greater joy may be conferred upon a heart deeply desirous of it. The Electress and my sister expressed their happiness upon learning of your safe delivery and your good health. . . . Adieu, my dearest heart, for God's sake take care of yourself, and of the young family, particularly the new-born infant, who at present has most need of care. The peace of my life depends upon knowing you in good health, and upon the conviction of your continued affection for me. I shall endeavour to attract it by all imaginable passion and love, and I shall never omit any way of showing you that no one could be more wholly yours, dear Caroline, than is your

GEORGE AUGUSTUS.

III

THE CROWN COMES TO HANOVER

Hanover lacked blitheness in the spring of 1714. Grave faces passed to and fro indoors. Preoccupied groups entered or left the Palace in serious talk. There were many callers and much business to be done. Only Fritzchen and his sisters, now three of them, romped care-free, though the boy's seven-year-old dignity had acquired tutors and a list of precepts formulated by Grandpapa Elector. Lessons claimed their share of every day, and indicated his superiority to little girls of 5, 3, and 1. Anne, a determined young miss, stood up to him well, but Amelia and Caroline counted themselves his contented admirers. Their parents seemed unsatisfactorily aloof. As well they might.

They expected important news from England, news which might promote them to an independent existence, news therefore, that concerned the old, old topic. Should a member of the Electoral Family go to England? The family suspected that Queen Anne's conscience had lately suffered more twinges from her enforced harshness towards the Pretender, her half-brother, than from her coldness for themselves. Her Tory ministers secretly courted that serious young man. Rumour harped upon his coming to England, supported by French arms. The prospect agitated Hanover's Whig friends because the Queen's health was poor. If the Pretender were in England when she died, possession might prove stronger than the law. They urged retaliation to ministerial intrigue.[1] But the Elector's inclination counselled action only if the Queen directly attacked his family's rights. The Whigs wanted their legal candidate safely in England. The Electress, now 83, no longer wished to go there save as Queen, but George Augustus was her natural substitute. His own succession to the English Crown being still remote, Queen Anne need not feel disquieted by his presence. He and Caroline, eager to escape parental control and do good work for the family, applauded the idea, but opposition came from the Elector, who based it on other reasons but was really jealous of his heir.

The Whigs, unaware of this personal complication, conceived a hopeful plan for bringing George Augustus to England. As Duke of Cambridge he had a right to be summoned to take his seat in Parliament. His writ of summons reposed in the Lord Chancellor's office. Nothing simpler than for Schütz, the electoral envoy, to demand it, and then the Prince could come at once. To her grandchildren's delight, the Electress Sophia took a sporting interest in the plan. She wrote to Schütz about the writ on 12 April 1714, but did not make clear whether she expected him to demand it, or simply to ask why the Lord Chancellor retained it.[2] This slight distinction became vital in time. Unconscious of any ambiguity in her letter, the Electress with George Augustus and Caroline waited hopefully for the reply. Waiting on the events of English politics had been their irksome lot these past four years.

When the Tories came into power in 1710, peace fled

48

from Hanover.[3] Petty irritation with Godolphin's ministry paled before the dangers to the English constitution
and the European balance of power which the change
foreboded in Hanover's opinion. The fair words spoken
by the new ministry, and the suave emissaries it sent over,
never allayed suspicions of its true intentions. Before this,
Tory and Whig had united in passing the Act of Settlement which legalized Protestant Hanover's succession.
Both parties agreed in fighting Louis XIV when he broke
his word by accepting the Spanish crown for his grandson,
and then proclaimed James Edward Stuart King of
England. The Elector and his mother had behaved im-
partially towards those 'vile enormous factions'; Marlborough's label for Whigs and Tories. However, the long
war produced a cleavage in the parties' foreign policy.
The Whigs and the Allies, who included Hanover, still
agreed that all Spain must be won for the Habsburg
Archduke Charles, Caroline's former suitor, but they had
no clear plan for achieving a peace which fulfilled this
condition. The Tories were prepared to solve the dead-
lock by a peace partitioning the Spanish empire between
the Austrian and French candidates. Their policy suited
British interests but entailed breaking promises given early
in the war. To Hanover and the Whigs it was heresy.
And the Tories were miserably divided over the Protestant
Succession; one group accepted Hanover's claims, another
wavered, and a third section was openly Jacobite. Naturally
Hanover was distrustful.

Their suspicion was justified. The English Government
opened secret negotiations with France, and confronted
its allies with peace preliminaries which betrayed the

objects they had formulated together. The Elector's protests were dismissed as Whig propaganda. The Government seduced England by a press campaign and deserted its allies in the field, to sign the Peace of Utrecht in 1713. The Empire, of which Hanover made a loyal unit, fought on for two years. The Tory ministers had achieved their object—peace, but only 'by becoming fellow-conspirators with French statesmen and Jacobite agents'.[4] Knowing that Hanover disapproved of their peace policy, Oxford and Bolingbroke plunged deeper into their Jacobite schemes; Oxford trying meanwhile to persuade Hanover of his good faith. But after three years of evasions, Hanover felt certain that both men were in touch with the Pretender, though the documentary evidence of this treachery long lay hidden in Jacobite and French archives.[5]

The stolid Elector still would assign neither money nor troops to extend his influence in England and to watch over his cause from Holland, nor would he send his son, who, as a prince of the blood, had 'so many just pretexts and reasons for coming' that no Englishman could reasonably object to it.[6] George Augustus and Caroline resented the fact that he would have allowed his brother, Duke Ernest, to go over, but that dissatisfied the Whigs.[7] The Elector, therefore, craftily pleaded affection for his 'only son and the only hope of his family', as the reason for debarring the Prince from such a precarious mission.[8] The most he would do for his anxious friends was to impress upon Baron von Schütz, his new and inexperienced envoy to St. James's in 1713, that he must co-operate with the chief Whigs.[9] The Electress still counselled Schütz to be impartial in his dealings with the parties.[10] Sadly enough he followed the Elector's precepts, to raise a storm of criticism which burst chiefly upon the Electress.

His reports painted an alarming picture. The Queen received him correctly but coldly.[11] At Christmas she nearly died. The Whigs renewed their pleas for George Augustus to come.[12] The Dutch Pensionary Heinsius thought he should go but the Elector was still adamant.[13] 'A Hanovre on est trop indolent sur l'affaire et je me trompe si l'Electeur n'est pas bien aisé d'en être quitte avec honneur,' wrote a shrewd observer at his Court.[14] When Queen Anne opened Parliament in January 1714, she censured those who maliciously supposed the Protestant Succession in danger. But Lords and Commons had grown uneasy over her ministers' intentions. The Government only gained slender majorities when both houses debated the topic. Happily for the country's peace, Oxford and Bolingbroke squandered their energies in a fight for personal supremacy, but, unhappily for the Hanover family's quiet, the Whigs then bethought themselves of the writ as the simplest way of bringing George Augustus to England. Schütz wrote urging him to start forthwith, but he was not his own master.

When they saw the Electress's letter the Whigs' good humour grew. For Schütz, obedient to the Elector's command, consulted with no fewer than ten eminent lords well disposed to Hanover.[15] All agreed that he should *demand* the writ of the Lord Chancellor. Schütz's own inclination, too, interpreted the Electress's words as an order to proceed. His request embarrassed the Lord Chancellor, who replied that no answer could be given before consultation with the Queen, but Schütz must not regard this as a refusal. That night a Cabinet Council meeting debated the request in the Queen's presence. Bolingbroke angled for her favour by agreeing with her that the writ should be refused. The law was plainly against them, as Oxford (who thereby lost his battle with Bolingbroke) and the other ministers pointed out. Schütz received the writ, but was told that the Queen considered his request as a personal affront, and that she ought first to have been privately consulted. He was forbidden to appear at Court, and learnt that his recall had been demanded. Whereat he took his secret departure from London, hoping to justify his conduct at Hanover, whither he had sent descriptions of the public joy occasioned by his request for the writ. 'The bells were ringing for some days past and healths drunk to his (the Prince's) good journey.'[16] Lord Townshend, one of the foremost Whigs, offered his congratulations, describing his party's despair at the Elector's previous refusal to send over the Prince, but Schütz's demand 'I can assure you is thought of by everybody, both friends as well as enemies, to be the first step that your court has made that looks as if you are in earnest about the succession'.[17] He added that it would be fatal to depress spirits raised to such expectation.

Hanover, meanwhile, endured Thomas Harley, the fourth special envoy from England, with scant patience. Besides conveying the stock assurances of his Queen's love for the family, and her offer to pay the Electress a private pension (which was refused, with the comment that as Heiress Presumptive, Sophia would only accept one upon the joint resolve of Queen and Parliament), he was ordered to inquire whether they wished any further

measures taken for the safety of their succession. As a
gambit for compliments the inquiry was misplaced. Harley received a formal answer to his last question signed by
the Elector and his mother.[18] They requested: the Queen's
endeavours to secure the Pretender's retirement from Lor-
raine to Italy, a revenue to be settled on the Electress by
Act of Parliament, and the establishment of a member of
their family in England. To obtain the Elector's assent to
this last item was a signal triumph, one which made
Schütz's news from England the more exasperating.

The Electress, after all, had only intended Schütz to
inquire about the writ and not demand it.[19] She was
horrified over the wrath her innocent letter let loose upon
her family. But after the first astonishment waned over
the precipitate turn of affairs, opinion at Hanover resented
the absurd fuss caused by Schütz's action. When the
Queen was so free with wordy love for the family, why
did the thought of one of them coming to England induce
a frenzy? If Schütz insulted her by omitting a private
consultation, why had not the Lord Chancellor given him
the hint? Meanwhile Marlborough, Townshend, and
Cadogan praised the Elector's wisdom; they begged him
not to defer his son's departure an unnecessary day.
Hanoverian Ministers shared that opinion. They observed
signs of trimming amongst the Tories. Lord Oxford's
paper announced that his party, far from deploring the
Prince's coming, would welcome it.[20] So the astute
secretary, Robethon, and the experienced diplomat, Bothmer, thought 'let him go'.[21] Leibniz from Vienna congratulated the Electress: 'In my opinion nothing could
be more timely, for this has happened just as the nation

begins to open its eyes and, numbers of the chief Tories having detached themselves from the ministry, it is essential to let the nation feel that Hanover both has affection for it and care of its interests.' To Caroline, he wrote that Schütz resembled a general who won a battle without waiting for orders to go into action.[22]

'Let George Augustus go,' the Electress told her son. 'Let me go,' the Prince pleaded with his father. Caroline tactfully, but firmly, echoed their advice in personal interviews with the Elector. An insistent crescendo drummed upon his ears. A few days before this crisis he had signed a statement urging the necessity for this very thing. Now, because its fulfilment threatened his peace, and because his son would appear the hero of the hour, he refused.

He told Harley shortly after that Schütz had acted without orders, dismissed the matter from his mind, and went off to hunt. Schütz, returned to Hanover, was refused an audience and sharply reproved:

It has caused Our particular disapproval and surprise that you used Our Mother's gracious name in this affair. You should have understood from Us personally, that in matters touching Us or Our Son, you had to observe Our and no other order, and to execute it alone.[23]

What matter if this rebuff showed little consideration for his mother's feelings? What matter if his ministers and English supporters were discouraged? All had been schooled to obey his wishes. He wished for peace. Open enmity between Prince and Elector followed. No seat in the Privy Council; no addition to his income, though he fathered four children; no regimental command, and now no journey to England.[24] His father was monstrous, thought the Prince, and Caroline agreed.

At this painful juncture the electoral family moved out to Herrenhausen for the summer. 'Here have I been in Herrenhausen since yesterday afternoon, and have admired everything, for it is quite a novelty to see all my pictures and paintings again. I wonder whether yours and the King's are like you: I believe it seems a century since I last saw you, and people alter a little all the time. My feet still carry me right round the garden without getting tired, which pleases me very much, for I love walking along these shady paths,' the Electress wrote to her granddaughter in Berlin.[25] But Caroline thought she looked frailer. The events of the past few weeks had strained her indomitable spirit. They still discussed the possibility of George Augustus's going to England, but it seemed unlikely after the Elector's repudiation of Schütz. In the first week of June a courier arrived with three letters from Queen Anne. Bolingbroke counted them revenge for his defeat at that midnight Cabinet Council meeting, though he was already richly revenged by gaining the Queen's favour. Caroline described their tone as 'd'un violences digne de Mylord Bullenbrock'.

The letter to the Elector showed restraint, but the Electress and George Augustus received strong expressions of Anne's displeasure at the thought of the Prince's coming over, which, if persisted in, she threatened, would prejudice the family's succession.[26] From her fierceness, the Pretender himself might have proposed visiting England.

The Electress felt depressed by these letters, as if Queen Anne's hate could really work upon Parliament to alter the Act of Succession. 'This affair will make me ill, I shall never get over it,' she said, losing her detachment, 'but I shall have this gracious letter printed, so that every one may see that it will not have been my fault if my children lose three crowns.' A few years before she would have simply eased her feelings by penning Leibniz an ironical commentary. Now her depression sent her to bed the day the letters came. Caroline answered Leibniz's letter of May:

. . . The Prince Electoral is greatly obliged by the strong interest you take in his affairs; it could be wished that every one shared the same feelings; it is the fault of neither the Prince nor all honest folk here; he has moved heaven and earth, and I have spoken about it very strongly to the Elector. We were in a state of crisis until the day before yesterday, when the Queen's courier arrived with letters for the Electress, Elector, and Electoral Prince, which are of a violence worthy of my Lord Bolingbroke. The Electoral Prince, as a result, is practically in despair about going to take his seat in the English Parliament according to his right. I do not know how the world may judge our conduct. I do not regret the loss we may personally suffer from it so much as having in some measure to abandon the cause of our religion, the liberty of Europe, and so many brave and honest friends in England. I have no other consolation than to know that everything humanly possible has been done to obtain permission for the Prince. The Electress supported him in this, and they want to send the Queen's letters to England. I can find no comfort apart from the belief that Providence orders all things for our good; your prefaces to La Théodicée have been a great help to me. Never has a sorrow seemed so insupportable as this one. I fear for the Prince's health, perhaps even his life. . . .[27]

It was not he who died. Caroline thought that by June 8th, two days later, the Electress seemed calmer. She was well enough to dine with the family in public, and she spent the afternoon doing her work and writing to her niece the Duchess of Orleans. The evening was fine and the Electress, loath to miss her airing, suggested a stroll.[28] Leaning on Caroline's arm, she discussed the topic uppermost in her mind. Marlborough had been sent copies of Queen Anne's letters; what would the English public think of them? On the still summer air the sound of other voices floated to them; the Elector, too, was out. The gardens soothed them all. Fountains plashed softly, the last sunbeams slanted amongst the greenery, and the day seemed drawing to a peaceful end. But suddenly a cool gust rustled the trees. A few raindrops began to fall. The little group quickened pace to reach a sheltering pavilion. 'Take care, you're going too fast,' Caroline cautioned the Electress. 'I can well believe it,' came the laughing reply. The next moment she sank lifeless into Caroline's arms. The Elector, hearing cries, hurried to them, and seeing his mother unconscious, put some *poudre d'or* into her mouth. Gently they carried her home. She had died as she had wished, in her beloved gardens, without doctor or priest. 'Let death snuff me out like a candle' she used to say. Death had heard and been kind.

Caroline mused sadly over the second friend she had lost. She had been blessed in both her dear mentors. Queen Sophia Charlotte's enthusiasms kindled her mind; the Electress's wisdom gave it poise and breadth. She had welcomed Caroline into the family as a bride. Their single phase of coolness past, they had achieved a delightful friendship. Together they had enjoyed Leibniz and listened to Handel. How jolly the Electress had been with Fritzchen and the girls; how pleased that time she returned from the Göhrde, and he had made her a serious little compliment in French. 'Her surprising mental vigour, strengthened by an enviable physical activity, kept her erect, bubbling over with the joy of life. Like renewed youth it sometimes coursed through the octogenarian, and made her sing at table, essay a minuet, or follow the hunt through thick and thin in a light chariot. But the real solace of her old age, besides her extensive charities, was more and more her correspondence.'[29] She kept in close touch with her numerous relations, scattered in almost every German Court. 'Madame' in France, her English, Dutch, and Italian friends plied her with letters. Her own memoirs, written long years ago to keep up her spirits whilst her husband went to Venice, showed her perception and humour.[30] Now she was gone, leaving Caroline to carry on the torch of liberal interests, so cheerfully tended during the past sixty years.

And Caroline, at 31, had fitted herself for the mission. Small-pox had stolen her bloom but admiration still greeted her appearance. Her mental capacities inspired compliments which, by their number and prosiness, saved her from too great a self-esteem. Marriage had added a store of practical wisdom, gained from mothering four sturdy children and managing her restive husband. To her he came like a sulky child when his father denied him some request; he strutted before her a martial hero wreathed in laurels or, fancying a lighter part, posed as worldly-wise with a brief flirtation. For, being denied a public stage, he was something of an actor at home, expecting the appropriate responses from Caroline, who gravely gave them and was rewarded by his unvarying

THE ELECTRESS SOPHIA

(*By* ANDREAS SCHEITS, 1706)

attachment. Bred up convinced of his innate superiority to women, he was spared the pain of perceiving that his sober actions were sometimes due to wifely counsel. As yet her influence remained a secret, but it would be significant in the position which would one day be theirs in England. The Elector guessed at it and, incapable of revising his own notions about women, despised his son the more. He told his confidants, for instance, that he dared not admit the Prince to the council of war because he 'blabs everything to the women'.[31] Nine years more of trifling occupations had certainly cultivated the Prince's good points very little. A General who had long known him criticized the Elector's training of him, but admitted that he was variable, suspicious, and formed opinions without proper cause; all signs of thwarted energies. The better aspects of this 'strangely mixed character', in the same judge's opinion, showed him witty, capable, and lively. For his future in England he possessed two excellent qualities. He burnt with ardour to go there and his memory was truly royal.[32] His grandmother's death gave him opportunity for peacemaking with his father, which he grasped at once, and tranquillity ensued, helped by a stiffening in the Elector's attitude towards English affairs.

To notify Queen Anne of his mother's death, the Elector sent over Bothmer, a shrewd diplomat, incapable of being intimidated by Bolingbroke or overruled by the Whigs. In revising the list of Regents, the Elector nominated thirteen Whigs to outnumber the Tory ministers in that select body which would govern England after Anne's death until his arrival. His reply to Queen Anne's petulant letters administered a neat rebuke:

It is so essential to me to cultivate the honour of your good graces, that it is natural to imagine that the presence of one of the princes of my family in your kingdoms could never have any other design than to confirm a good understanding between the two courts and to render your Majesty all possible services.[33]

Lord Clarendon eventually brought over the Queen's answer to the memorandum. She curtly rejected the Elector's suggestions, made at her own request.[34] Her rudeness, however, was not destined to exacerbate relations between the two courts, for she was nearing her appointed end. Lord Clarendon delivered his message on August 4th. On August 7th he composed his dispatch about the audience, and on that day Lord Oxford was dismissed from the Lord Treasurership, after a bitter scene with Bolingbroke in the Queen's presence. Five days later the Queen died, a lonely woman, deprived of a husband's consolation, estranged from old friends, bewildered by brawling ministers. Thus was Bolingbroke cheated of his triumph, and the country saved the civil war that might have been caused by his calling over the Pretender.

During the Queen's brief illness, the Whigs and the Middle Party, supporting Hanover but owning allegiance to neither Whigs nor Tories, acted swiftly. Through the instrumentality of the Privy Council, they took measures to ensure the legal succession, and Bolingbroke, without plans of his own, tamely concurred.[35]

All was in readiness when rest came to the Queen at Kensington that Sunday morning, August 12th. The red brick battlements of St. James's gazed down upon fast gathering crowds, come to watch history being made. The great of the land hurried there. Inside the Palace

Bothmer and Kreienberg helped to draw up the Proclamation, which bore 127 signatures, showing it to be a national act. The documents naming the Regents being opened, the chosen men were sworn into their solemn office. Bolingbroke, as simple Secretary of State, did not rank amongst them. The Regents first made their appearance before the expectant people thronging the Palace, then the rich pageantry of proclaiming the new monarch was played. Tory threats had faded unfulfilled. Whig anxieties were ended. The Regency Act had done its part valiantly, and the 'High and Mighty Prince George, Elector of Brunswick-Lüneburg,' had entered upon the peaceful possession of his new dominions. Seldom had fate thrust honour upon one so undesirous of it as the Elector. His conduct during the period of waiting for the English crown has often been extolled for its prudence. But prudence was scarcely a virtue in him who would have renounced that crown had occasion offered itself. In keeping his son at Hanover this summer of 1714, he acted against the unanimous advice of English politicians, his own ministers, and his family, anxious to hearten their supporters in England at a critical time. The Elector preferred to depress these adherents, and repudiate his envoy rather than risk disturbing his peace or giving his son an opportunity. Queen Anne's death, closely following his decision, prevented any bad consequences arising from it. Who dare prophesy what might have happened had Bolingbroke's spell of power been longer?

By contrast with the stirring English scenes, the news came soberly to Hanover. The first to arrive was the ambitious young Whig James Craggs, who spoke of

Queen Anne's grave state, and of the measures taken by the Privy Council. This mission later brought him the reward of ministerial rank. Next day, August 17th, Bothmer's secretary, Gödeke, came to tell the Elector he was King.[36] Hearing the news only after he returned from dining with the Kielmanseggs, Lord Clarendon disturbed the Electoral repose to greet George Louis, but received cold thanks for his tactless courtesy.[37] After his plain speaking on the Queen's behalf he could scarcely have expected a good reception. Lord Dorset, sent by the Regency to make official declaration of George I's accession, was received in the Orangery at Herrenhausen two days later. The new King, replying to his daughter's congratulations, thought more about Hanover than England:[38]

> I am deeply touched by your compliments upon my accession to the English throne. It is my wish that it shall afford me new means of showing you my affection, to which I hope distance will not prove any obstacle, since I intend to be often in this country.

Caroline and George Augustus greeted the change gladly. The King after all had passed fifty. It was hard to forsake the home and work of a lifetime, but they relished a career in England, land of riches and warm Whig friendship. Unlike him they had troubled to learn English. To be sure, Caroline spattered her talk with French idiom and German expressions, while George Augustus lacked a certain purity of accent. However, the effort was what counted. England, to Caroline, was the country of Bacon, Locke, Wollaston, and Newton happily still alive. A gorgeous vista of books, discussions, and vital contacts whetted her eagerness. Schoolmarm perhaps, but the constraint and pettiness of Court circles made impersonal pleasures a precious escape. She laughed with George Augustus over her intellectualism, but she helped him the better for it. And she had need of her serenity now, for the King, with his knack of spoiling the best anticipations, declared that Fritzchen must stay at Hanover as family representative. To make the child of 7 the puppet of Court ceremonial was cruelty. Besides, Duke Ernest was staying to preside over the Privy Council until his hopes of the Osnabrück bishopric matured; but the parents had to waive their feelings in deference to what the King considered were Hanover's prior claims upon their boy.[39]

He arranged that Caroline should bring over her girls after he and George Augustus had made certain that the unstable islanders harboured no designs against him. The English Privy Councillors had secured his kingdoms against attack in two days' work, but he took a leisurely month before he left Hanover. Bernstorff his electoral prime minister, Robethon the secretary, the chief court officers, and of course lean Mademoiselle Schulenburg, went with him. But it took Madame Kielmansegge till autumn to appease her insistent creditors. The retinue gained a picturesque touch from his two Turkish pages, Mustapha and Mahomet.[40] Forgetting his reserve as he left Herrenhausen, the King spoke these feeling words, 'Farewell, dear place, where I have spent so many peaceful hours. I leave you but not for ever: I shall see you again from time to time.' After a ceremonial ten days at The Hague, he set sail for England aboard the yacht *Peregrine*, escorted by twenty-two warships, four frigates, six other yachts, and baggage ships. On September 29th they came safely to English waters, heading for Greenwich, where all the great of the land waited to greet a German King.

Just after the King left, Leibniz returned from a long stay in Vienna. Caroline at once asked him to stay at Herrenhausen until she went to England.

'I am very glad to enjoy as much as I can the good graces of such an accomplished, intelligent princess, who even wished to discuss the Théodicée with me, if you can believe it. She has read it more than once . . . it seems a great deal when such a princess, surrounded by everything that might dissipate the intellect, pays so much attention to matters as lofty as those treated by my work. If I were free to obey her Royal Highness I should accompany her to England,' the philosopher wrote to a friend.[41] Caroline tried hard to obtain him this permission, knowing how much he wanted to meet Sir Isaac Newton and the Deist, Dr. Samuel Clarke, but her father-in-law disapproved of talk, however elevated, which did not produce results. He paid Leibniz as his family historiographer. He wanted to see fat volumes about his ancestors produced by the pen of this genius whose mind ranged the problems of the universe. Leibniz, in common with other great intellects, experienced the misery of being beholden to men who despised him as an eccentric idealist. His women friends, the first Prussian Queen, the Electress, and Caroline, glimpsed something of his vision and gave him the sympathetic admiration which genius needs if it is not to dissolve in bitter frustration. Caroline valued his counsel at this time because he had familiarized himself with English politics ever since the Electress became

Heiress of Great Britain. He felt sure that a splendid future awaited Caroline's gifts. He told the Empress's mistress of the robes:

> During my stay at Herrenhausen I have admired the equability and honour, the kindness and moderation, which this princess maintains amidst such great prosperity.[42]

In spite of the gloomy conviction that the untrustworthy Englishmen would soon banish their new King or chop off his head,[43] good news reached Caroline from England.[44]

Few stories betrayed the King's first impressions of England. Being a wise man he knew that silence was better than adverse comment. But he could not resist one shrewd poke at the English, who for all their proud ways seemed to him more grasping than his well-schooled Hanoverians. 'This is a strange country,' he observed drily, 'the first morning after my arrival at St. James's, I looked out of my window and saw a park with walls and canal which they told me was mine. The next day Lord Chetwynd, the manager of *my* park, sent me a fine brace of carp out of *my* canal; and I was told I must give five guineas to Lord Chetwynd's servant for bringing me my own carp out of my own canal in my own park.'[45] It was a salutary point of view for people who exclaimed throughout the reign against German greed. Caroline was also amused to hear that the King found time for sociability amidst his manifold new duties. Out of politeness he accepted the hospitality of his most august subjects, so that he and the Prince attended several parties, which passed off with more fun than the hosts had expected.[46] Lord Rochester consoled the Prince in his separation from wife and family by inviting him to meet Queen Anne's maids of honour, wherein he gauged the Heir Apparent's taste to a nicety.

There was no longer reason for Caroline to tarry at Herrenhausen. The Duchesses of Celle and Wolfenbüttel came to bid her God-speed. Her brother insisted on going part of the journey with her, knowing that the future held scant chance of their meeting one another.[47] Hanover expressed regret at losing her in lofty but prosy strain. Her admirable qualities had made her 'the darling of the People'. Besides 'a sweet temper and beautiful inclinations', she had 'a majestic mien'; 'her extraordinary sense, her greatness of soul and her exemplary conjugal affection . . . raise her character to the highest degree'.[48] Baby Caroline upset plans by being unwell and had to be left with Fritzchen for the present. Caroline said good-bye to this bright-eyed young son early the morning she left, thinking their parting cruelly unnecessary. It was October 12th. Nine years had gone since she faced her unknown future at Hanover. With her brother beside her she had driven into electoral history. In his company she passed out of it to see what England held for her.

IV

PRINCESS OF WALES

TEN days after leaving Hanover on her only sea voyage, Caroline sighted the busy port of Margate, whose 'exceeding industrious' natives were 'amphibious creatures; both fishermen and ploughmen, both husbandmen and mariners'. According to the seasons, the seas yielded them up cod, herring, and mackerel for their own use, whilst on the chalky soil at the gates of the town they raised corn and garden seeds for the London market. Then began Caroline's first English journey, through the lush Kent landscape, heavy with offerings of hops and rich green produce, and past towns that had known Roman and Saxon history.[1] At Rochester her exuberant Prince waited with the Dukes of Argyll and Somerset to complete the journey with her. Londoners, inspired with good nature towards this new dynasty for the free shows it provided, packed the streets to greet the smiling family party, bowling past with a fine escort of Life Guards. The excited little princesses bobbing about in the open coach raised delighted cheers.[2] Citizens had known no royal nursery since Charles I's days, for the family of Queen Anne and her Danish spouse were but 'seventeen short-lived evidences of their public zeal and private affection'.

When Caroline arrived contented at St. James's she had seen as much of England as she would ever see. Kensington, Kew, Richmond, Hampton Court, Windsor, and the big houses in their vicinity, bounded her movements henceforth. King and Prince grew familiar with the blessed routes to the coast whence they took ship for the Continent. Sometimes they ventured to Newmarket for the races, or essayed a brief tour in the south-eastern counties. But to the Hanover family, England principally meant the metropolis of London.

The rest of their fertile, lovely kingdom they knew not: the woodlands and coppices; the well-tilled arable land, winding country roads infested with dangers that made travel arduous; the rivers flowing past green rural scenes and lively market towns. All these sights they missed, and, living in London, saw a wonder quite untypical of England. Like an octopus it sucked to itself the best of the country's toil and produce, but distributed its foreign merchandise and manufactures in return. Close on three-quarters of a million people lived or sweated in London. Only Paris could be compared with it for size and wickedness. The unskilled, labouring hordes teemed in odious slums, immersed in toil and crime and procreation. Overcrowded, underfed, denied sanitation and social services, their sorrows and their joys were crude. Gin-drinking, bull and bear baiting, watching death agonies upon Tyburn gallows, gazing at repulsive human freaks exposed for show, these they counted pleasures. No wonder that London mobs were deemed the world's most menacing; but decades passed before people probed for the causes. The trained craftsmen and rich merchants in Wren's new city enjoyed a comfortable sufficiency of life's good things. At the top of the scale, Society glittered in its classical squares and stately mansions set aloof in spacious grounds. Dress, food, and amusement at cards, masques, and theatres loomed large in leisurely lives. A clubbable age sought its news sheets and gossip at coffee-houses. One was either born into this privileged set or remained forever an outcast. Church and Law provided the exceptional few with the means of entering these exclusive portals. And yet at times the polite veneer wore thin.

Caroline met these rare beings for the first time at the Drawing-room on the night after her arrival. As she made her entry at about seven o'clock she knew that their curiosity outmatched her own, but happily she had mastered the technique of public appearances; her timing was usually admirable. An abrupt hush froze the bubbling conversation while batteries of critical eyes were trained on this new Princess of Wales. People took stock of her as the evening passed. They saw her talking easily to those around her; her foreign accent and idiom struck the ear piquantly. Her appearance and alert expression proclaimed her to be no royal marionette. When she settled down at the piquet table, players deserted their basset and ombre to form a gaping ring.[3] Already at the table was redoubtable Sarah Marlborough, with a lifetime of crises and quarrels behind her, and many more to come. Her self-assertiveness was always apparent in the presence of royalty, but Caroline seems to have provoked no aggression that evening, otherwise a Court diarist would have recorded it for posterity. Sarah's scenes always had news value. Caroline retired at 10 o'clock, earning approval for staying so long. The King never outstayed his boredom for more than an hour.

The Court was amused by Caroline's passion for walking. Soon after her coming, one confided to his diary that 'Prince and Princess walked quite round the Park',[4] and another day they strolled from St. James's to Kensington. Physical exercise had not been considered a noble amusement since Charles II's day, but these royal perambulations by the formal Dutch canal or along the avenues of St. James's Park quickly became fashion parades so that Prince and Princess could scarcely move for crowds. A harassed official urgently minuted for money for gravelling the paths which suddenly had to carry so much illustrious traffic. But soon Caroline complained that the Park 'stank of people' and took her walks round by Kensington.

Caroline's first task was to choose her household. Far-seeing ladies had corresponded with her for years past, offering their services in hopeful humility. Now humility was not so perceptible as fawning and back-biting. The King had experienced such importunity that he considered his new subjects the most grasping people in the world. The great Marlborough, a bad offender, was one day astonished by his Sovereign inquiring whether the Archbishop of Canterbury had no relations. 'Certainly he has,' was the puzzled reply. 'Queer,' murmured the King, 'he was two hours with me and asked me for nothing.'[5] Caroline redeemed a promise made by the Electress in appointing debonair Mrs. Howard a woman of the bedchamber, for that lady had long ago turned towards the rising sun of Hanover to improve her fortunes. Lord Chancellor Cowper's wife obviously ached for a place. She had been one of the wise correspondents but now hid her hopes under a pious resignation. Caroline ended her suspense by beckoning her up at a Drawing-room and saying, with a twinkle in her eye, that M. de Bernstorff, one of the King's principal German ministers, 'who was never in love in his life before,' had succumbed to Lady Cowper, so that Caroline had entrusted him with a message for her, which proved to be her appointment as a lady of the bedchamber.[6] Lady Cowper soon made herself an indispensable member of the household. She kissed hands upon her appointment; and 'the Princess when I had done it took me up and embraced me three or four times and said the kindest things to me far beyond the value of any riches'.

Caroline had gained one good friend, and made another of Mrs. Clayton, whose practical mind fitted her to become Caroline's informal secretary. They shared a taste for theological discussions, and together followed Church affairs. Lady Cowper and Mrs. Clayton were cronies, the sedate couple who disapproved of the giddy parties that went on in Mrs. Howard's rooms, where the twelve sprightly maids of honour gathered. Caroline smiled upon their pranks. Their high spirits drew young wits to her receptions and kept the Prince amused. The men could never decide whether Mary Bellenden was lovelier than Molly Lepel, and permitted themselves agreeable verses dwelling upon their perfections. The Prince plumped for Mary, while Molly's subtle charms impelled Voltaire to compose a polite trifle in her honour, depicting himself as the languishing lover.

The Coronation took place on October 20th, within a week of Caroline's arrival.[7] There being no Queen, neither Caroline nor the peeresses walked in the procession, but from her place in the Abbey she watched all England's power and wealth assembled to crown a German King, who needed to have the rites explained to him in hoarse whispers of indifferent Latin, causing it to be said that much bad language passed that day. When the crown was set upon the Sovereign's head, the peers put on their coronets and acclaimed him so vociferously that astonishment momentarily displaced the boredom on his features. It was four o'clock when the crowned King returned to Westminster Hall for the final spectacle. Three hours elapsed before he had done with feasting and reached St. James's, a weary man. Afterwards a notice in the *London Gazette* lamented that 'several Pieces of Plate, as Dishes, Trenchers, Plates, Knives, Forks, Spoons, Salts together with Pewter of all Sorts which were provided for His Majesty's Coronation Feast have been taken away from thence and are yet concealed',[8] and the souvenir hunters were urged to return their trophies. Though the day passed off peacefully in London, except for accidents resulting from two stands collapsing, there were Jacobite riots in several big towns.

Caroline first visited the City on Lord Mayor's day* when every citizen turned out to indulge his love of pageantry. Civic dignitaries forgot for a few brief hours that those bustling upstarts, the Bank of England and the East India Company, were undermining their importance. As the Royal family watched the processions from a Cheapside balcony they appraised Wren's new city; the

* October 29th, until the adoption of the Gregorian Calendar shifted it to November 9th.

72

neat tall houses set back in broad streets, paved for walkers, and here and there slender steeples rising skywards, with St. Paul's dome riding majestically above them all. The King offered to knight his linen-draper-host of the balcony, and looked incredulous when that worthy refused the honour because he was a Quaker. At Court, perpetual squabbles raged for every vacant office, while here was a man who rejected knighthood. He and Caroline had been told that the Lord Mayor had borrowed a wife for the day.[9] This hired Lady Mayoress appeared at the banquet decked in black velvet and looked annoyed when Caroline did not salute her with a kiss. Caroline's ladies had long debated this thorny point of etiquette. Lady Cowper with some difficulty convinced the King that of course their hostess was the Lord Mayor's proper wife. Those who said differently were only joking. Though he could not imagine why people thought it funny to mislead him, he could well believe that the good Lord Mayor, if he had set about borrowing a wife, would have chosen a more beautiful lady.

A spate of entertainment ended with the celebration of the Prince's birthday next day, when every courtier appeared in new clothes. The Prince opened the ball with Caroline, who 'danced in slippers very well'.[10] That she chose low-heeled shoes rather than the spiky, wooden-heeled variety was characteristic. She appeared finely dressed at big functions, as every one agreed, and her presence gave them the distinction they lacked under gouty Queen Anne, but she never aspired to be a leader of fashion. Caroline wore her hair simply dressed, falling to the shoulder in two slender curls. For public occasions she decked her stiff, low-cut bodices with glittering gems. Her waistline was disciplined by severe whaleboning in the habit of the time. It remained obediently trim long after her figure had changed from slim to fine. Skirts, gathered up in side-bunches, exposed to view the gorgeous petticoat, chief adornment of feminine costume. Caroline preferred hers made from bold flowered silks; often choosing a white ground big-patterned with gold, silver, or bright devices. Sleeves billowed lightly to the elbows in foamy lace or muslin flounces. The patch, the fan, and the paint pot were indispensable aids to feminine allurement, though Caroline eschewed the first and used the others sparingly. Like the late Queen of Prussia she took snuff. Out of doors women donned hooded red 'cardinal' cloaks, or for riding affected saucy adaptations of masculine dress, set off with rakish three-cornered hats. In a colourful world, men outspent their wives to enhance the gay picture. They paid anything from £30 for their full-bottomed wigs, which presently gave place to the neater bag-wigs, and pig-tailed variety. They spent fabulously on lace cravats, loose-knotted round the neck; on ceremonial swords, which came to be worn less; and on diamond-studded, square shoe buckles. Frilly-fronted muslin shirts peeped over waistcoats of many colours and lovely patterns, ending a few inches short of knee-length coats, with enormous turn-back embroidered cuffs. For show, men exhibited the ribbon and badge of the highest Order they possessed; they used snuff-boxes for effect; and for making gallant gestures carried their three-cornered hats indoors with them.

As workaday life ousted festivities, Caroline planned her

time wisely. To achieve the success she hoped for, she perceived she must appear as English as possible; observing certain conventions without losing her easy manners. She saw that these scornfully insular people despised foreigners, resented condescension and disliked familiarity. The difficulty of securing their critical approbation appealed to her. Pious Queen Anne had spent much time over church observances. It seemed that her subjects, though not over-religious themselves, judged hers a fitting example, and deplored His Hanoverian Majesty's contenting himself with a weekly appearance at rites which he understood imperfectly.[11] His unemployed chaplains grumbled at their few opportunities for delivering rousing sermons. Neither could Caroline persuade the Prince to do his duty more often, though she herself regularly attended morning prayers, and her behaviour at Sunday services was judged the 'devoutest in the world'.[12] It was only later that her bad habit of talking during prayers developed.

Just a month after her arrival, Dr. Samuel Clarke, Rector of St. James's, Piccadilly, called at the Palace and presented her with his works.[13] The doctor was a learned and delightful person, but one of his books, called *The Scripture Doctrine of the Trinity* made the orthodox murmur of heresy.[14] In it he maintained that the Father alone was supreme God. Rejecting the Athanasian Creed's elaborate interpretation of the Trinity, he saw Jesus rather as the Messiah; he stressed the reasonable, rational aspects of religion and passed lightly over all dogma and supernatural phenomena. Worse, he later prepared a revision of the Prayer Book, deleting the offending Athanasian and Nicene Creeds, and re-phrasing all passages which accepted the triunity of the Godhead.[15] This was Caroline's new mentor. Three days after his visit, she exclaimed, whilst discussing clerical personalities with High Church Lady Nottingham, 'Here's Dr. Clarke shall be one of my favourites; his writings are the finest things in the world.'[16] Shocked Lady Nottingham replied that his latest works were tainted with heresy. Mrs. Clayton and Lady Cowper intervened to snub the High Church hypocrite, by bidding her quote offending passages from his works. 'Not I indeed. I dare not trust myself with the reading of such books,' was the lame reply. No wonder that the Bishop of London thought it his duty to wait on Caroline with an offer to explain anything she did not comprehend about the established religion. Nettled by his tactless way of stating the purpose of this visit, she bade Mrs. Howard 'Send him away civilly: though he is very impertinent to suppose that I, who refused to be Empress for the sake of the Protestant religion, don't understand it fully.'[17] Dr. Clarke continued her regular visitor, one day bringing with him Sir Isaac Newton to expound his philosophical system. Caroline had already acquired Lord Bacon's complete works. Nor did she relax her efforts on behalf of her old friend Leibniz, but she could not shake the King's resolution to keep him working in Hanover.

Caroline never let her private activities encroach upon what she rightly conceived to be her duty of seeing and being seen by as many people as possible. She could not undertake public engagements with the King unwilling, but she held regular Drawing-rooms, admitted company before dinner and kept an informal circle in her apartments when she did not go out. Then there were always tables for basset and piquet, which latter game she preferred, though she enjoyed an occasional gamble at hazard, and was not squeamish over high stakes.[18] These gatherings allowed her to chat easily with her guests, discovering their several tastes; and to inspect the rarities which were soon offered for her opinion. When the King and Prince were not due at their customary and separate supper parties, they appeared briefly in her rooms.

The King counted on his supper contacts to compensate in some measure for his unsociable habits, and so he behaved affably, saying a 'world of sprightly things', and applauding the Italian Duchess of Shrewsbury's jests, which often exceeded the 'bounds of decency'. But such occasions did not atone for disinclination to see company during the day. He ate, worked, and slept in his bedroom and the adjoining cabinet, served at table by his Turkish pages, at toilet by his German valets, and at business by his faithful trio, Bernstorff, Bothmer, and Robethon.* His English officials drew their salaries but kicked their heels in dissatisfied idleness.[19] Men could only see him by appointment, which invested the meeting with formality. Latin was the conversational medium with those of his ministers who spoke no French. Though the Prince and

---

* Baron de Bernstorff, formerly Hanoverian Prime Minister, continued to enjoy the King's chief confidence until 1720. His open contempt for the political capacities of the English made him hated. Count von Bothmer was the sagacious diplomat who had ensured the King's peaceful accession. Continuing after 1714 in the mainly ornamental post of Hanoverian envoy to St. James's, he concentrated on foreign affairs. He lived and died at No. 10 Downing Street. The Huguenot Jean de Robethon served the King as that enigmatic character, the ideal private secretary, whose superiors owed him more than he let them guess. His official papers, divided between the British Museum and Hanover, bear witness to his quiet but pervasive influence.

Caroline had their German friends like the Countess of Bückeburg, Augustus Schütz, one of the Prince's staff, and Phillip von Hattorf at the Hanoverian chancellery, they kept them discreetly in the background, letting their English lords and ladies perform the duties they were paid for. Lady Cowper at the end of her first week's waiting expressed herself as 'so charmed with' Caroline's 'good nature and good qualities, that I shall never think I can do enough to please her'.[20] Courtesies such as standing sponsor at christenings, and presenting the Huguenot church with a set of Communion plate, disposed the nation to feel warmly towards the first Princess of Wales it had known for many centuries.

Playgoing ranked chief amongst the royal recreations, though the stage did not merit such advertisement. The King stole off twice a week to Drury Lane or Lincoln's Inn Fields, and peeped at the players from the back of a private box.[21] The Prince and Caroline went less often, but even when they saw the same piece on the same night as the King, it was observed that His Majesty evaded them. Amongst the earliest plays Caroline saw were *The Tempest*; Betterton's comedy *The Wanton Wife*, which she liked as well as any, it being 'not more obscene than all comedies are'; Addison's acclaimed but mediocre tragedy of *Cato*; a farce called *The Emperor of the Moon*; and a play dedicated to the Prince, not inaptly, since it was entitled *The Wonder, a Woman keeps a Secret*.[22] They also visited the opera, then wilting under a severe attack of Italian pieces, starred by Farinelli and Niccolini, over whose rival merits ladies provoked fierce arguments. Handel had been in England since 1712. Though Caroline

KING GEORGE I, AND THE PRINCE AND PRINCESS OF WALES

(*From a print by J. SIMON*)

was his faithful supporter, later prevailing upon her economical Prince to pension him £1,000 a year, his operas
waned in popularity after some initial successes, with the
gratifying result that he turned to oratorio. The King's
lack of English caused the theatre proprietors to concentrate upon spectacles that pleased the eye; on dances,
farces, decorative effects, pantomime, and 'other things
which divert the senses more than the mind'.[23]

Londoners often saw their Prince and Princess out on
the Thames in a stately, multi-oared barge. Sometimes
the young princesses were taken with them to see the busy
river traffic. Since London Bridge made the only span
across the river, citizens daily used the tiltboats plying
between the banks. It was exciting to watch small craft
shoot under one of the bridge's narrow arches, because
the current at the change of tide piled up the waters so
high, that calm judgement was needed for a safe passage.
Above bridge, placid green turf of the riverside palaces
edged the banks. Below bridge glided the endless procession of merchant craft, 'a continued forest of ships of all
nations, the surest proof of the opulence of the city'. The
Prince and Princess generally chose the smooth delights of
a river passage to Hampton Court or Richmond Lodge
in preference to the bumpy country roads. Once the rich
young Duke of Newcastle offered in their honour 'a very
fine cold treat of above 80 dishes' upon his newest twelve-
oared barge.[24] His guests ate to the strains of the orchestra
from the Haymarket Playhouse, and afterwards attended
a ball at his house in Lincoln's Inn Fields.

When the new Parliament met in March 1715, the
Whigs rejoiced in a fat majority. Caroline and two of her

little girls watched the Prince take his seat in the House
of Lords. Clad in his robes, he walked behind Lord
Chancellor Cowper and his new friend the Duke of
Argyll, who bore his crown on its stately velvet bed. After
his writ of summons and patent as Prince of Wales were
read, he was placed in a chair to the right of the Throne
with his family beside him.[25] His treasurer, the efficient
but uninspired Sir Spencer Compton, was chosen Speaker.
At the State opening the Lord Chancellor read the King's
Speech while His Majesty sat dumb in all his panoply.
Then the Commons hunted down their Tory quarry.
General Ormonde, Lord Oxford, and the Earl of Bolingbroke were impeached for high treason while the less
guilty Stafford escaped with 'high crimes and misdemean-
ours'. Mercurial Bolingbroke's nerve failed him. He fled
the country into the Pretender's camp; which was what
the Whig Government hoped the others would do, for
there were signs that the country disliked this violence
over such an old score as the Treaty of Utrecht.

The only semi-official duty permitted the Prince and
Caroline was to receive the foreign ambassadors or depu-
tations come over to compliment the King on his accession. Alas! these honeyed descriptions of their merits
signified little. The Dutch Ambassadors, being firm
Protestants, extolled Caroline to the skies. 'In your most
tender years you despis'd with so much courage and firmness those dazzling grandeurs which combated the duties
you ow'd to conscience that there's nothing too great
for the Protestant religion to expect from so noble a soul.'[26]
Amidst the flow of superlatives the uneffusive King was
hymned as 'the prop of empire, and the world's delight',

or greeted 'Hail, happy genius of the British Isle'. The Prince's growing dissatisfaction was a little stemmed by being nominated a Governor of the South Sea Company, a parcel of whose lucrative stock he had acquired. The Company named its first ship *The Royal Prince* in his honour and fêted him on board her.[27] When, a few years later, the second ship bore the King's name, His Majesty was also elected a Governor. Then the Prince lost his taste for business and resigned his post.[28]

For the English crown had worked no miracle upon the family animosity. The King remained like an iceberg. If he could not avoid being in the same room with the Prince, he ignored him. Fading, too, were those visions of career and power that cheered the Prince before he left Hanover. When the leading Whigs had urged him to come to England, he and Caroline had supposed that they liked him personally. Consequently he was aggrieved to find them as ready as the German ministers to lend approval to the King's usage of him. There was little that even a cordial sovereign could give his heir to do in these times, which antedated the monarchy's conscientious round of public duties, but ministerial tact and some harmless State secrets would have contented the Prince. Instead, the ministers behaved ungraciously even in small matters. Once Caroline desired of Walpole and Townshend that the husband of her friend Mrs. Clayton should be made Secretary to the Treasury. They received her request politely but it remained ungranted. Presently it emerged that Walpole intended this financial plum for his brother Horatio, which he brusquely told Mr. Clayton, vowing that for all Caroline's influence Horatio should have the place. He forestalled her approach to the King, who normally made the appointment, by obtaining a warrant from His Majesty empowering him to fill the vacancy.[29] Naturally Caroline felt the rival attraction of Tory theories, and an oppressed Heir Apparent saw political opposition as his only outlet.

Two betterments they gained over the bad old days at Hanover: social leadership and an income of £100,000 a year derived from the Civil List. But the King tempered these joys by forcing them to squeeze into St. James's with him. This mellowed brick Tudor hunting-lodge was spatially unequal to the honour of being the chief Royal residence in London. The King's Germans grumbled with cause at its abominable inconveniences, accentuated by two households sharing them. Only after a public quarrel with the King were the Prince and Caroline sent to seek the blessings of their own establishment. None of them liked St. James's any better than Dutch William had done. The King escaped to Kensington or, in summer, to Hampton Court, whenever his affairs permitted it.

As the people perceived their invisible monarch's apathy towards his new country, their tolerance evaporated. They came to look upon him merely as an unpleasant substitute for a popish King. His ugly women friends repelled them. Lanky Mademoiselle Schulenburg, who had been created Duchess of Kendal, was quickly dubbed 'The Maypole', while Baroness Kielmansegge, overtaken by affable corpulence, became 'The Elephant'. Gossip freely credited both these ladies and the chief German ministers with prosperity acquired by selling their influence with the King. In London, the changed temper showed itself by various means, some not without their humour. On St. George's Day, memorable as the anniversary of Queen Anne's coronation, rowdies indulged their favourite pastime of window-breaking. They detained passers-by to give the old cry 'God bless the Queen and the High Church'. Insolent rogues wore habits of deepest mourning for the King's birthday on May 28th, reserving their new clothes for the next day, the anniversary of the Stuart Restoration. The foot-guards thought the shirts issued them as part of their new outfit on the Royal birthday too coarse, so they pitched the offending garments into the King's and Marlborough's gardens. Meanwhile, the British Ambassador's efficient spy system in Paris collected proofs of Jacobite activity. Parliament, forewarned, prepared counter-measures, and the days crept on with increasing tension, until early in September the Earl of Mar set up the Stuart standard at Braemar. The '15 had begun, only to peter out through inept leadership.

The Prince's best friend, the Duke of Argyll, appointed Government commander, had been superseded by Marlborough's former chief-of-staff Cadogan, after an acrimonious exchange of letters with the Secretaries of State over the scantiness of troops sent him. Many thought the episode an ugly manoeuvre plotted by those who distrusted Argyll's friendship with the Prince.[30] As a rich landowner and powerful chieftain, the Duke could secure his Prince docile voters for a Parliamentary Party of his own. Back in London at open enmity with the ministers, Argyll's continued intimacy with the Prince angered the King. Caroline doubted whether the proud, irascible Scot was worth the additional complication in their lives.[31] Not that she loved the Government. She and the Prince deplored its decision to hang the rebel ringleaders when public feeling favoured mercy. The Prince listened to their trials, presided over by the compassionate Lord Chancellor Cowper, who had to pronounce sentence of death.[32] Caroline intervened on behalf of thirty-year-old Lord Carnwarth, who was related to her physician, Sir David Hamilton. Receiving a letter from Carnwarth she was 'much moved and wept', promising her influence if only he would confess, instead of feigning ignorance while his injudicious mother showed herself a violent Jacobite.[33] When the House of Lords, spurred on by Lord Nottingham, passed a petition seeking the King's mercy, the plea could not be overlooked, though King and Ministers were furious at having the final responsibility for the rebels' fate thrust upon His Majesty.[34] Lord Carnwarth and three others were reprieved, leaving two scapegoats. The tender-hearted Tory Nottingham and his relations were dismissed their posts, which, securing them a total of £15,000 a year, should have insured them against feeling pity for rebels.[35] Thus was another step taken towards the evolution of party government.

Caroline's conception of a monarch's function demanded at least his close supervision of affairs. She was so irked to see the King careless of his prerogatives that she scolded him for letting the German triumvirate, plus Townshend, Stanhope, and Walpole direct all business. In her opinion these Whigs were taking the Royal power into their own hands. As long as this process continued she preferred the Tories, who held a more dignified conception of monarchy.

The civil treatment she met with from moderate members of that party strengthened her inclination to their theories. But the King, confronted with the perpetual struggle to understand the piles of documents requiring his consent, gave up the unequal task, and signed them, ignorant of what they enacted, thus allowing great power to pass into the hands of his advisers.[36] Caroline rebuked him for growing lazy: 'Sir, I tell you they say the Ministry does everything and you nothing.' 'This is all the thanks I get for all the pains I take,' he replied blandly, and changed the subject.[37]

The ministers in their turn grew nervous over the rising numbers of the Prince's friends.[38] They also mistrusted public temper, made restive by the impeachments of Tory ministers and seven months of rebellion followed by the severe treatment of the rebels. To postpone the General Election due in 1718 and thus to conserve their own power, they devised the Septennial Act, extending a Parliament's life from three to seven years.[39] Caroline listened to the Commons debating the Bill and was chagrined that it slipped through so easily.[40] Resenting the interest his son's court showed in politics, the King sent Bernstorff to school the Prince and Caroline, who were unrepentant. Once, indeed, Caroline reversed the parts by telling him that she thought him 'an old fool to be led by the nose by Mr. Walpole and Lord Townshend'.[41] He privately urged Lady Cowper to offset the schemes of 'ill people that influence the Prince and Princess by telling her of the Whigs being against the King's prerogative'.

However, with the coming of spring in 1716, the King resolved to visit Hanover, which promised Caroline and the Prince a free summer. He dismissed the Cabinet's

objections to his absence, and Parliament revoked the
stipulation in the Act of Settlement that he must seek its
consent every time he left England. The Prince hoped to
be nominated Regent. Even the seductive prospect of
seeing Hanover could not induce the King to agree to
that without a struggle.[42] Bernstorff and Robethon
shared his distaste for the idea. Not until June did the discussions mature; then the whole month passed in wrangles
and letter-writing, for the ministers and the friends of both
parties busied themselves in the matter, each suggesting
whatever best suited his private schemes; until there were
not two but a score of tempers to reconcile in common
agreement. Marlborough suggested that six other Regents
should act with the Prince, secretly planning to pack this
council with his supporters. But a special committee of
the Cabinet Council found no precedent for this, or for
restricting the Regent's powers.[43] So the King submitted
to the English reverence for precedent by letting his son
act for him alone, but he determined to limit his authority.

The ministers thought that the Prince would be tract-
able but for the headstrong Duke of Argyll. After acrimonious messages between father and son, the King finally
dismissed Argyll and his brother Lord Islay from their
public appointments. The Prince refused to part with his
friend until threatened that the Duke of Osnabrück,
Ernest Augustus of Hanover days, would be fetched over
and named Regent. At last the Prince told Bernstorff
that he had 'resolved to sacrifice everything and please and
live well with the King'. Just to ensure this promised
docility, the King debarred him from making any high
civil or military appointments; from taking decisions over

foreign policy; and from giving the royal assent to such bills as Parliament passed if it met before the King's return. And the Prince was styled 'Guardian and Lieutenant of the Realm', instead of Regent, which title implied great power from its usage in France, where the Regent Orleans ruled for young Louis XV. The King's letter announcing these unwelcome facts ended with the exasperating assurance that his 'regard for his descendants and for possible future dangers to the Crown did not permit him to allow his son such full powers as his confidence in him would have justified'.[44]

Then a holiday spirit asserted itself, and those bound for Hanover took genial leave of their friends staying in England. The King, merry as a schoolboy, spent his last evening in Caroline's apartments. The next morning, July 7th, dawned cheerfully bright, auspicious omen for his trip, and he wasted little of it in smoky London. By ten o'clock he had driven to the Tower and there taken boat for Gravesend, where his yacht awaited him. Bernstorff and Robethon were homeward bound too, but Bothmer, as the Hanoverian envoy to St. James's, remained at his post. Earl Stanhope, Secretary of State for the North, went with the King, leaving Walpole and Townshend to conduct affairs in England. To his military laurels, Stanhope had added a diplomatic reputation since becoming a Secretary of State, so that many people considered him abler than his fellow Secretary Townshend. The Prince accompanied his father on board. Before the assembled company they said cordial farewells, to show that they parted friends,[45] and then a cheerful 'Guardian and Lieutenant of the Realm' returned to London to hold the centre of the stage awhile.

V

STRIFE

Busy months followed for the Prince and Caroline. To be rid of the frigid King was exquisite relief. Responsibility appealed to them as a fresh adventure offering problems to be mastered. They had thought over their policy during the days when it was uncertain whether the Prince would be appointed Regent, but their greatest asset was their determination to make his Regency a success. As soon as London heard that the King had landed in Holland, a Cabinet Council assembled to hear the Prince's Commission read. The ministers felt the contrast between the King's apathy and the Regent's briskness. Because he spoke English, Cabinet meetings proceeded with greater dispatch under his chairmanship. The Cabinet met on the same day each week and the Dutch mail day was altered to fit in with it.[1] The Prince studied his papers assiduously. 'I am not sure they are not more for the people's perusal than his own', Walpole commented suspiciously.[2] 'We are here chained to the oar and working like slaves' he wrote to Stanhope in Hanover. But both he and Townshend were pleased by the civil treatment that the Prince and Caroline accorded them.[3] The Prince's dislike for them had proceeded from their serving his father so well as to neglect him, but when he found them helpful he modified his feelings. They faced the

difficulty of steering a middle course between courting
the Prince too much and thus offending the King, and too
little, thus leaving the way open for the Tories to gain the
Prince.

Once the Prince had acquainted himself with his work,
it was needless to wilt in London envying the King his
sylvan joys at Herrenhausen. Caroline wanted country
air because she was hoping for another son to keep her
three little girls company. One fine morning towards
the end of July, the family party crossed the river to Lam-
beth and there took coach for Hampton Court. Sheltering
in parklands, it was the perfect country palace. Regal
avenues converged upon the grounds. Wren's scarlet-
bricked east front stared out upon a formal, semicircular
garden. There primness reigned in walks, grass plats, and
queer-shaped beds tricked out with dwarf box, which
traced a profusion of twists and twirls and stops. A dozen
stiff little fountains spurted each a single jet skywards, and
father fountain spurted a bigger one. Northwards lay the
'wilderness', one corner of which contained the maze.
Round the gardens flowed the Thames, and pleasant riverside walks led to the bowling greens.

Caroline and the Prince lodged in Wren's wing, built
for William III. Its suite of State apartments looked on
to the Great Fountain garden and parks beyond. A year
ago Sir James Thornhill had decorated the Queen's State
bedroom, an imposing apartment thirty feet high. On the
ceiling he painted Aurora rising from the ocean in her
golden chariot, surrounded by the usual obese cupids and
attendant figures. In the cornice above the bed, a portrait
of King George hovered like an evil genius, facing his

grandson Frederick above the window. Caroline and the Prince looked at each other from the remaining walls. For his labour Thornhill was paid at the rate of £3 11s. a yard 'including all gilding, decorations, and history painting'. This crude method of reward earned him £475 10s.[4] The Queen's Gallery next door was eighty feet long and twenty-five feet wide, with seven superb windows that reached nearly from ceiling to floor.

The anniversary of the King's accession on August 1st gave occasion for an opening flourish to the stay at Hampton Court. The Prince and Caroline entertained vast congratulatory crowds at dinner. Surrey's Grand Jury travelled from Kingston to pay its respects.[5] The bailiff of Kingston had gone to Hampton Court a Tory: pictures of Ormonde and Sacheverell decorated his parlour walls. But he was so delighted with the princely reception that when he came home he took them down immediately and removed them to his 'repository of excrements'. A wonderful tribute to royal affability! Country folk wandered in the Palace gardens as they pleased. During her walks, Caroline often stopped to 'talk to a country lass in a straw hat, with the same gracious air' that she showed towards 'persons of the first distinction'.[6] These good subjects jostled each other for the best places to watch the Court at dinner. Though their Royal Highnesses tired of an exhibition savouring of meal-time at the Zoo, their patience was repaid by the gapers returning home 'wonderfully pleased' by the free access. The Prince organized races for the girls of the neighbourhood. Winners gained a smock, quilted petticoat, or sarsenet hood for their fleetness and losers were consoled with ten shillings and a pair of scarlet stockings. The sports ended with a free treat of biscuits and wine.[7]

In the morning Caroline and the Prince went on the river in crimson-decked barge, or, when energetic, he hunted the stag. After dining in public Caroline spent her afternoons quietly, while her maids of honour frolicked with their beaux. On cool evenings she walked long in the gardens, then strolled to one of the pavilions by the bowling-green for games of ombre or loo which kept her till past ten o'clock. Those who were not in attendance made up gay parties in Mrs. Howard's rooms. Two hardships these lazy young maids of honour complained of, 'l'excès des promenades et d'être obligées de monter si haut pour venir à leurs chambres'.[8]

To their surprise the Tories met with friendliness when they ventured to Court.[9] Since 1714 they had been treated as traitors, this ensuring that they should not be considered as an alternative Government to the Whigs. Neither Caroline nor the Prince loved the Whigs well enough to keep up the pretence. They made a point of being civil to men who were equally the King's subjects with the Whigs, hoping to win their loyalty if indeed it were really in doubt. Some of the leading Tories who lived near Hampton Court shyly proffered hospitality to the Prince. Since he always enjoyed festivities in his honour, he accepted invitations from Whig and Tory alike.[10] He graced a dozen or more fine dinners, for the nobility felt proud to entertain the King's son.

The Whigs disliked seeing their spell broken. Like suspicious old women they attached significance to innocent actions. Walpole gloomily prophesied that by Michaelmas 'the company here will be two to one of the King's enemies'. He pointed out that Argyll 'comes constantly to Court, appears in public, and has his private audiences, and not without influence'.[11] Yet was it politics that brought the Duke to Court? Amongst Caroline's maids of honour was one Jenny Warburton, a country lass of good family but not bred up in court ways. She made *faux pas* which amused her companions. They teased her unmercifully about the Duke. What sweeter than 'frizillations' with Jenny at the 'parties of pleasure' and little private balls which he and the Prince organized? In their holiday mood it was doubtful whether the two men discussed any more serious topic than a pretty face. But the matter of how to treat Whigs and Tories was not so simple as Caroline and the Prince thought. Reasonable though the idea was of hoping to attach the Tories to their House, the King was so completely 'King of the Whigs' that their new policy created uncertainty. It angered the King, and gave the Tories hope that Prince and Princess would work against the Ministry when they only intended to show themselves free from party prejudice.[12]

News from Hanover showed the King 'to have forgotten the misfortune that befel him and his family on August 1st,* 1714'. After a few days at Herrenhausen he left to take the waters at Pyrmont, where he was diverted 'by exceeding simple pastimes', 'martial music or the rural sports of peasants and country lasses dancing before his windows'.[13] The end of August found him back at Herrenhausen, in good health, shooting partridges round

* Old Style.

about the estate.[14] Northern politics were tiresome, but Stanhope shared his views, and much might come from France, now hoping for a British alliance.

Caroline envied the King's seeing Fritz. She eagerly questioned people who had passed through Hanover for the latest news of him. 'The Princess sent for me in private and asked me a thousand questions about her little Frederick,' wrote one of them.[15] Lord Polwarth, on his way to take up a diplomatic post in Denmark, stopped three days at Hanover, and admired 'the finest young prince in the world'. The Wortley Montagus, travelling *en poste* to Constantinople, also paused at Hanover, and Lady Mary sent home a glowing description: 'without either flattery or partiality . . . our young prince has all the accomplishments that it is possible to have at his age, with an air of sprightliness . . . or something so very engaging . . . in his behaviour. . . . I had the honour of a long conversation with him (alone) . . . and I was surprised at the quickness and politeness in everything he said.'[16] For a lad of nine these were promising qualities. Through Caroline's insistence, a young Mr. Nichols was engaged to teach him English.[17] With these second-hand impressions Caroline had to satisfy herself. Her own health caused some anxiety, for her pregnancies were often tiresome, and Lady Cowper told Mrs. Clayton in mid-August that 'The Princess has been mightily out of order. She was in great danger of miscarrying. . . . She has taken some things Sir David Hamilton gave her and I hope she is out of danger this time, though I wish she would take a little more care of herself,'[18] thinking no doubt of the long walks that her ladies found so tiring.

Their affability had made the Prince and Caroline so popular that public bodies prepared complimentary addresses, but since they implied criticism of the King, the Prince intimated after the first one that such addresses should be presented to his father, 'so that there will be no more of them'.[19] The Whigs saw in the attempt fresh evidence of Tory machinations to drive a wedge between father and son, and distract those well disposed towards the Royal Family; but there was no reason for supposing that Tories could suddenly command a majority on every town council.

At the end of September the Prince made his first English progress.[20] Setting out on a Monday he came by noon next day to dine with the Duke of Richmond near Chichester. He slept that night in Lord Scarbrough's hospitable home outside Havant. Wednesday brought him to Portsmouth, chief goal of his tour. The civic dignitaries welcomed him and staged a military review for his pleasure before the sailors entertained him. He inspected the shore equipment, docks, magazines, and fortifications. Later he boarded a guardship and bomb vessel. The homeward way took him through Farnham, which turned out the mounted dragoons to salute him, and Guildford was ablaze with lights in his honour. Two nights after he left Portsmouth, Caroline greeted him back at Hampton Court, delighted to hear of the pleasure his journey had given.

She liked the peace and freshness of Hampton Court so well that she wished to lie-in there, but officialdom disapproved. 'The days are getting very short and the roads bad for those who have to come and go and those who stay here find a double *ménage* inconvenient.'[21] Early in October she nearly miscarried and so the Court was detained, to the annoyance of some restive spirits anxious for town comforts. She was well enough to travel by the end of the month. On a 'wonderfully fine morning' in October she left Hampton Court with the Prince and her ladies in their barge and 'nothing in the world could be pleasanter than the passage'.[22]

A week later, on Sunday, November 4th, her labour began.[23] The Prince sat up all night with members of the Cabinet Council waiting for news, but the labour was difficult and morning brought no progress. Thereupon Caroline's ladies urged that her physician, Sir David Hamilton, should take over from the hag-like German midwife who tended her. The Prince would only consent 'if absolutely necessary'. Caroline 'would not hear of it', which was misplaced modesty. French Princesses had preferred trained accoucheurs to midwives since Boucher delivered La Vallière, and made the profession fashionable for his sex.[24] Caroline spent a trying Monday and Tuesday disturbed by clatter in the courtyard below and noise from neighbouring rooms. The Council took fright when she fell into a violent shivering fit. They sent her old friend, the Countess of Bückeburg, to the Prince with their request that Sir David should take charge. The Prince, knowing that Caroline's labours were usually difficult, 'was angry' at it. The insulted midwife caused 'hurly-burly' by refusing to proceed unless the Prince protected her from the English 'high dames' who 'threatened to hang her if the Princess miscarried'. The Prince swore to the astonished Dukes of Bolton and St. Albans, who chanced to enter the room, that he 'would fling out of the window whoever . . . pretended to meddle'. Every one then coaxed and cosseted the old German. Lord Townshend 'ran and shook and squeezed her by the hand and made kind faces at her'. On the Friday, when Caroline was too ill to recognize any one, she bore a dead son. Prudery had cost her a babe and nearly her life. However, she rallied steadily and felt strong enough to read her correspondence two days later.

The King's prolonged holiday was causing ministerial discomfort.[25] The Prince was angered by the prorogation of Parliament, and the King was irritated at being pressed to fix a date for his return or else to increase his son's powers. Walpole and Townshend in London could not share Stanhope's wish for the quick conclusion of an Anglo-French alliance which he had negotiated from Hanover. Townshend's oversight twice failed to furnish the English plenipotentiary with sufficient powers to sign the treaty. Sunderland, a dissatisfied cabinet colleague, had ingratiated himself at Hanover and intrigued against the brothers-in-law. Finally Townshend received a curt dismissal from his Secretaryship of State. He refused the proffered palliative of the Irish Viceroyalty. Tories rejoiced at this proof of Whig disunity, but the Prince and Caroline saw that it boded them no good personally. The King was not grateful for their successful regency.

As his freedom neared its end, the Prince reviewed troops while he had the chance. Two regiments of foot guards drilled before him in St. James's Park, and later he inspected the Princess's regiment of horse, which made such a 'fine appearance' that he nominated it for the honour of guarding the King upon his landing and progress as far as Greenwich.[26] As Prince of many another European house, his love of soldiering would have made him popular, but the English hated militarism. After every war they clamoured for the army's disbandment, regardless of hardships inflicted upon the men in their search for civil employment. Sneering jokes were poked at the Prince for his little weakness. However, he delighted his countrymen by his courage in remaining unruffled when a madman made an attempt on his life at Drury Lane Theatre one night.[27] His assailant was sent to Newgate and the next spring attacked his bedmaker and wounded two warders, whereupon he was removed to the condemned hold and passed out of history.[28] Shortly before this incident the Prince assisted in quelling a fire that broke out in Spring Gardens at five o'clock one morning, and he sent £1,000 to sufferers from another destructive outbreak at Limehouse.[29] A newspaper observed that he was 'truly a guardian' and the year ended with the people feeling more affection for the Royal Family than they had done since the reign began.

In the last days of January an unwilling Elector of Hanover came back again to rule in England. He was met by the Prince at Blackheath. He 'descended from his coach and received His Royal Highness with open arms and took him into his own coach,' which brought them both to London.[30] After this paternal greeting, the King resumed his old coldness towards his son and daughter-in-law. They were aware that he resented their popular regency, but as he declined to discuss matters personally, they could only wonder what tales of their disloyalty he had been fed with.

An uncomfortable spring and summer passed in this state of semi-hostility, so apparent to the outside world that rumours spread of the Prince's looking for a separate house or summer home.[31] But when July came round again the disgruntled party moved to Hampton Court for a holiday which was to contrast sadly with the previous summer's happy interlude. The King himself recovered a measure of 'ease and tranquillity'[32], holding informal dinners, when 'the freer the conversation the more to the King's mind', bidding bowls players finish their game 'by the light of a lanthorn', ending his days by supping with his lean Duchess, and a 'seasonable bedtime'. The uninspiring routine suited Caroline, who was expecting another baby, and preferred the country ease of Hampton Court to St. James's. She felt less nervous of scenes when the Prince could work off his spleen in a hearty hunt. By keeping to their own rooms, they avoided thrusting their company upon the King, whom they never saw until chapel time on the Sunday after their arrival, when they escaped after perfunctory greetings. When the King essayed an innovation by visiting Cambridge and Newmarket in October, she and the Prince returned to London.[33]

Before then they had watched the fissures in the Whig party widen to an ugly gap.[34] Helped by mellow vintages, Stanhope and Sunderland had reconciled themselves to Townshend and Walpole. Divergent ideas of England's northern policy soon caused the friendly intoxication to vanish. The brothers-in-law thought Stanhope had acquired a Hanoverian outlook from his Hanoverian holiday. They gave him only formal support, while some of their followers spoke and voted against his measures. Townshend, the nominal leader of the mutinous faction, was again dismissed. As the firm acted in unison, Walpole resigned next day despite the King's repeated efforts to retain his more valuable services. Four other ministers and a number of their friends departed into opposition. The party schism was complete. In the Commons, the Walpole Whigs exceeded the Tories in enmity to the Government.

The Prince and Caroline distrusted the reconstituted Whig Ministry. Since the King's return Walpole and Townshend had mildly supported the Prince, but their supplanter, Sunderland, maligned him more than any one. Stanhope was the head of the Government, but Sunderland's new favour with the King, and secret league with his mistress, the Duchess of Kendal, and with Bernstorff, made him influential. Distrust of him was general. 'He bought all men as he could get them, some by places, others by promises and many by more secret ways.'[35] The King, however, felt happy because his advisers shared his dislike of the Prince, and in Stanhope he recognized a master of foreign policy. But trouble was brewing. As the mutinous Whigs gathered round the Prince, their natural leader, the ministers grew fearful of his future power.

At Court the situation became ridiculous. Men talked of the King's party and the Prince's party as if they were enemy armies drawn up in battle array. Two households under the same roof could not continue in this mute hostility. Nine months had passed since the King's return when a spark fell, firing pent-up tempers, and people murmured that he had been biding his chance to pick a quarrel. The innocent cause of the wrangle was Caroline's new baby, born on November 9th, 1717. To her great joy it was a boy. No one was 'so transported as the Prince of Wales', who sent to inform the King at Hampton Court of the good news.[36] No personal letter accompanied the message, which gained Carr Hervey, its bearer, £1,000 from the King. However, a duke conveyed back to St. James's His Majesty's felicitations. Two days later he civilly visited Caroline, but repulsed his son's attempted greeting, and so the Prince never thanked him for coming. The parents wanted to call their son Louis, and ask the Queen of Prussia and the Duke of Osnabrück and York to stand sponsors with King George, who should have assented. Louis was his own name, the Prussian Queen his daughter, and the Duke his brother. Perversely he decided to name the child George William, and to appoint the Lord Chamberlain Newcastle and the Duchess of St. Albans as his co-sponsors. The parents felt provoked. Though usage held that the Lord Chamberlain might be a godfather to a Royal infant, there was no positive rule in the matter, and the Prince's dislike of Newcastle was too much common property to have been unknown to the King. The Prince could scarcely preserve a formal deference towards his father. On a rare visit to Court he made his bow and withdrew.

A tense party gathered round Caroline's bed for the christening ceremony, and directly it was over the King left the room. Now, thought the Prince, this odious

Newcastle should hear of his displeasure. Coming close to the Duke, the irate father shook a quivering finger in his ugly face, saying with his foreign accent, 'you rascal, I will find you'. The overwrought Newcastle mistook the German turn of phrase for 'you rascal, I will fight you'. No duellist by inclination, he hurried off to take counsel with his friends.

He consulted Stanhope and Sunderland. There the news should have stopped, because three Cabinet ministers had settled more difficult incidents than this, but no, they must needs confer with Bernstorff. They realized that once he knew, the matter would come before the King, and in telling him made themselves suspect of wishing to embroil the Prince with His Majesty. They had all suffered from the Prince's temper, and he was a thorn in their side politically. Of course the King was informed. He regarded his son's supposed words as a deliberate insult to himself, and he, too, became incapable of dealing with his private affairs. Instead, he summoned a Cabinet Council meeting, thereby investing a trivial affair with needless significance. Report credited him with opening the proceedings in these ominous words. 'If I were in Hanover I would know what to do. Since I have come here to rule according to the laws of this country, I ask your advice in this matter.' The counsellors suggested the obvious course of finding out what the Prince really had said to Newcastle, but now it was hedged about with formality.

Three august officers of the realm, the Dukes of Kingston, Kent and Roxburgh, interviewed the Prince, who was annoyed at being questioned so pompously about words intended for Newcastle alone.[37]   He emphatically but rudely denied that he had challenged Newcastle. Further incensed by the envoys' reception, the King disregarded his son's statement and placed him under arrest.

The town exulted over the scandal. The yeomen in the guard chamber had actually debarred an astonished lady-in-waiting from attending upon the Princess. The King's harshness to his wife made people wonder what he would do with his arrested son, who meanwhile tendered him an explanation and apology. 'If I have had the misfortune to offend His Majesty, contrary to my intention, I crave His pardon and pray Him to be persuaded of the respect with which I am . . . &c.' A further note assured the King that the Prince would show no more resentment to Newcastle. Only a man resolved on punishment would have rejected these overtures. The ministers told the King that the Prince's further confinement constituted a breach of the Habeas Corpus Act, about which the Opposition Whigs would make a fine clamour. So the Cabinet Council met to approve the King's decision to banish his son from St. James's. The Prince heard that he must leave forthwith. Caroline might stay on in complete seclusion if she wished, until her strength returned. They would have regarded their expulsion as a happy release, but the message continued:

It is my pleasure that my grandson and granddaughters remain at St. James's where they are . . . the Princess is permitted to see them when she has a mind and . . . the children are permitted from time to time to go to see her and my son.

A fiendish scheme! The penalty hurt Caroline more than the supposed culprit, but the King was a family despot who prided himself on showing that no slight to his power would go unpunished. The possibility of there being two sides to any dispute never occurred to him. Nor was he unique in demanding absolute submission from his family. All over Europe, fathers experienced the delights of parental omnipotence, plus the hatred it inspired. Peter the Great beheaded his heir. The King's irascible Prussian son-in-law was hardly restrained from following that precedent. But English monarchs had been more tolerant to their families. Charles II was an easy brother and a jovial uncle; James II was no domestic martinet; Anne doted on her fat Danish Prince, and fussed lovingly over the single child spared her until he too died. Consequently the nation resented this German King, with bad morals of his own, chasing his son from his house.

Caroline never considered parting from her husband, although going with him entailed immediate separation from her little family. Already made a stranger to her eldest son, it was agonizing to have the other children taken from her too. Like refugees, she and the Prince crept to the Earl of Grantham's house late one December evening. No sooner arrived there, than she collapsed in a heavy faint, while for two hours the Prince sat and cried like a child, and they both continued ill for some days. Caroline's fainting fits and violent throat pains alarmed the doctors summoned by her anxious host. Her husband subsided with a feverish 'inflammatory distemper, with bumps in his face somewhat like a rash'.

The King determined to forget that such a troublesome person as the Prince existed. Foreign ambassadors were forbidden to visit him if they wished to appear at Court. For the enlightenment of their own sovereigns they received a report which no longer accused the Prince of challenging Newcastle, but only of using 'very injurious language to him'. The King, finding his explanations 'unsatisfactory', and 'having besides, many reasons to be discontented with the Prince's conduct in several other particulars', had revoked his royal privileges. He was denied beefeaters round his chair or coach, guards before his door, salutes and deference of any kind. Members of his household had to decide between continuing in his service and losing their other public or military employment. Though they were staunch, the Prince and Caroline found themselves shunned for a time. Ministers, members of the King's suite, and the polite world, passed by Grantham House. 'Formerly the Prince had his own party, but now he is forsaken,' wrote a diplomat to his colleague. The King rejoiced at no longer hearing tiresome talk of the 'King's Party' and the 'Prince's Party'. But the Duchess of Orleans in Paris thought that he 'would do well to end the matter, for it can only cause a hundred impertinent things to be said, and reopen ugly old stories which were best completely forgotten'.[38] The 'excellent new ballads', quips and jests invented by the nation proved her right.

Men expected the King to rescind his son's banishment soon, and took hope from Bernstorff's visits to Grantham House. When time passed without bringing a settlement, they said that the German's 'harsh, inflexible humour' made it difficult. The Prince could never accept the rumoured terms: a surrender of his patent allowing him £100,000 a year; he was never to act as Regent again, nor to choose his servants without the King's consent. But he forfeited much sympathy when his letters to the King appeared in print.[39] He and Caroline denied complicity in their publication. Some misguided follower might have hoped to gain his master's goodwill thereby; or one of the King's underlings might have arranged the printing as an ingenious way of discrediting the Prince. Men were not over-nice in choosing their methods to trounce an opponent. The King ignored his son's denial, and thought no more about reconciliation.

Freed from an imminent return to St. James's, Caroline and the Prince looked about for a house of their own. They relished the experience after spending thirteen years in communal quarters. For £6,000 the Prince bought Leicester House, a two-storied brick building, separated from the public square by a courtyard, and having a pleasant Dutch garden at the back.[40] Elizabeth, Queen of Bohemia, the Prince's great-great-grandmother, once lived in the house, which was later used as an embassy. By its owner's courtesy, the Prince also bought the adjoining property to gain extra privacy and room. The prospective tenants were amused to think that in the previous reign the neighbourhood had been a haunt of duellists, footpads, and wild young bloods. They took possession in January 1718, their felicity complete save for the separation from the children. A few times the three little girls visited them at Grantham House, but Caroline felt too bitter towards the King to avail herself of his permission to go to St. James's just yet.

By setting up their own household, the Prince and Caroline stole some of the King's early triumph. Very soon the discontented Whigs visited Leicester House. Different causes had produced the Whig and the family quarrel, but the seeds of both were sown during the

Prince's Regency. A Prince sore with the King was the natural ally of politicians enraged with his ministers. Caroline stressed the benefits of association to prevent him from rejecting it in favour of impotent rage and aimlesss intrigue, which came to him more easily than co-operation. The new partners healed their old dislike for one another by the agreeable pursuit of impeding the King's government. The Prince attended the House of Lords regularly, and listened in the Commons to Walpole, whose debating skill, plus his financial wizardry and his knowledge of farming, scored many triumphs. No considerations of patriotism or consistency softened his indiscriminate but effective opposition. The Government was aware that its former colleague was now its most crushing opponent.

Caroline increased the significance of Leicester House by making its social life a brilliant antithesis to the gloomy Court. While the King cleaved to his seclusion, the coaches and sedan chairs, linkmen and footmen, besieged Leicester House bringing their gorgeous owners to her balls, routs, assemblies, masquerades and drawing-rooms. 'The most promising of the young lords and gentlemen of that party and the prettiest and liveliest of the young ladies formed the new court of the Prince and Princess of Wales. The apartment of the bedchamber woman-in-waiting became the fashionable evening rendezvous of the most distinguished wits and beauties.'[41] When they were not entertaining, the hosts went abroad to theatre or opera, splendidly attended. Caroline aimed higher than the popularity of mere numbers. Famous litterateurs like Pope, Gay, Tickell, and Swift (when in London), enjoyed themselves at Leicester

House. After young Lord Stanhope* had perfected himself in Paris as a man of fashion, he joined the Prince's household, and kept the Maids rippling at his witticisms. His dictum about Lady Kielmansegge amused Caroline. 'The standard of His Majesty's taste, as exemplified in his mistress, makes all ladies who aspire to his favour, and who are near the suitable age, strain and swell themselves, like the frogs in the fable, to rival the bulk and dignity of the ox. Some succeed and others burst.' His mockery spared none. His jests at her own expense soon reached Caroline, who told him bluntly, 'You have more wit, my lord, than I, but I have a bitter tongue and always repay my debts with exorbitant interest'.[42] At quieter times Caroline's serious friends visited her. Dr. Clarke came often for discussions, or to introduce a learned colleague. Venerable Sir Isaac Newton lived near by in St. Martin's Street.

Caroline realized that the King held the trump card in the custody of her children. Little Anne's precocious remark saddened her, 'We have a good father and a good mother and yet we are like charity children', which made her hearer ask whether the King never visited them. 'Oh no, he does not love us enough for that,' said Anne.[43] The incident made him see them for an hour, and enjoying the experience he repeated it. But he was bent on showing their parents his rights to their guardianship.

By his command twelve judges were appointed to pronounce upon the matter in January 1718.[44] His royal desire for justice taxed impartiality. Nine judges reported that 'after several conferences and deliberations . . . we are

* Known by this courtesy title until he succeeded his father as 4th Earl of Chesterfield in 1726.

humbly of the opinion that the education and care of Your Majesty's grandchildren now in England and of Prince Frederick . . . do belong of a right to Your Majesty as King of the Realm'. The stern minority quoted examples showing that a King must waive his rights in the father's favour during the children's youth, though their marriage needed His Majesty's assent. 'If any stress can be laid upon History, the case of Richard, son to Edward the Black Prince, will be an instance against the power supposed to be lodged by law in a grandfather.' Richard had lived with his father, who appointed his governors. After the Black Prince died, Richard 'continued with his mother to the death of his grandfather', when he succeeded as King Richard II. Neither did Charles II, as King, exercise any authority over his brother James's two girls. The judges also cited two Acts of Parliament which upheld the father's rights 'against all persons whatsoever'.

Next month, Prince George William, the guileless cause of the royal quarrel, ended his pathetic little life, which was menaced from the outset by a cough. He, too, was made the subject of a grand inquiry to prove that his separation from Caroline had not caused his death. Four physicians and two surgeons signed an account of the autopsy, which revealed an imposing array of defects. In the Robethon papers is a note in a different handwriting appended to a copy of the report, and a commentary signed by the chief physician.[45] The note reads: 'It appears from all this that it was impossible that the young prince could have lived'. Relieved by such evidence, they buried the babe in Westminster Abbey. But Caroline was not comforted.

Her dismay deepened when the King underwent a rare

attack of Anglomania. One of the few Germans in her household was Baroness von Gemmingen, a trusted old friend who stayed on at St. James's as the princesses' governess. The King now dismissed her, appointing the dowager Lady Portland in her place at a salary of £3,000 a year to direct a large staff.[46] Lord Glenorchy became Master of the Horse with an equerry, clerk, and sixteen stable servants under him, but the King decided that separate carriages were unnecessary for his granddaughters, whose household expenses were mounting up. Lady Portland quickly cautioned Glenorchy not to dissipate the money set aside for stable expenses. It must provide essentials for which no allowance had been made. The King had lately created Prince Frederick Duke of Gloucester, and now asked the Prince of Wales to provide the £40,000 necessary for the children's two households.[47] The Prince refused, and in his turn took legal opinion, which sheepishly supported him, having so recently pronounced the King guardian of his grandchildren. He told the King that his greatest pleasure would be to see Frederick complete his education in England. When that event began, he would happily provide for his son.

Lady Portland's vigilant programme for the princesses reassured Caroline, whose own untutored youth made her prize regular instruction, however formidable. By eight o'clock her little girls had dressed, said their prayers and breakfasted. Next they walked, then read for an hour with their governess. An hour for learning by rote and an hour for prayers still separated them from a well-earned dinner. Afterwards they might 'jouer au volonté ou se promener en parlant des choses raisonables' followed by more reading or clavichord lessons from Handel, who gave them rare pleasure in music. If the weather was kind, a second walk ended their day.[48] As a result of this hot pursuit of knowledge, Anne averred that the Duke of Bolton resembled her globe with a blue zodiac above it. On grandpapa's birthday all three little girls danced for him, amidst great applause. Their life glowed with military colour. Motionless beefeaters stood guard, dazzling generals stalked the palace corridors, every common soldier's uniform splashed the scene vividly. When the King went abroad, the guard changed in their honour, and all the stiff statesmen and exotic ambassadors paid them grave court.

Best of all they loved seeing their mother. After those early months of separation she came regularly or, when she could not, sent them little notes addressed to Anne as the eldest.[49] 'I had hoped to see you, but your Father, who sends his love, would not let me come until you have taken your medicine. I await that time impatiently. You know too well how much I love you.' Little Caroline was once in trouble: 'Caroline, I pray you quit your indolence which prevents you from expressing your pretty thoughts and makes you act as if you had neither feeling nor reason'. Anne, on the other hand, received praise for her well-written letters. Indeed, she wrote and spelt better than her mother.

A ma chere Mama,
 La Caroline se port fort bien ce matin et a fort bien dormie, j'espère que vous vous portes bien aujourdhui et que vous seres en etat de venir ce soir ce qui nous fera beaucoup de plaisir. Anne.[50]

Caroline found the Duchess of Orleans a sympathetic confidant during these distressful times. The Duchess had always disliked her phlegmatic cousin, King George, and censured him over the quarrel, fomented, to her thinking, by his Germans. Caroline's shortest letters filled five double pages; her fattest varied between thirty-five and forty-three pages, which kept the Duchess busy deciphering. 'Our dear Princess of Wales is very defective in her spelling, but it is not surprising, since she taught herself to read. I am used to it now, but at first I found it difficult to understand what she meant.'[51] Indeed, Caroline's phonetic French showed a fine contempt for the proprieties. Her rendering of English names was often a pure joy. The royal abodes figured in her letters as Kinsinthon, St. Jemes, Richement and hampthancoui.[52] Lord Hervey became harway; Hereford, herforth; Grafton masqueraded as graffthan. A correct rendering was a surprising exception, but her faults at least gave her style a spontaneity lacking in the sonorous epistolary manner then in vogue.

Relieved of the family holiday at Hampton Court, the Prince and Caroline fixed on Richmond Lodge, 'neat and pretty', as their summer home. After the Civil War, Richmond Palace fell into decay, and the Lodge became the chief residence in the Park. The beautiful views and grounds attracted Caroline. A fine avenue linked it to the town half a mile away, another slipped downhill to the river, which was overlooked by a terrace. 'But, above all, the woods, cut out into walks, with plenty of birds singing, made it a most delicious habitation.' It was not too far from London, though 'footpads know that people return very late from such places, so the roads are very unsafe'. And Caroline felt the charms of Richmond town, which suited eighteenth-century style, tempering beauty with man's handiwork in the most becoming way. Riverside meadows were filled 'with jolly children skipping in them'. The hills 'shimmering in the verdure' showed a sprinkling of elegant villas. 'The pleasant open town' took pride in its trim green, bordered by houses of the best quality. In Richmond gathered men 'of all professions and religions', hospitable alike with their books and their wine.

When the King first heard that the Prince and Caroline fancied the Lodge, he churlishly sent word to Grantham, in whose keeping it was, that it would be forefeit if he lent or sold it to the Prince.[53] His objections were overruled. Early in May 1718 the Prince and Caroline started their first of many summer holidays at Richmond.[54] After six stormy months, Caroline looked forward to the new baby who would compensate a little for the children kept from her. The winter's strain had taxed her more heavily than she realized, and the bustle of moving did harm. One day, less than three weeks after her arrival, a passing storm caused a violent thunderclap overhead. A large elm-tree crashed down near Caroline's window, and her hopes of a baby were shattered.[55]

Fresh surroundings helped her over the disappointment. At the Lodge she played hostess to a merry country-house party. One Mr. Penkthetman quickly built a theatre for the royal diversion.[56] It was in use before the summer ended, and his enterprise gained it at least two royal visits. Caroline's lively Maids of Honour found holidays away from Richmond a dull penance. 'If my Lord Lumley does not send the coach he shall never have the least flirtation more with me—next Wednesday the coach must come or I die,' wrote one to Mrs. Howard, sending her love 'to all the he and she flirts at Richmond'. The Prince was among them, captive to Mary Bellenden's sprightliness.[57] But she would have none of him; and so he suspected a rival, bade her name him and asked her not to marry without his privity. Then he would consent and 'be kind to her husband'. When time was ripe, Mary's wisdom or guile made her marry first and tell afterwards, but the Prince, ever gallant, retained her Colonel Campbell in his service, and sanctioned her own appointment as House-keeper at Somerset House.

The Prince tempered flirtation with more active sport. Caroline did not share his zest for either, but she was grateful for the time to pursue her reading, discussion and correspondence. Her own fresh air she took walking and gardening, which gave scope for her creative faculties as well. She was already noting where her new grounds needed improvement. Her husband's clockwork regularity admitted accurate forecast of his wishes, though she knew the wits joked upon the theme: he did business, ate, slept, even made love to time, they said. This zeal for routine slowly obsessed him until he judged a man by his punctuality. The Prince felt in his element at Richmond, with its parks for hunting and hacking. One fine May day saw him 'ride out to take the air in Surrey', which had such tonic effect that someone complained of hunger, so the Duke of Argyll led the party to an inn on Ham Green, kept by an old servant of his. There they satisfied themselves with 'eggs and bacon and other wholesome fare' to the amount of 5s., but the Prince pressed as many guineas into his host's hand, and left behind him a zealous supporter.[58]

Caroline often went to Kensington that summer. Sometimes she saw the King as well as her daughters.[59] The Press of the day was gifted with the intuition of its modern successor. Bernstorff was credited with visiting Richmond and Lord Hervey was said to have taken a letter to Kensington; the next step, therefore, was to herald the forthcoming reconciliation. One well-informed paper stated that the Prince had offered to pay for his daughter's establishment.[60] No pleasanter corroboration of this optimism is forthcoming than a report, written by or for Mr. Secretary Craggs, upon the King's conditions for peace.[61] The Speaker, Sir Spencer Compton, was selected as an acceptable envoy. He informed the Prince of certain conditions to which the King felt sure he would assent, as proof of submission from a good son. Summarized, they read:

1. To fill no places in his household without the King's pleasure, and to retain in his service no one disagreeable to His Majesty.
2. To sever relations with any one whom the King declared was disagreeable to His Majesty.
3. and 4. To treat the King's servants, particularly the Dukes of Newcastle and Roxburgh, in a civil manner.
5. To acquiesce in the King's right to guardianship of his grandchildren.

The Prince asked leave to ponder these truculent terms, but was given only an hour. When Sir Spencer returned, the Prince expressed anxiety for peace, but not on such terms. Some conditions he judged impossible, others he had complied with already. By accepting the last one he might render himself liable to pay away the whole of his income. In his report, the Speaker declared that the Prince wanted peace, but gave his own opinion that it could never be achieved by signing conditions.

In August the King went to Hampton Court with his grandchildren, and his good humour showed that he did not worry about the failure of these negotiations.

PEACE WITHOUT HONOUR

EARLY in 1719 the Prince and Caroline saw how effectively their political supporters pressed the ministry.
Stanhope and Sunderland felt menaced by a variety of
hostile groups: the Prince's friends; the Tories and Jacobites; and now even the King's German advisers, who
resented the curb lately applied to their influence in English
affairs.[1] Exaggerated fears of the Prince's power in the
future, coupled with the King's alacrity to hurt him,
fathered their strange Peerage Bill.[2] It proposed to limit
the House of Lords to 235 members for ever, so that the
Prince, when King, could not create a single peer. His
father's consent to this curtailment of the royal prerogative
can 'be accounted for', Speaker Onslow suggested, 'by his
. . . suffering himself, from his want of knowledge of the
Constitution, ever to be governed by those he employed'.
Stanhope privately agreed. 'I think we must carry it [the
Bill] now or never, since it will probably never happen
again that a King and Ministry will be for it.'[3] Though the
Bill passed two readings in the House of Lords, public
opinion condemned it. So Stanhope changed his tactics.
He moved postponement of the Bill. The King prorogued
Parliament and soon afterwards went to Hanover, after an
interval of two years. This time the Prince was neither left

Regent nor nominated one of the thirteen Lords Justices appointed to rule the country.

From Hanover, Stanhope told Newcastle that the King would 'not . . . be baffled a second time' over the Bill. When the new session came, it passed the Lords without fuss. The Opposition in the Commons was ready to throw up the fight, convinced that the Government's well-drilled voters always triumphed in the end. Only Walpole's courage saved the Prince from mortification. By a magnificent speech during the second reading, he galvanized support, and the Bill was rejected by a majority of ninety-two votes. Had it become law 'the House of Lords would have become firmly entrenched as a narrow oligarchy, subject to no restraint from King or Commons—a permanent obstacle to progress'.[4]

In the Spring of 1720 the Commons innocently passed the measure that paved the way for that gigantic hoax, the South Sea Bubble. Eager to reduce the public debt, they allowed a plausible financier to pay £7,500,000 for the privilege of taking it over. He incorporated it with the stock of his South Sea Company, expressing his pious conviction that the bottomless riches of South Sea trade would expunge the whole debt within twenty-five years.[5] This triumph, pregnant with disaster, did not relieve the ministers. The King had grossly exceeded his Civil List, and the ministry was functioning like a machine starved of oil. Just then Sunderland discovered a madcap scheme of Bernstorff's to supersede Stanhope and himself by an alliance with the Walpole Whigs and the leading Tories.[6] The King was to be told that his present advisers planned to overthrow the constitution and rule alone or with a

117

puppet monarch. A bad attack of nerves convinced the
ministers that Bernstorff would succeed. Their easiest
counter-stroke seemed to be to win Walpole first.

He responded sympathetically to their approaches, unwilling to fritter away a promising career out of office.
Under the prevailing system the Government usually
found convenient means of renewing its majority at elections. Walpole insisted that the Royal quarrel should be
patched up at the same time as the party schism. This condition was not prompted by sentiment over the past three
years' collaboration with the Prince. He simply wanted
no rival faction to embarrass the Ministry as his own had
done. Stanhope assented, for the royal friction had im-
peded his work. In the privacy of Horatio Walpole's
lodgings, situated in a 'by place', the leaders of both
sections hatched out their schemes, of which no whisper
reached the German ministers. The Walpole Whigs promised assent to the proposals for paying off the Civil List
debts. In return, three of them became junior ministers.
By accepting such meagre reward, they revealed how
pleased they were to cease a stultifying opposition. Stanhope and Sunderland congratulated themselves on out-
witting Bernstorff at an easy price. Each section agreed to
persuade its respective royal master to make peace with the
least possible fuss.

During the past winter Walpole had often visited
Leicester House and so had been the first politician to
realize the importance of Caroline's good will. To her he
now turned for co-operation. She was delighted to hear
his plans for peacemaking. In three years she had changed
her opinion of Walpole. She applauded his political

ability, which had gained her husband's followers more
tactical advantage than their obstructive policy deserved.
She suspected that the Prince by himself would have pursued a querulous course. Walpole too, had helped them
to a neat fortune out of South Sea stock, expatiating
meanwhile upon the financial unsoundness of the scheme,
from which he extracted fat sums for the glories of
Houghton. Lady Cowper, piqued by his upstart success,
thought that he 'engrossed and monopolized the Princess
to a degree of making her deaf to everything that did not
come from him'.[7] Walpole and Caroline agreed that the
Prince had better know nothing about the proposed reconciliation for a time. If he were to lay down impossible
conditions he would wreck negotiations. Walpole bluntly
justified their desertion of the Tories by saying that they
would accept a similar chance without scrupling to let the
Prince and Caroline benefit from their good fortune. The
argument told Caroline that Walpole's own motives did
not spring from purest charity; but desiring her children
back above everything else, she rated the royal reunion as
the most important part of the double reconciliation.

The King could not see why he must forgive his impertinent son. He had been at peace since the Prince's disgrace. Could not the Whigs come back without him?[8]
He was told that they would not. But by giving back
the Prince his beefeaters, his guards, and his children, the
most trifling concessions, he would have his debts paid,
gain Walpole's services and leave his son politically impotent! Meanwhile Caroline prepared her husband for
graceful submission. A mere formal apology would secure
him the satisfaction of placing his friends back in power,

the return of all his royal privileges and a tactical advantage with the King by his magnanimity in agreeing to the debt settlement.

The Prince shied at first at apologizing; and live at St. James's again he would not. Discussions dragged on for a fortnight. The King had never been so short-tempered. In an 'intolerable humour' he grumbled to Sunderland, 'Did you not always promise to bring me the Prince bound hand and foot?'[9] And he refused to part with his grandchildren, secure in the verdict which awarded him their guardianship.

Only one thing mattered to Caroline. 'You will hear of me and my complaints every day and hour and in every place if I have not my children again,' she told Walpole.[10] Her advisers' divided counsels made her course perplexing. Lord Cowper had been excluded from the secret Whig meetings because his integrity made him an uneasy companion in political manœuvres. Caroline insisted on his being told when the tentative proposals had assumed definite shape, because she valued his opinion and had no thought of discarding old friends. Both the Cowpers advised her to hold out for her children openly. Unless she regained them 'she would never have a faithful friend again nor be thought a good mother'.[11] Walpole favoured subterfuge and indirect pressure. He averred correctly that the King was 'inexorable if ruffled', and told Lord Cowper that he hoped presently to gain the children through the Duchess of Kendal's interest. 'She was in effect as much Queen of England as any one was.' The King's consent could be secured on grounds of economy, while harmless intimidation over a pension would persuade Lady Portland to resign her charges gracefully. Walpole, as the pivot of the peacemaking, held the advantage. Caroline saw the difficulty of changing his point of view. If she ignored his advice, and the negotiations failed, she would never get her children.

So the work of appeasement continued. The Prince was a little mollified by being excused from returning to St. James's, 'the true reason being because the King won't bear it—so 'tis artfully made a merit to the Prince to be suffered to stay where he is'.[12] The ministers prepared a respectful letter for him to send to the King. Then Walpole was left a clear field because little Princess Anne caught small-pox, and anxious bedside vigils diverted Caroline's thoughts from the complicated situation. The letter was finally drafted and the Prince pushed into signing it, and Lord Lumley hurried with it to the Palace. Permission came back for the Prince to wait upon his father forthwith. Walpole relaxed. He had triumphed in every particular.

The King was in his most ungracious mood. Replying to his son's expressions of sorrow he only muttered '*votre conduite, votre conduite*'. In five minutes the interview was over, and the Prince went to see his little girls before returning to Leicester House. The manner of that home-ward ride atoned for his father's cold reception. Beefeaters marched round his chair, and the crowds roared their pleasure over the royal reconciliation, which seemed more significant to them than the Whig party's reunion. Long months had passed since such a demonstration cheered the Prince. He arrived home red-eyed and grave as was his wont when particularly affected. The day passed joyfully. 'Guards before the door and square full of coaches; the

rooms full of company; everything gay and laughing.'
Lady Cowper offered her felicitations a trifle starchily but
the Prince gleefully imprinted five or six kisses on each
cheek, 'his usual heartiness when he means sincerely'.
'So, I think you two always kiss upon great occasions,'
Caroline laughed.[13]   All over the country the people made
merry upon this happy peace. One loyal captain 'testified
his zeal at the expense of his sobriety; for he was not satisfied to make his men drunk, but got drunk himself . . . he
celebrated the news in a manner that alarmed the country
people for he made them ring the bells all day and in the
evening made his troops draw up before his lodging . . .
and began the King and Prince's health . . . at every health
he made his troops fire a round of shot'.[14]

Next morning, a Sunday, the reinstated Whigs had an
audience with the King, who replied barely audibly to
their spokesman's greeting. Neither before nor after
chapel did he exchange a word with his son, but he saw
Caroline for over an hour that evening, while in an outer
room his Turkish page Mahomet regaled Lady Cowper
and Lord Grantham with stories of his desperate grief over
the death of his sister, Queen Sophia Charlotte of Prussia.
Caroline told every one 'how mightily kind he had been
to her'.[15]   But the King drily replied to his daughter the
Queen of Prussia's congratulations upon the Prince's
submission:

> Thank you for all the obliging compliments you make me upon
> my son's submission, which would have been better for coming
> sooner and without the persuasion of the party, which is also
> reconciled.[16]

The Prince led his household to the Drawing-room on

Monday night. The terrifying Lady Essex Robartes stood in the royal circle as they entered, so 'they all kept at the bottom of the room for fear of her, which made the whole thing look like two armies drawn up in battle array'. Though the Prince behaved 'prodigious well' the King only condescended to an occasional angry glance in his direction.[17]

Young Lord Stanhope informed Bernstorff and Bothmer of the peacemaking that had shattered their schemes. He piped, in the shrill treble which was his secret humiliation, that the Prince was expected at Court any minute to interview his father. Nettled by the surprising news, and the casual way it reached them, Bothmer said coldly: 'Monsieur, vous avez été bien secret dans vos affaires.' Stanhope replied unfeelingly: 'Oui, oui, nous l'avons été . . . le secret est toujours nécessaire pour faire les bonnes choses.'[18] Bothmer, who 'could not bear the insult of being given up by his old master, burst into tears'. Bernstorff plainly showed 'the great anxiety and anguish he was under'.[19] His hopes of retrieving favour by another swing of the political pendulum proved baseless. When the King next went to Hanover, Bernstorff went too, remaining there some years. There was pathos in the defeat. The King owed his peaceful accession largely to the devoted work of his German ministers. In 1714 they found themselves involved in a constitutional experiment beset with problems. Accustomed to the chief influence with the King, these trained diplomats would have needed a saint's resignation and a Solomon's wisdom to have handed over their authority to Englishmen who seemed crude amateurs by comparison. But disaster came from their foreign outlook and alacrity to sell their influence. The English revelled in their insularity and preferred to keep their bribe-money circulating in the country.

Exuberance marked the ministerial peace; 'great hugging and great kissing between the two old and the two new ministers. They walk all four with their arms round one another to show that they are one.'[20] And at first the Prince was satisfied with his regained privileges. Caroline's work was so neatly done that he imagined the peace was due to his unaided efforts. 'And now', he told Lady Cowper one day, 'I have the comfort of having done well; for if in this I had given up my friends, by G—— it had broke my heart . . . but now I can bring my friends in with honour. We have drove them to this peace.'[21] His generosity over the King's debts pleased him. 'Since he had helped to do this' he expected 'the same to be done for him when he is King.' 'To what purpose will be the fixing of the Civil List after this example?' Lady Cowper righteously asked herself.[22]

But his joviality dimmed as the months slipped by without giving him the influence which he thought he deserved. The King's frigidity he could cheerfully support. But he was pained by his friends' evasions over the matter of his being appointed Regent again when the King went to Hanover. Naturally he assumed that he would be named. The time for his father's departure approached, and he was still being fobbed off with excuses. When he did not even find himself amongst the Lords Justices, disillusionment was bitter. That 'great rogue' Walpole and the 'choleric blockhead' Townshend had served him a rascally trick. His old repugnance for the shameless pair was revived. Slowly he perceived the irony of his position. The re-entry of his friends into the party fold isolated him politically. As the forgiven penitent, he was powerless to side with an Opposition composed of open Jacobites and Tories sympathetic to the Stuarts. Possessing no interests apart from sport and a flair for intricate genealogies, his enforced leisure chafed him. That his grumble was legitimate could not ease his frustration, which left its adverse mark upon him. At 37 he had approached middle age, and lost youthful resiliency without gaining a philosophical outlook. Adversity merely soured him. Each year saw fewer glimpses of the buoyant Regent, until in 1727 he emerged as the pompous, petulant little monarch who struts across Hervey's pages like an irascible turkey-cock.

Though the King showed Caroline every politeness, she, too, was angry when she found Walpole's early confidence over getting her back the children had now dwindled strangely. Desultory talks with other ministers advanced the matter no further than their attempts to disclaim the original suggestion of separating her from her children. Vacillation and vague promises were all she could extract from any minister.[23] Bernstorff privately told the Cowpers that the King might allow the princesses to summer with their parents but that he would insist on their return when he came back from Hanover. His forecast was optimistic; the children remained their grandfather's hostages until he died. It seemed that Lady Cowper had written truly: 'Townshend and Walpole have agreed for themselves only, exclusively of all the world.' In fact, they found that they lost their commanding position when they rejoined the ministry in minor capacities. When they saw that the King intended only a formal peace with his son, self-interest showed them the wisdom of exemplary behaviour to avoid being suspected of intriguing against His Majesty a second time.

Caroline ruefully perceived that she would have done better to have acted upon 'the good old English saying, "the less you believe, the less you'll be cheated".' Familiar with at least part of the secret negotiations, she never imagined that Walpole owed the Prince any gratitude for his new office. And his subsequent behaviour exempted her from feeling obligation towards him. She and the Prince had indeed been used as the 'cat's foot' to please Walpole and Townshend. But she found no relief in petulant outbursts, nor did her sympathetic reception of the Prince's complaints necessarily imply agreement. Walpole's trickery revealed a coarse fibre but it also showed an extreme tenacity. For the present Caroline kept her counsel and watched events. The strange, mad turmoil of the next twelve months gave Walpole an opportunity which she saw him grasp brilliantly.

April 1720 ushered in the South Sea Act, the Whig reunion, and the royal peace. But its excitements paled before the summer's thrills and the havoc of autumn. 'South Sea fever' turned the nation into a pack of gullible moneymakers. The Prince, against the advice of Walpole and his treasurer Compton, accepted the Governorship of a copper company whose activities bore no scrutiny. Presently the South Sea Company's directors, concerned for their falling stock, induced the Lords Justices to suppress some eighty-nine shady companies. Before publishing the order, they tactfully sent the Prince word that his copper company figured on the proscribed list, 'which compliment His Royal Highness received very graciously and sent a message to the said company desiring them to choose another Governor'. His honour was saved and his fortune increased by £40,000, but the company went to its doom.[24]

The purgative came too late. 'Fortunes froze and assets melted overnight.' Panic was punctuated by shrieks for vengeance. The King was obliged to curtail his Hanoverian holiday and open Parliament, which forgot that its members' cupidity deserved much of the blame. Sufficient evidence emerged to incriminate four ministers and shake the throne itself. The ministry was finally wrecked by the untimely death of Stanhope, who had not been implicated in the scandal. The public raged against the King's German lady friends and their various nieces, for whose favour the South Seas directors had paid most liberally. One wrathful journalist so far forgot discretion as to proclaim, 'We are ruined by trulls, nay, what is more, by old ugly trulls', and was sent to cool his temper in Newgate. The task of clearing up the wreckage proved insipid after the sport of baiting ministers and directors. But the Bubble, truly named, left no permanent hurt upon the nation. The damage 'was incomparably less than would have been caused by a single campaign or the failure of a harvest'.

Walpole emerged from this madness a national hero. Unheeded he had prophesied disaster, then coolly profited from the gamble, and pursued his course as a junior minister without responsibility for the South Sea Act. When the Ministry was ruined and the King's honour clouded, the panic-stricken nation begged his help. It was the only time in his career that he heard a united appeal for his leadership. He responded with typical coolness, neither railing against sinners nor promising magic cures but devising common-sense solutions to the problems. A year before had seen him a cautious bargainer for minor office. Now he was master of the country. His favour and influence with the King increased steadily during the rest of the reign.

.   .   .   .   .

Matrimony and indiscretion had stolen Caroline's best known Maids of Honour. Beautiful Molly Lepel married Lord Hervey and Mary Bellenden made her impecunious Colonel Campbell a devoted wife. Rash Sophy Howe took a worthless lover. The successors to this trio never attained equal liveliness or beauty, or perhaps it was that once-busy pens had no heart to extol the newcomers. Mrs. Howard remained in the household. Poets, soldiers, wits, and politicians offered this pale goddess their devotion. It was based not on passion or love, but on gallantry. It was a delicate ritual that the exquisites of this age performed with relish. At her shrine rose the incense of friendship offered by Pope and Peterborough, irrepressible Johnny Gay, genial Arbuthnot, caustic Chesterfield, charming Bathurst, and the most famous of deans—Swift. To their bows she swept her lowest curtsy; answered their letters and sighs with easy distinction; never, in short, mistook gallantry for passion or spoilt artistic philandering by a clumsy touch of real feeling.

Fashion approved such playful exercises but also decreed monogamy dull. Any correspondence like Lady Mary Wortley-Montagu's showed how faithfully its dictates were obeyed. Her letters prattled maliciously about the latest love affairs diverting the town. The Prince, incapable of finesse, preferred the second method of being fashionable. Had he not shown his discrimination in pursuing Mary Bellenden? At intimate meetings with Mary, Mrs. Howard had made a discreet third. Possibly her famous tact had softened the young lady's snubs to the Prince and subconsciously aroused his gratitude. When Mary showed herself unkind, the cosy meetings continued with Mrs. Howard as the chief attraction. Sometimes Mary was there too, pleased to be relieved of advances she found tedious. After her marriage 'these visits became uninterrupted tête-à-têtes with Mrs. Howard'.[25] Every evening, the Prince spent three or four hours in her lodgings. Sometimes he paced up and down, watch in hand, waiting for nine o'clock to strike and signal the time for his interview to begin. Soon the Court realized that he had attained his object as a man of the world. Another royal liaison had come to pass.

Perplexed society wondered why Mrs. Howard exposed herself to gossip by such a connexion. She shared no taste with the Prince. No excited flush or coquetry ruffled her serenity to show her in love. Even the Prince seemed better pleased with himself than with her. Many people supposed that desire for power must have been the motive which induced her complacence. Accordingly they courted her with a deference which they hoped would repay them presently. The truth was more prosaic. Mrs.

Howard had many friends but no money, and a dissolute husband who made conjugal life impossible. Her 'Reflections on Marriage' recorded that bitterness had been her only marriage portion. Her reputation needed more for its sustenance than the bedchamber woman's salary of £300. She may have hoped for power from her liaison with the Prince, though her temperament made that unlikely, but she certainly must have expected the profit which Lord Hervey, on Caroline's authority, stated she received. Life on £2,300 a year was a rosier affair than subsistence on £300.

Her friends all noticed her detachment,

> So very reasonable, so unmoved
> As never yet to love or to be loved.

This aloofness, which fitted her to receive their gallantry, also explained her acceptance of the Prince's unplatonic attentions. Schooled by her unhappy marriage, she seemed to feel no need of spiritual union. Since the Prince, for other reasons, left her detachment unassailed, she accepted his advances at their correct value. They lost her no friends. The playful devotion and the gay parties continued. She bought an estate at sylvan Twickenham, near Pope's Strawberry Hill. Her admirers busied themselves in making it the perfect setting for her.[26]

Caroline perceived the reasons for this 'liaison of convenience'. Her husband's gratified preening, combined with the absurd regularity of his visits to Mrs. Howard, told Caroline that passion had little place in their relationship, which simply proved his manliness. A mistress reigned in nearly every European Court. Had not her step-father died from small-pox caught from his? Hanover had been no exception. Caroline's luckless mother-in-law, Sophia Dorothea, became the Prisoner of Ahlden through thinking she might behave as her husband did. Though Caroline knew the Electress Sophia only in her peaceful widowhood, she was familiar with the Elector Ernest Augustus's reputation both in Venice during Carnival time and in Hanover, where the Platens provided his family with successive mistresses. The Electress Sophia had early learnt to cultivate her own interests as an antidote to unprofitable moping; just as her daughter, Queen Sophia Charlotte of Prussia, let intellectual pleasures compensate for King Frederick's infidelity. The only alternative was a spiritless self-effacement.

As a young wife Caroline had not achieved their detachment, so she consulted a wise old statesman, who said that jealousy or scenes were no cure for unfaithfulness, with which many wives had to bear.[27] By ignoring it she would find her own power growing. She took the advice; and legion were the great ladies of a later era who did likewise. But Victorian wives were helped by the convention of reticence on this topic; officially they were ignorant of the 'other woman' and preserved their dignity unimpaired. Reserve being alien to the Prince's nature, he kept no amorous secrets from Caroline, convinced that these indelicate confidences showed her that she ranked first in his affections. Later this made moralists accuse her of pandering to his desires, but Lord Hervey indubitably expressed contemporary opinion when he wrote that Caroline, realizing the Prince's vanity must show the world that he kept a mistress, 'wisely suffered it'.[28] His

131

realistic age neither expended sympathy on virtuous wives nor expected objections from them. 'Only girls or fools' moped over conjugal infidelity, Caroline once exclaimed bitterly, for at heart she could not subdue all jealousy despite her outward calm.[29]

She hated any one bringing the Prince's indiscretions to her notice.[30] Once a nurse to the young Princesses hoped to curry favour by telling Caroline that the Prince had ogled her. Caroline cut short the story and dismissed the woman without the privilege of revisiting the Royal family, which all old nurses enjoyed. Another time Mrs. Howard had just received a *billet doux* from the Prince when Caroline summoned her to attendance. Stuffing it into her bosom, Mrs. Howard went at once. In curtsying, the note, unknown to her, slipped from its hiding-place. When Caroline found it she called Mrs. Howard back, handed it over and coldly bade her to take more care of her secrets in future. She made a note of the men who courted this lady, and they duly saw their mistake, for the wife, not the favourite, possessed the power, which she shared with none. When Mrs. Howard eventually retired from Court, Caroline could not conceal her relief, though she knew that there would probably be a successor.[31]

Her second little family was a great pleasure to her during the seven years that passed between the reconciliation and her husband's accession. In 1721, she gave birth to a fine boy, christened William and later created Duke of Cumberland. At four years old, William started his military career by formal entry as a grenadier in the 2nd Foot Guard regiment. The new recruit, clad in correct

WILLIAM, DUKE OF CUMBERLAND

(*From a print by* J. SIMON)

equipment, did duty at Leicester House. That same year Caroline took him to be installed Knight of the Bath. This Order was re-established because Walpole 'knew the persuasive value of a ribbon as well as a handful of silver'. By then, William had two sisters called Mary and Louise.

Caroline still had no say about Frederick at Hanover. However, the King replied conscientiously to the frequent reports sent him concerning the lad, who was not robust during adolescence.[32] He had several feverish attacks and other ailments that responded to bleedings. He was prescribed a diet of asses' milk and allowed to wear stays strengthened with whalebone, instead of steel which pressed painfully on his nerves. Most perturbing were his recurrent attacks of glandular pain, which made Caroline wonder whether he would be a properly developed man. After his eighteenth birthday in 1725, the King allowed him 8,000 crowns a year for his pocket expenses, and appointed him an adult's household instead of governors. Talk of marrying him to his Prussian first cousin Wilhelmine had begun these two years past. His uncle and aunt of Prussia were anxious for some definite understanding, but King George would not be hurried.

Caroline was interested by a new experiment being tried in England. While Edward Wortley-Montagu was ambassador to the Porte in 1717, Lady Mary sent home accounts of how the Turks 'ingrafted' the small-pox to render it harmless.[33] A minute wound was infected with pus taken from a small-pox sore, to produce a mild attack of small-pox, which gave immunity and rarely proved fatal. 'Everywhere thousands undergo this operation and the French ambassador says pleasantly that they take the small-pox here by way of diversion as they take the waters in other countries,' wrote Lady Mary, who felt enough confidence in the practice to let her doctor, Charles Maitland, inoculate her son. When Master Montagu returned home, Caroline inspected his scratches, thinking how relieved she would feel if her own family could be immunized. Small-pox had killed both her father and stepfather and nearly stolen her Anne. In England it claimed about seventy-two victims in every thousand of the population, and disfigured scores of others. When Maitland successfully inoculated little Miss Montagu in 1721,[34] a few daring spirits submitted to the operation, but most people thought Lady Mary an unnatural mother. Clergy discanted upon the impiety of meddling with the ways of Providence. Doctors foretold fatal consequences.

Caroline, however, was unperturbed by the clamour and considered that further experiment would be useful, so she begged the lives of six condemned Newgate criminals who had not had small-pox.[35] She persuaded Maitland, grown diffident from abuse, to inoculate them and invite eminent doctors as witnesses. He succeeded perfectly and dedicated a diary to the Prince and Caroline describing his patients' progress. This encouraged Caroline to have six charity children inoculated. Five took successfully but the sixth was discovered to have had small-pox before and hidden the fact in order to gain the promised reward. Caroline summoned Sir Hans Sloane for discussion, feeling that she would be willing to have her family inoculated.[36] Sloane gave his opinion in favour of the practice but he 'would not persuade or advise the making of trials upon patients of such importance to the public. The Princess then asked me if I would dissuade her from it: to which I made answer that I would not, in a matter so likely to be of such advantage. Her reply was, that she was then resolved it should be done.' Amelia and Caroline were inoculated in April 1722 'without danger at the time or the least ill symptoms since'. The next year Maitland went to Hanover and inoculated Frederick, who gave him an anxious few days but made a good recovery. Maitland received £1,000 for his services.[37] Caroline's courage revived waverers and confounded the gloomy prophets. Inoculation became an established practice. The Secretary of the Royal Society, Dr. Jurin, published yearly statistics of its success,[38] and thirty years later Lord Chesterfield airily told a Parisian friend: 'not one in a hundred has died of it . . . nobody whatever is disfigured by it. . . . I know your priests . . . exclaim against it as a deadly sin. . . . Ours did so too at first, but we have let them talk on and have not done the less for their outcry.' Less than a century after 1721, Jenner discovered vaccination to be safer than inoculation in giving immunity, and the battle against small-pox was won.

Caroline had more time for her own pursuits when Leicester House ceased to be the centre of Opposition intrigue. Her receptions still drew the wits and writers, whose potential importance Walpole overlooked, to his later disadvantage. She appreciated living in exciting literary times. The publication of Pope's *Iliad*, spread over eleven years from 1715, made its author classical at 29, and brought him £9,000. For relaxation she had Defoe's full-blooded novels, composed with a vigour which is usually abated in writers of nearly 60. He presented *Robinson Crusoe* to an avid public in 1719 and 1720, and in the next four years regaled it with three other romances, numerous novels, and his *Tour through Great Britain*. Gay had produced *Trivia*, his epic of London street life, and was at work upon his *Fables*, which he dedicated to Caroline's daughters. When Dean Swift reappeared in London in 1726, Caroline invited him to visit her. With his studied rudeness, Swift made her ask ten times before he accepted, so he said. London was agog over Peter, the 'wild boy' found in a German forest. Dr. Arbuthnot had his keeping and showed him to Caroline the same night that she met Swift. 'I told her' said the Dean, 'that having sent for a wild boy from Germany, she had a curiosity to see a wild Dean from Ireland.'[39] They had a long discussion about Ireland's troubles, which were a current topic in the year after the episode of Wood's halfpence. Caroline's intimation that she would like to see the Dean settled in England revived his hopes of long-deferred preferment, but they were ill-founded while Walpole was predominant in the Ministry.

London relished *Gulliver's Travels*, with its political allusions, published that autumn. Dr. Arbuthnot wrote to Swift that he had just seen Caroline laughing over the passage of the hobbling prince, which was a dig at her husband's Tory leanings.[40] Swift described how, of the two parties in Lilliput, one wore high and the other low heels. The King used only the low-heeled party for his government, but his son had a tendency towards high heels, so he wore one heel higher than the other, which made him hobble. 'From the highest to the lowest it is universally read, from the Cabinet Council to the nursery,'

Swift's friends reported to him. When Mrs. Howard thanked him for some Irish plaid he had sent Caroline, her letter was full of Gulliverian allusions. Caroline ordered some more plaid 'the height of the Brobdingnag dwarf multiplied by two and a half'. Swift replied to Mrs. Howard:

> I am sorry I have no complaint to make of her Royal Highness, therefore I think I may let you tell her that every grain of virtue and good sense in one of her rank, considering their bad education among flatterers and adorers, is worth a dozen in inferior persons.[41]

Early in the autumn of Swift's London visit, the young Voltaire arrived to stay with a rich merchant friend. He met all the celebrities, and found much to praise in his host's country. When his poem, *La Henriade*, appeared in 1728, it was dedicated to the new Queen, Caroline, and prefaced by an imposing list of 344 subscribers, headed by their Majesties.[42] Amongst his *Letters concerning the English Nation* is one on Inoculation, wherein he extolled Caroline's services.[43]

Uneventful years took a little of the bitterness out of the royal family's relationship. Caroline and the Prince sometimes looked in at Kensington on their way to or from Richmond. Occasionally the Prince went over to Windsor for some shooting with the King. If there was no cordiality between them, at least there was no fresh friction. His Majesty had entered on his most English phase. His German advisers lost their overruling influence after 1720, while Walpole's expanded with each passing year, to the content of the King, who valued his efficiency. In November 1726 death ended his wife's thirty-two years of weary imprisonment at Ahlden. A curt notice in the

London Gazette announced the fact to the public. No official notification was made to foreign sovereigns, and the Court did not go into mourning.

Seven months later the King left for Hanover, when Caroline and the Prince were in residence at Richmond as usual. He slept the night of June 9th in the Dutch town of Delden.[44] In spite of feeling unwell, he pressed on his journey with his usual tearing speed, accompanied only by Townshend. Those who were not obliged to be in attendance on him preferred to travel at a more reasonable pace. Not long past Bentheim he had a stroke. As no doctor could be found the journey continued to Osnabrück, his brother's home. By late evening when the party arrived there, the King was unconscious. He died at one hour past midnight, on June 11th, 1727. Townshend's dispatch announcing the demise reached Walpole at Chelsea three days later.

Fittingly they buried the King at Hanover, which had retained his warmest feelings. To remember him as a family man is to recall his dourest aspect. As a monarch he abided loyally by England's constitution, and his judgement was sound enough to trust the high abilities first of Stanhope, then of Walpole. Had he tried 'to be a King', like his great-grandson, his descendants might not be here now. The best of Hanover's Electors, he was certainly not the worst of England's Kings.

PART II

1727-37

VII

QUEEN CAROLINE REIGNS

RICHMOND drowsed in the hot afternoon. Upstairs in the Lodge Caroline knotted pensively to the sound of her husband's slumbers. There was a clatter of hoofs in the courtyard below. 'Mon Dieu, that noise will wake the Prince,' she thought. A minute later bulky, breathless Sir Robert Walpole burst upon their royal privacy.[1] The sleepy Prince sprang from his bed with breeches in hand, to be greeted as 'Your Majesty'. His outraged dignity scarce believed the reason for the salute. He demanded proofs from that 'rogue and rascal' Walpole. Townshend's dispatch told him the truth, but induced no cordiality towards its bearer. Walpole asked for directions: the Privy Council must be summoned and the King's Accession speech drafted. Prompt decision was a kingly virtue. The answer flashed back: 'Go to Chiswick and take your directions from Sir Spencer Compton', and His Majesty glanced slyly at his wife, hoping that she had noticed his promptitude. Caroline's eyes never left her work. Silence was a woman's part when men talked business together. The King's order revealed his intentions, which scarcely surprised Walpole, who had been too good a servant of his late Majesty's to expect power in the new reign.

King and Queen took coach for Leicester House.

London crowds, having heard of the Accession, greeted the smiling, bowing monarchs with thunderous huzzas. The square was so thronged that their coach could scarcely crawl towards the royal portals. With this cheerful din ringing in their ears, they proceeded indoors to find every room packed with well-wishers, eager to kiss hands and murmur zealous professions. Members of the King's own household looked especially jubilant, as men do who anticipate increased favours, but a thoughtful sobriety marked the faces of the old King's friends. George II's familiar epithets for his father's chief ministers came ominously to mind. Sir Robert Walpole, 'that great rogue'; his brother Horatio, ambassador to France, 'dirty buffoon'; Secretaries of State, the Duke of Newcastle, 'impertinent fool', and Viscount Townshend, 'choleric blockhead'. For His Majesty was pleased to express himself freely. When Sir Spencer Compton presently emerged from his first audience, he returned to his coach through ranks of bowed heads, like the sheaves in Joseph's dream. He and Mrs. Howard were the new idols, so it was thought.

Dim misgivings already clouded the minister-designate's mind. By then he had received the King's message from Walpole with a flustered surprise which in turn astonished the newsgiver. Could His Majesty really have left Compton unwarned of the office he intended for him? Walpole wondered. As Treasurer to the Prince, Speaker, and Paymaster of the Forces, the grave, methodical Compton enjoyed opportunities for experience by which his limited capacity never profited. He lacked the initiative and self-reliance necessary in a statesman but was naturally pleased to be thought one. Faint courage sustained him as he heard Walpole's frank admission of departed power, coupled with a plea for protection in return for help during the interregnum. Compton graciously promised his favour. Together they attended a committee of Ministers convened to settle formalities concerning the Accession council meeting and Proclamation. Too bustled to draft the King's speech, Compton privily gave Walpole the task, though precedents were to hand in old *Gazettes*. The meeting approved Walpole's effort, which Compton recopied in his own handwriting and submitted to the King. Another snare awaited him. Walpole followed Compton to Leicester House and found him agitated because His Majesty wished, against Compton's advice, to alter passages in the speech. Perhaps Walpole could persuade the King? He did, while the annoyed monarch glowered at both men. Compton had blundered twice and the Queen was one of those who heard it without surprise.

As the proceedings of the Accession council meeting neared their end, Dr. Wake, Archbishop of Canterbury, handed the King a sealed document which had been deposited in his safe keeping. It was the late King's will, ordered to be delivered thus, to ensure that it should be read. All waited expectantly for His Majesty to divulge its contents, which might prove sensational because father and son had hated each other. The King pocketed the document and strode from the room. No official statement was ever issued to quell the resultant gossip. Since the King must have had reasons for opening his reign with a felony, men invented promising ones. The truth has only lately refuted their tales of filial villainy.[2] The new accession was proclaimed next day, June 15th, when crowds at

Leicester Square, Charing Cross, Temple Bar, Cheapside, and the Royal Exchange, cheered their sovereign lord King George II. Members of Parliament took their oath to him and Parliament was prorogued until the 27th, when its most vital duty would be to pass the Civil List.

During the four days that elapsed before the Court moved to Kensington, Leicester House was packed from morning to night, but when Walpole appeared his presence 'emptied every corner he turned to'. Onslow, soon to be chosen Speaker, paying him a tactful visit of condolence, so unmanned him that he burst into tears and cried out that his friend's kindness 'had drawn a weakness from him which his enemies never could do'.[3] Meanwhile Compton opened levees and benevolently received the whole world's importunities. Unlike Walpole, he had always courted Mrs. Howard, it was whispered significantly. When Lord Malpas, Walpole's son-in-law, was summarily dismissed from the Mastership of the Robes, they daily waited to read Compton's appointment gazetted. On Sunday, the 18th, Horatio Walpole appeared unbidden from Paris, pleading as his excuse Cardinal Fleury's urgent wish that he should carry greetings to His Majesty.[4] The King's wrath softened to pleasure when he heard of Fleury's sincere hope that the good relations between their two countries, so vital to the peace of Europe, would continue in unchecked harmony. Graciously the King wrote Fleury an autograph letter saying that he cherished no keener desire than amity with France. Horatio's mission was of his own making, assented to by Fleury because the present English ministry suited French policy. The

Queen smiled over the successful ruse; arguments were coming nicely to hand for her planned verbal attack.

She wanted the King to start his reign with a strong government. Her dynasty had not yet struck root in England and must eschew political experiments. The motley Opposition aroused her contempt.[5] The Jacobites, with honest Shippen as their leader, preserved an allegiance to the Stuarts which the Tories had long since forsaken. Led ostensibly by Sir William Wyndham, the Tories moved to Lord Bolingbroke's bidding, which damned them with the Queen. After he had bought the Duchess of Kendal's favour for £12,000 two years ago, a bill had been passed restoring him his property and rights as a citizen, but not as a peer. His French wife boasted to Caroline that he had only entered the Pretender's service as a spy to earn his pardon in England, a statement so odious and untrue that Caroline thenceforth despised them both.[6] Bolingbroke combined with Pulteney's discontented Whigs (for Walpole preferred compliant rather than clever colleagues) to pester this man who had barred his re-entry to the House of Lords. Caroline detested their year-old paper, the *Craftsman*, for finding fault with her family's foreign ways. The Whigs in power must carry on the government, but the King's antipathy to Walpole made him prefer Compton as its leader. Caroline could stifle personal animosity to secure an important object. She knew Compton for a mere figurehead compared with Walpole, who had extricated the country from financial chaos in 1721, and since guided it to sound prosperity. His mastery of the Commons made him invaluable. When he spoke to the King and her to acquaint them with the present state of affairs during these opening days of their reign, she found him sensible, lucid, and frank.[7] Walpole, therefore, was her candidate for leadership; tact and patience were her weapons when she talked with the King. As concealment was no part of her policy towards the downcast minister, Walpole soon learnt that she was his ally, and moulded his plans accordingly. The public, still expecting Compton's appointment, was only faintly perplexed over the delay in announcing it.

How had Compton been doing? the Queen asked her husband, to find him peevish with the man's diffidence over facing the Commons and drawing up the provisions of the Civil List.[8] King George liked ebullient confidence in his advisers, to smother his own indecision. With him a quick decision usually meant a wrong one, and time to ponder produced confusing alternatives. Compton would improve, the Queen reassured him, but certainly the Civil List was important. Compton had only suggested the same sums as in the last reign; an absurd idea when the King had a large family, while £100,000, the King's own income as Heir Apparent, was excessive for that stripling Fritz. Humbly the Queen suggested alternative leaders, Pulteney, Newcastle, Wyndham. She could not have expressed the objections to them more succinctly than did His Majesty. Then perhaps Walpole should be retained for the present, countered the Queen. Uncertainty about his future would make him docile; his vast fortune keep him from picking; and his long experience be useful to Compton. What, Compton take his orders from that fellow? the King grumbled, to be reminded that he had done so already. Thus the King came to see how subtle he would be to make his father's minister do his business. He had no thought of being a ministerial puppet like the late King. No, his ministers should obey him, just as office clerks or private soldiers heeded their superiors. He, their King, would survey policies, interview every one, and issue his decisions.[9] Under such a system Walpole could not be pert. At least he might talk to the fellow about his Civil List. At this the Queen was well content, for Walpole was his own best advocate.

Walpole came sensibly to the point. Experience had taught him that love of money is common to most human beings. His rivals, Pulteney especially, had made extravagant offers, but unlike him they could not be certain of an obedient Commons. He told the King that the Civil List might be fixed at £800,000, produced by certain taxes, leaving His Majesty to provide whatever he judged fit for his heir.[10] If the funds showed a surplus, as well they might in these prosperous times, the King should enjoy it instead of handing it over to the Sinking Fund, as had been the practice during the last reign. This was a skilful bait. For the Queen, Walpole proposed an establishment of £60,000 a year; £20,000 more than Charles II's Queen had enjoyed or than Compton had intended for her. Her jointure he thought might properly be £100,000, just double what any Queen had had before, and with the use of Somerset House and Richmond Lodge. The King was in high good humour. With an eye to economy where his own pocket was affected, he suggested that Queen Caroline would be well content with a yearly allowance of £50,000. And so it came to pass. When the House met on June 27th it assented obediently to Walpole's proposals, privately thinking them excessively generous, but they could afford to be liberal with the nation's money. Blunt Jacobite Shippen alone protested. As the House's *enfant terrible*, he was forgiven his honesty.

The document relating to the Queen's jointure contained devoted tribute to her qualities. The King 'having a perfect knowledge and sense of the early and never to be forgotten instances which Her Majesty . . . hath given of her zeal for the Protestant religion and welfare of these kingdoms, and of her continued exercise of every royal virtue whereby she hath merited and engaged herself to the inviolable affection of His Majesty and the duty and gratitude of his people',[11] desired to settle on her 'a certain and ample revenue'. Made emotional by success, His Majesty took Walpole by the hand—'Consider Sir Robert, what makes me easy in this matter will prove for your ease too; it is for my life it is to be fixed, and it is for your life'.[12] Thus Walpole knew his services were to be retained, and Queen Caroline's reign had begun.

In mid-July the ministers were re-appointed to their places and in August Parliament was dissolved. Compton's snowball popularity melted overnight when his helplessness was known. His ineptitude had lost him the game, but defeat was softened for him. Raised to the peerage as Baron Wilmington, and later created Lord Privy Seal, he seemed as pleased by these tactful honours as if he had been the King's sole minister.[13] Mrs. Howard shared his eclipse and, possessing keener sensibility than Compton, felt it more acutely. Though she had never aspired to power, she judged that people would be contemptuous of a mistress without it.[14] Walpole was the Queen's nominee. Her

KING GEORGE II

(*By* LOUIS FRANÇOIS ROUBILIAC)

own friend, Compton, had been quietly retired, and when she found the King more perfunctory to her than formerly, she meditated leaving Court, but never quite took the decision.[15] Habit held King and mistress in its grip. On her husband's inheriting the Earldom of Suffolk in 1731, she was made Mistress of the Robes, and matters drifted slowly to their appointed end.[16]

Before George II's accession, the world was ignorant of Caroline's influence, but now men who had taken pride in courting Mrs. Howard found how accurately the Queen had diagnosed her husband's liaison. Wilmington himself, the Dukes of Dorset and Argyll, Lord Islay, perceived that their astonishing prince gave his leisure hours to a pretty woman but kept his business confidences for his wife.[17] He bestowed such confidences not consciously to seek advice, but to show his skill, for he warmly admired his own good parts. His failings forced dissimulation upon the Queen. She found that smiles and deference gained her ends better than logic or opposition, but her methods were exposed to the glare of publicity. As the world came to know that the forceful, trenchant Queen ruled both kingdom and King, it composed lampoons and libels, ballads and satires upon a theme which it found fruitful and ridiculous.[18] The *Craftsman* lashed most stingingly, and one of the many lampoons observed:

> You may strut, dapper George, but 'twill all be in vain;
> We know 'tis Queen Caroline, not you, that reign—
> You govern no more than Don Philip of Spain.
> Then if you would have us fall down and adore you,
> Lock up your fat spouse, as your dad did before you.[19]

Until repetition inured the Queen, such attacks smarted,

and made her nervous lest the King should believe them. But he saw only an obedient, humble wife, who divined his opinions to a nicety. He once enumerated the real governors of this country in other reigns. Charles I was governed by his wife; Charles II by his whores; James II by his priests; William by his men, and Anne by her women favourites; his father by anybody who could get at him. To complete his catalogue, which showed penetration, he asked triumphantly, 'And who do they say governs now?'[20] The story ends there, for the King desired no answer to his rhetorical question. Indubitably, he was the first monarch since Queen Elizabeth to rule his country for himself!

Yet that phrase concerning Caroline's jointure spoke the truth. 'She hath merited and engaged herself to the inviolable affection of His Majesty.' He snubbed her before other people, but always left her Regent. He kept mistresses, but wrote her letters of forty or fifty pages when he was in Hanover, and daily spent hours in her company when he was at home. He teased her for being a pedant, yet let none of her learned friends lose by her death. After she died, he would not suffer her rooms to be touched again, and made exact arrangements for his own burial beside her. And the Queen gave him her unfailing loyalty and tolerance. It was their tragedy that Lord Hervey spared their relationship neither sanctity nor privacy. Few marriages would survive with dignity such ruthless prying.

Two matters concerning the King's parents demanded prompt attention. The first revived memories of his mother's unhappy love affair forty years before. Her lover, Count Königsmarck, had entrusted a sealed casket of her

letters to the keeping of a faithful family official called
Hansen, whose heirs regarded them as a potential gold
mine.[21] Neither Sophia Dorothea nor her mother could
pay their fantastic price, so the prospective vendors anonymously approached the Hanoverian Government, who
informed George I, suggesting that someone should be
appointed to inspect the letters. The King characteristically
replied that he left the person who wrote the letters to buy
them. His wife retaliated by denying their authenticity.
But Baron von Görtz, the Hanoverian minister-negotiator,
kept the affair going, and two months before the old
King's death, George II handed over the money demanded
for an inspection. The confidential secretary from Celle,
who undertook it, pronounced the letters valid beyond
doubt, and urged their speedy purchase. The sellers asked
25,000 thalers, but obligingly intimated that they *might*
accept a fifth of the sum, which George II agreed to pay.
Records do not specify whether the purchase was completed, because at once another lot of this indiscreet correspondence appeared for sale at an exorbitant price. Filial as
the King had shown himself, he shied at disbursing his new
wealth to cover up his mother's old indiscretion. He
showed his loyalty to her memory in a less expensive way.
The day after his accession he hung up her portrait in his
dressing-room. In time, Frederick the Great's sister, the
Queen of Sweden, pilfered some of the second batch of
Sophia Dorothea's letters. She sent them as an affectionate
memento to her brother, who stored them discreetly in his
secret archives, where they are to-day. The rest of this set
found a safe resting-place in the Swedish University of
Lund. The letters proved that Sophia Dorothea, all those

years ago, had fully consoled herself for her husband's neglect. And who shall blame her?

His father's will gave the new King more trouble.[22] By its wording the elder George showed that he resented his electorate being subordinated to England as keenly as Englishmen resented the connexion with Hanover. George II and grandson Frederick were each to rule as King-Elector. Then the 'German lands' were to be separated from England if Frederick, or another of George I's male descendants being King-Elector, left two sons. The eldest would be King, the second inaugurate a dynasty of Electors, and free Hanover from English domination. George I knew that this plan involved constitutional difficulties. The Emperor told him so in 1716, when the King forwarded a copy of his will for safe deposit in the Imperial treasury. His English ministers endorsed the verdict, ignorant that the plan of separation which he asked them to discuss had been embodied in his will. King George I, however, left his will unaltered. Perhaps he hoped that by the time he died the benefits of separation would appear so desirable as to produce a solution of the difficulties resulting from the constitutions of both England and the Holy Roman Empire.

The new King consulted his Hanoverian Privy Councillors about the will, and received a third verdict against its feasibility. Both his Governments agreed that he should suppress it. One copy Dr. Wake had considerately handed over. The Duke of Brunswick-Wolfenbüttel held the second copy. Happily the two families were on the best of terms. Caroline had often corresponded with the Duchess about their many German friends and relatives. The

Duke sensibly agreed to receive £100,000 for returning
the will unopened. A neat military pact camouflaged
the bargain. The King's new friend, Cardinal Fleury,
flattered by such delicate confidences, agreed that His
Majesty had taken the proper course. There remained the
Emperor's copy. Four years passed before the King judged
it tactful to negotiate for its return. Then in 1737 he sent
all three copies to his Hanoverian archives, where they
came to be overlooked for two hundred years. His grace-
less subjects had meanwhile invented the most felonious
reasons for his silence over the will. The Queen privately
must have heard a good many people called blockhead,
fool and puppy for spreading such scandals. Outwardly,
however, the King preserved a stoical calm. It was the
more impressive for its rarity.

A crowded summer at Kensington sped quickly by.
The King renewed his old pleasure of reviewing troops,
and the Queen eased his labours by receiving applicants
and sifting papers for his attention. The special envoy from
Wolfenbüttel described one of these receptions.[23] The
Queen's chamberlain, Lord Grantham, led him to Her
Majesty, whom he found in a room furnished completely
in white, with black hangings. The bed fitted the colour
scheme. Her Majesty, with a lady-in-waiting behind her,
was seated at the far end of the room. Lord Grantham
stayed by the door. The Queen graciously heard the
envoy's speech and received his letter, assuring him of her
tenderest affection for the Duke and Duchess of Wolfenbüttel. She bade him convey her warmest greetings to
them, and then the two spent half an hour discussing the
affairs of the Duchy and of the Empire, before the Queen

ended the audience. As the envoy withdrew, he over-heard her tactful remark: 'I should like to see him more often. I am very glad he is here.' The Prussian Envoy determined to win her confidence so that matters would progress quickly when he had any proposal to put before the King, who otherwise was inclined to give short, un-helpful answers.[24] The Queen's trust in Philip von Hattorf, minister in London for Hanoverian affairs, had not escaped him.[25] Unlike George I's German trio, Hattorf used his increased influence so modestly as to leave most people unaware of it. The Queen could trust his discretion even when His Majesty declared that he would discharge any German in his service who dared to meddle in English affairs.[26] The King dismissed Lady Portland as governess to his elder daughters, who now needed more grown-up arrangements made for them.[27] He decreed that Anne, an accomplished girl of eighteen, should be styled Princess Royal. Extensive preparations went forward for the Coronation in October. The King loved a good show pro-vided he was cast for the lead, and the Queen appreciated its value as propaganda.

When October 11th came, she showed herself a better player than he. She was the first Queen Consort to be crowned since Anne of Denmark, through whose daughter the King derived his right to that day's splendour. A century had passed since then. Going in procession from Westminster Hall to the Abbey and back, the Queen walked well forward under her canopy, so that the crowds could see her fine clothes; the pearls gleaming on head and shoulders, her petticoat studded all over with diamonds.[28] She walked gracefully, smiling on all as she passed. Her daughters held up the tip of her train. Their stiff-bodied, silver tissue gowns, their diadems and purple, ermine-edged mantles, vastly became them. Contrary to his intentions, the King was almost hidden from view because he kept so much under his canopy.[29] The splendid rites with which England crowns its Kings passed in full beauty. A few days later the Queen was stricken unromantically with gout. She gave out that her leg had been badly kicked in the Coronation procession, which subterfuge did not deceive some knowing people.[30] On the anniversary of the Coronation next year she had gout again, but appeared at the festivities in a special easy chair.[31] Thereafter these recurrent attacks were seldom allowed to impede her work though they sometimes impaired her joviality.[32] On Lord Mayor's Day the newly crowned Sovereigns maintained tradition by dining at the Guildhall, whither their coach was drawn by eight cream horses, 'the beautifullest creatures of their kind', with purple trappings and tail ribbons; visible proof of the King's taste in horses.[33]

The Queen had the pleasure of seeing Walpole meet the new Parliament in January 1728 with a good majority. Their smooth co-operation was giving the Opposition a cohesion it lacked as long as Pulteney and his Whigs thought they might dislodge him, but this increasing stability did not yet disturb Queen or minister. Onslow was chosen to succeed Compton as Speaker. No controversial domestic issue cropped up. Abroad, the tension between England and Spain slackened. For a year they had sparred over Gibraltar, as the outcome of uneasy regroupings amongst the European Powers. George II's peaceful accession, his resolute navy, and Spain's own faithless ally, the Emperor, showed that country its stupidity in breaking itself upon a barren rock. Hostilities ceased two months after Parliament met. The current panacea for soothing frayed nations was applied. While the Court was summering in the country, a congress assembled at Soissons to pass a year in bickering and feasting.[34]

After Parliament rose, Richmond's privacy refreshed a busy Queen, but only reminded the King of his enforced retreats there.[35] Before long he bustled them off to Hampton Court as a fitter setting for triumphant majesty. To humour him, his courtiers discovered a convenient passion for stag hunting. 'We hunt with great noise and violence, and have every day a tolerable chance of having a neck broke,' Mrs. Howard plaintively told Lady Hervey. Vast fields, numbering nearly 800, charged off in battle array to plough up the countryside. Once an astonished stag fled from Windsor across the river, to be slaughtered by this army on the terrace of Lord Lincoln's house. The King made amends by breakfasting with his lordship.[36] When the Queen found him flushed and red-eyed from his sport, she praised his vigour, but His Majesty must not let kindness in amusing others trespass unduly upon his valuable time, she gravely suggested, to be countered by the usual 'Pooh and stuff'.[37] However, the Court was thereafter thankful for some abatement of its exertions. From Windsor, whither the Court moved late in August, their Majesties honoured the Duke of Newcastle with a visit at Claremont. As Secretary of State and born electioneer, the Duke deserved royal favour, though the Queen smiled secretly over his flustered ways. Her daughters christened him 'Permis' because he prefaced every remark by *est-il permis?*[38]

Windsor loyally greeted the Coronation anniversary by decking itself in fairy lights and letting off a profusion of fireworks. At the Castle there was a splendid ball.[39] But the Queen was aware that the public did not see its King often enough, and it was poorly repaid in shows for the money devoted to his upkeep. At a masquerade soon after his accession, some unknown lady tapped him on the shoulder to tell him as much.[40] The nation would never love him if he hoarded his revenues. Let him make more display, marry his children, then he would find himself popular, said this masked heroine before she vanished into the crowd. His inexpensive tastes and the habits of a lifetime made her advice hard to follow. The Queen had a brilliant idea. During the summer at Hampton Court, when her husband acted as Regent, one of the most popular spectacles had been their dining in public. This royal custom was honoured by a wealth of tradition and picturesque ceremony. Best of all it was an inexpensive, if inconvenient, way of being seen by subjects who felt as if they had been admitted to the family circle. She easily persuaded the King to revive it that autumn. Every Sunday in London, crowds thronged the Palace to gaze at the royal dinner in progress, which 'the people here very much love doing', reported the Prussian Envoy, who pronounced the idea a *coup de maîtresse*, and the Queen was satisfied with her start.[41]

Ever since the Accession the Queen had pondered the second counsel given by the masked lady, but mating royal children was a complicated pastime. Fritz, now turned 21, was still at Hanover. When the Queen thanked the Duchess of Wolfenbüttel for some kindness shown him in

1727, she wrote of him as 'le plus cher de mes enfants', but George I's inhumanity had made them strangers for fourteen years.[42] There was the added embarrassment of Fritz's evident affection for this grandfather, after whose death he wrote to his sister Anne:

> I am sure that you share the grief I have felt since the death of our dear grandfather. I should be lacking in filial duty and the most ungrateful of men if it had not caused me great sorrow, for he treated me with especial affection and friendship. I was so overcome by sadness when they told me the news that I could not leave my bed for two days and fainted twice. My only consolation in this sad affliction is the knowledge of my dear parents' goodness. I flatter myself that I shall always conduct myself in a manner deserving of their esteem and friendship for me. I pray you dear sister, as you are by them, to remember me often to Their Majesties.[43] . . .

This letter exhibited priggish pre-occupation with his own emotions, but Fritz, of course, was writing to a virtual stranger, and apparently judged such affliction highly becoming.

His marriage and his coming to England absorbed hours of discussion. There was the friendly family plan for marrying him to his Prussian first cousin, Wilhelmine, and one of his sisters to the Prussian Crown Prince Fritz. George I had approved of the idea, but told his daughter and son-in-law, the Prussian sovereigns, that there was no hurry. The grandchildren were all very young. So he never rounded off the Treaty of Charlottenburg or Hanover with a family pact, but said that he would settle at least the English Fritz's marriage when he went to Hanover in 1727.[44] Then he died inconsiderately before he could keep his word. King Frederick William instructed Wallenrodt, his new Envoy, to promote the marriages as 'the best and surest way of uniting the two countries'.[45] On his way to England, Wallenrodt saw Frederick at Hanover. They both thought how natural and nice it would be for him to pay a little visit to Berlin before he left for England. His Prussian uncle and aunt were agreeable.[46]

In England, Wallenrodt perceived Queen Caroline's decisive influence. True to his intentions, he asked an audience of her as the quickest method of forwarding his King's commands. Both she and the King felt well-disposed towards his mission, little as the King liked his cousin King Frederick William. Politically, however, Prussia had strayed from virtue, by letting her traditional ally, the Emperor, weaken her friendship with England and France as expressed by the Treaty of Hanover.[47] The Emperor's bait had been to promise King Frederick William his heart's desire, the reversion of the western Duchies of Berg and Julich. No diplomatic breach with England followed, but that country considered Prussia guilty of bad form. When Townshend, the Secretary of State for Northern Affairs, learnt that the Prussian King desired the marriages, he saw his chance of making Prussia return to her duty. As a diplomat, Townshend lacked finesse. He adored spirited gestures: countering one set of alliances by making stronger ones; showing Europe that England feared nobody. In fact he resembled King Frederick William in many ways. It never occurred to him that schoolroom methods were fatal with an irascible monarch, who perhaps felt guilty over his defection, but would certainly never admit it. Accept Frederick William's overtures for the marriages, and pleasant political results would have ensued. The King of Prussia, like Townshend again, was a genuine soul who acted honourably as long as his pride was humoured.

Queen Caroline learnt of her Government's policy in this matter, and promised her support. She was excessively busy when she granted Wallenrodt an audience in September 1727. Only three months had passed since the Accession; the Coronation lay a month ahead. She was sorting the threads of State affairs, interviewing, and writing with an effortlessness which told the King that he was the very hub of all the activity. Her tact being consumed by her husband, she could spare none for the psychological problems of her brother-in-law, Frederick William.

Wallenrodt came to her rooms at Kensington at seven o'clock on September 22nd.[48] Their amicable interview lasted two hours. The Queen expressed herself as wholly favourable to the marriages, but she said briskly, 'ne commençons pas le roman par la queue; let us first settle (political) affairs and the marriages will be a natural conclusion'. Unhappily, Berlin took just the opposite view. When Wallenrodt asked leave for her Fritz to visit Berlin, the Queen returned to the theme of settling first things first, 'I cannot say more now.' Wallenrodt reported the interview to Berlin. A nettled answer came quickly back:

We learnt from your letter of September 22nd/October 2nd how your audience with Her Majesty the Queen passed off. You can easily judge how little pleasure it gave us, for it appears that we are to be forced into closer engagements and treaties with that Court, and that they hope to use the marriages as a lever to that end. They will be completely deceived by such an opinion, for we find no such advantages in these marriages to engage us to postpone the interests of our House, or to enter into difficult conditions. . . . It would therefore be best for you to think no more about this affair, still less to mention it again.[49]

Wallenrodt died suddenly on October 24th.[50] Thereafter the Prussian King flared into rude marginal comments whenever dispatches from England mentioned the marriages. He began to make conditions. 'If I get land or property with the marriage then all will be well; but don't forget: half of Celle and the town of Lüneburg.'[51] Queen Caroline, of course, did not see these comments. She still wanted her Fritz to marry Wilhelmine, provided that he were willing, for she and the King decided that the final choice must be his.[52] When he came over to England he agreed to the plan, but its fulfilment appeared ever more uncertain. Disputes between Hanover and Prussia made George II and Frederick William hate each other more heartily. The Prussian King was inquisitive about George I's will. His crony, the Austrian Seckendorff, aided by his own trusted minister, Grumbkow (in Austrian pay), bound him more closely to the Emperor by a secret treaty in December 1728. He produced impossible suitors for his daughter Wilhelmine and was enraged by his wife's objections to them. The Seckendorff-Grumbkow combine prevailed upon Reichenbach, the chargé d'affaires in London, so to doctor his dispatches that it appeared that England sought to make Prussia a satellite in her own political orbit.[53] This duplicity Walpole discovered by the effective method of opening the Grumbkow–Reichenbach correspondence. But it so far worked upon King Frederick William's susceptibilities as to make him unwilling to have an English daughter-in-law, who might scheme against him. His Queen, Sophia Dorothea, bravely kept the talk going, but when she wrote to Caroline in 1728 she mentioned only English Fritz's marriage to Wilhelmine, which she hoped could soon be definitely arranged.[54] Caroline replied that the King was perfectly willing provided his Prussian Majesty would ask for one of their daughters to marry Crown Prince Fritz.[55] At this unpromising stage the matter rested, but the intriguers in Berlin worked on. At the same time discreet agents searched other Courts, procuring portraits and reporting upon other possible brides for English Fritz.[56]

Meanwhile the King debated when to bring him over from Hanover.[57] A clause in George I's will decreed that a prince of his house must always reside there as Regent.[58] His Majesty, when Heir Apparent, boasted of his affection for England, but scurvy treatment and long separation had re-awakened his love for Hanover.[59] Now that he was King, he found himself as eager to go there as his father had been; better able to appreciate the paternal concern for the electorate's welfare, though still unwilling to follow paternal precedent in making a child the puppet of court ceremonial. The King's uncle, Duke Ernest Augustus, had been Bishop of Osnabrück these many years past. The only substitute for Fritz as family representative was six-year-old William, Duke of Cumberland. Neither parent dreamt of sending him over.

Then the King had unlimited faith in his Commons' generosity or Walpole's wizardry. He had been voted a handsome Civil List, quite proper too for a King with so many calls upon his purse, and left to his own discretion about Fritz's allowance. If he chose his time carefully, waiting perhaps until his reign had proceeded further along the brilliant course he destined for it, the Commons might gratefully make separate provision for Fritz.[60] And deep in his heart was the uneasy knowledge that an adult heir would prove a nuisance, because his own experience had taught him how little scope the English constitution afforded to a Prince of Wales.

Throughout 1728 his Ministers pressed him to send for Fritz.[61] That winter it became urgent that Fritz should arrive before Parliament met in the New Year, because Walpole's spies found that the Opposition was canvassing support for an address petitioning the King to bring him over.[62] It was also making ugly but pertinent remarks about the King's thrift. The Ministers frankly informed His Majesty that they were not in a position to procure further revenues. The King fumed until the Queen soothed him as best she could.[63] Fritz, as Prince of Wales, could not be left indefinitely at Hanover. Better that he should receive his initiation into statecraft under the King's supervision whilst he was still at a formative age. Since the most important provision of the late King's will was invalid, his present Majesty did not sin by disregarding another item. He could look after Hanover when he visited it. She pressed such arguments quickly home. By the beginning of December, Colonel de Launay and the Marquis de la Forêt had proceeded to Hanover in the greatest secrecy to bring back a surprised Fritz.[64] The official reason for this mystery was to avoid swarms of petitioners in both countries begging places in his household.[65] In reality it thwarted the Opposition plans without giving time for alternatives.

The furtive party endured a wretched homeward journey.[66] They nearly foundered in a snow-covered marsh, which they mistook for firm ground, but found to be but water and ice. They slipped off a dyke into a canal. A miserable cockle-boat took them out through ice floes to the Helvoetsluys packet-boat. And Fritz's design to surprise his parents was defeated by an officious fellow sending news to London of his being landed. He reached the capital on a gloomy December night, and was conducted straight to the Queen's apartments.

Fritz grown an elegant young man! What absurd tricks time played, for there stood the child she had left at Herrenhausen, now looking like her husband when she first knew him. He had the same neat figure, shapely limbs, and lively air. His sartorial elegance and agreeable manner brought the George Augustus of 1705 to life again. His mouth, more pouting, favoured the late King; those prominent Guelph eyes all three of them had. Independence gave Fritz greater address than the King possessed at his age. He liked talking, and he talked well, the Queen noted, but what was behind his easy ways time would show. The King had changed much since the period that Fritz so vividly recalled to her. However, he greeted his heir civilly, agreeably surprised by the young man's deference.[67]

He duly admitted Fritz to the Privy Council and created him Prince of Wales. The Court liked its young Prince. Such crowds flocked to pay him their respects that His Majesty felt a trifle restive. Too much fuss was bad for young puppies. However, he gave a Court ball in the Prince's honour, and Fritz stayed at a masquerade until early morning. At dinner in public, and in chapel, he sat opposite his sisters to the King's right. The Queen made William unwillingly resign his proud privilege of leading her to her place. Why should this 'German brother' do it? William asked Mama sulkily. His attitude showed the natural family jealousy towards a stranger whom the public, pleased by a new plaything, treated as a hero. When the Prince went sightseeing to the Tower and Somerset House, he could hardly proceed on his way because of the friendly crowds. On appearing to see *Henry VIII* with the rest of his family, he was so loudly cheered, that he said nothing in his life had pleased him so much as those huzzas.[68] Again the King felt displeased.

The Prince shared his sisters' table but was granted his own household officers—men whom the Ministers wanted to please. Later their selection was made a grievance, but the Prince, as a stranger to England, could not have chosen his own staff. The King at first allowed him £2,000 a month, which, with the revenues of the Duchy of Cornwall, gave him the adequate income of about £34,000 a year.[69] Public opinion considered the provision mean because the King's own income as Heir Apparent had been £100,000. His Majesty might have silenced criticism by giving his son £50,000 from the start, and explaining that their differing circumstances at the outset of their careers as Heirs Apparent made him withhold the rest for the present. Fifty thousand pounds was the Queen's income. Therefore the King probably reasoned that if she could make it cover her greater expenses, £34,000 was ample for Fritz. That the Queen could never save a penny of her income was apparently no argument for making a discreet and generous gesture towards Fritz.

George II unfortunately never discovered the joys of being a willing giver. He loved money not for what it bought, but simply to gloat over, yet he could be generous at times. He relieved sufferers from fire, distributed £1,000 annually amongst the poor of eight parishes, and responded to tales of distress that reached him. Then he spoilt the good impression by habitually grumbling to Walpole about the prices he paid for his household officers, as if he were being overcharged for so many chairs and tables in a carpenter's bill.[70] He avoided filling places promptly so as to save the salaries.[71] He gave presents to the Queen, such as Richmond Lodge and several sets of horses, 'which he used as much as she, that Her Majesty, having the nominal property of them, might be at the expense of keeping them'.[72] If he alone had suffered from his later parsimony towards Fritz, it would have been just, but the Queen was constrained to defend stinginess she could never justify, and herself came in for the cruellest blasts of filial resentment.

During the session of 1729, the King obliged Walpole to see that Parliament made good an alleged deficiency of £115,000 in his Civil List funds.[73] The 'deficiency' was notoriously caused by a faulty method of accountancy. Also, the wording of the Act concerning his Civil List left it doubtful whether Parliament was obliged to compose any true shortage in his funds. However, the Commons once more humoured their miserly little monarch, but poked fun at him privately, while Fritz forgot his deference in some witticisms.

In 1728 the King's eagerness for Hanover was conquered by his indecision over Fritz. If he went there, he must either take back the lad with him or be worse pestered.

Now in 1729 the royal will had overcome this dilemma, so to Hanover His Majesty would go. His Ministers and people deplored this revived Germanophilia, but always found the King unmoved by their arguments against his visits. If Parliamentary business bade fair to delay his start, he called a plague upon his prating subjects: 'the devil . . . may take the Parliament and the whole island provided I can get out of it and go to Hanover'.[74] If Europe blazed with war, he announced, 'I am not afraid and I have a sword. For all your fine reasons, I shall go because I want to'.[75] And he always went. The Queen never accompanied him. It was tacitly understood between them that he wanted a bachelor fling, in the style of his grandfather's Venetian holidays, while she preferred queening it in England.

A buoyant King appointed his *chère* Caroline sole Regent, without limiting her powers as his had been curtailed in 1716, and departed jubilantly to Hanover in May.[76] The Queen would have been a hypocrite to pretend that she did not esteem this triennial relaxation.[77] Her time was her own. She could do her work openly. Mail days brought the separated spouses bulky letters from each other, which gave them both sincere pleasure, and only the forsaken kingdom felt restive. Five days after the King's going, the Queen held her first Council meeting at Kensington. Her commission of Regency was read, after which the Prince of Wales and all others present 'had the honour to kiss Her Majesty's hand'.[78] Of course Fritz had not lacked 'friends' to tell him that he was slighted in being passed over as Regent, but their grumble was flimsy considering that he had only been six months in England. His mother's pre-eminent authority was apparent to every one. After a few formal sulks, he joined in the social round with infectious good spirits.

Each post and special messenger from Hanover carried a mass of official correspondence for the Queen's perusal. Indeed the King's holidays multiplied the secretarial work. Townshend with the King, and Newcastle at home, wrote to each other by every mail, enclosing for their respective Majesties' information copies of correspondence they had received and written. Each continued to transact the business of his own department of State, though Townshend wrote occasionally to the Ambassador in Paris, who came within Newcastle's province, and often to the English plenipotentiaries attending the dying Congress of Soissons. Diplomats who communicated direct with him sent Newcastle 'duplicates . . . to be laid before the Queen pursuant to His Majesty's orders'. Letters between the two Secretaries of State dealt almost exclusively with foreign affairs because the King 'left all domestic matters to the Regent'. Townshend requested that documents marked 'Private' should be seen only by the Queen and 'those Lords of the Council who are consulted upon the most secret foreign affairs'. Decisions on policy were left 'entirely to the Queen with the advice of the Lords of the Council'. During June her diplomacy averted an incident with Portugal, which laid an embargo on a British ship in the Tagus. Her firm but friendly representations to the Portuguese minister were successful in getting it raised. Townshend wrote that 'the King likes extremely what Her Majesty said to the Portugal envoy'.[79]

Apart from this slight alarm, the Queen met with a

slack time politically. The chief business claiming her attention was the negotiation proceeding at Seville, where William Stanhope, Ambassador and Plenipotentiary, worked in the hope that direct contact would succeed where the desultory parleys at Soissons had failed.[80] Helped by Fleury's kindly mediation, and a skill not again evident in his career, Stanhope signed peace with Spain. The Treaty of Seville was as remarkable for the possible grievances it evaded as for its positive terms. Spain withdrew assistance from the Emperor's Ostend Company, which had threatened English commerce since its inception in 1722. The three other signatories, England, France, and Holland, recognized Don Carlos's claims to the Duchy of Parma. Though the Emperor had already done likewise his consistency was mistrusted, at which he took offence and sought for allies of his own. The Treaty avoided mentioning Gibraltar or settling the rights of British merchantmen on the American seas. However, it gave England peace, repaid Fleury by improving relations between the two Bourbon dynasties, and made Stanhope a peer. As Lord Harrington he soon blossomed out into a Secretaryship of State.

Don Carlos, Don Philip, and Don Luis* were the darling sons of the termagant Spanish Queen Elizabeth, whose maternal exertions for their futures were exceeded only by the Emperor Charles VI's paternal care for Maria Theresa. These fond parents fluttered the peace of Europe more than once, and perpetually complicated the diplomatic game. Dynamic Queen Elizabeth heeded no rules

---

* This son, later Archbishop of Toledo, is not to be confused with her eldest stepson Luis I (1707-24).

and gave no warnings but plunged Spain into whatever action seemed most promising to her motherly objects. Good fortune smiled upon her opportunism, but shunned the pathetic Emperor although he observed the legal proprieties. It was this earnest Habsburg who, as titular King of Spain, had courted Caroline. He never won the Spanish throne, but succeeded his brother Joseph I as Emperor in 1711. History would have been quite different if Caroline had married and brought him, not George II, the sons he so urgently desired. Instead, he was concerned that his possessions should pass undivided to his daughter, despite the Salic law debarring female succession. Nations sold him their assent to the arrangement for fancy prices. And fatherly Charles believed their promises, though he sometimes overlooked his own part of the pact. Under his narcotic emotion the Austrian army and treasury wilted, so that his daughter, Maria Theresa, eventually found a fine set of signatures less comforting than soldiers and shillings. Even that cipher, Louis XV of France, plunged half Europe into war for a foolish piece of sentiment. His desire to find his father-in-law a convenient crown cost fifty thousand soldiers their lives in one year. But the Prussian King Frederick William eschewed emotion to cherish his troops and territories instead. Whisper 'Berg and Julich', or 'twenty giant grenadiers', and his little eyes glinted with longing. The Dutch States bickered themselves into impotence. In England, Caroline's King longed to unsheath his rusting sword in some heroic cause. Well might a subject moan that the 'tranquillity or distress of whole nations' depended upon the personal whims 'of those mortal deities, their Princes'.[81]

However, the partnership between the Queen and Walpole was a guarantee that solid sense would shape England's policy. These two worked together perfectly. The Queen liked the fat, jovial man with his coarse hunting metaphors and his private generosity. Even more did she admire the statesman's clear head, quick judgement, and easy management of others. Though their motives differed slightly, their object was the same: to strengthen her dynasty. She was prompted by natural family affections, he by the desire to see his policy for trade and peace fructify. Both of them loved ruling. Walpole freely admitted his debt to her. In those first days of the reign she had the power to make or break his career. Their former relations gave her just cause for the latter choice, but dispassionately she rejected it. She was the pivot on whom depended the success of his advice. Where it might take Walpole six weeks to convince his obstinate master over some plan, the Queen could do his business in six hours. No sentiment tinged their relationship. Each saw the other's failings, but they achieved a sound friendship as between two business partners.

To mark their accord, the Queen took her family to dine with Walpole at Chelsea, and was amused by his respect for ceremony.[82] He waited on her himself, entertaining his other guests in a separate room. Subtly he flattered her connoisseurship by arranging for his best pictures to be brought from Houghton House for the party.[83] Sir Robert spent his South Sea riches well, thought the Queen; so well indeed, that after his death his collection was snapped up for the Hermitage at St. Petersburg, and thereby lost to his slothful countrymen forever. Another

evening found the royal party at Cliveden, where they
were diverted in spite of Lady Orkney's anxious fear that
the dinner was ill-dished and the tables badly set; 'the
greater the goodness in the Queen to be so very easy',
wrote Lady Orkney. 'We all agreed Her Majesty must be
admired; and, if I may use the term, it was impossible to
see her and not love her.'[84] At Claremont with Newcastle,
Fritz set them all drinking bumpers to his mother's health,
until she laughingly broke up the dinner to walk in the
gardens till candle-light; then played quadrille, while Fritz
called for the fiddles to accompany the dancing in the next
room. When she later watched the dancers, the Queen
commented on how easily Sir Robert moved; 'his dancing
really became him, which I should not have believed if
I had not seen', noted her hearer. Another cheerful round
of bumpers ended the night's pleasure, and with it some
of the guests' sobriety. Queen and Prince chaffed the
thrifty Duke of Grafton into asking them to his hunting-
seat near Richmond. 'He fended off for a long while,
saying his house was not fit to receive them. . . . But His
Royal Highness, who is very quick at good inventions,
told him he would bring tents and pitch them in his
gardens, so his Grace's excuse did not come off.' Hunting
near Windsor, expeditions to Richmond, days at Hampton Court, brought September round quickly. The King
landed at Margate on the 11th. When the outriders
reached Kensington, heralding his approach, the Queen
and her family walked right to St. James's Park to meet
him.[85] Their Majesties embraced heartily, and drove back
to Kensington followed by their suite and cheered by their
subjects.

The King opened his third Parliament in January 1730
'with a very excellent speech' stating that he and his allies
'had concluded an absolute peace with the Crown of
Spain'.[86] Soon the Commons staged a piece upon a
favourite Opposition theme. Most sessions opened with
this little play about the numbers of the army or foreign
troops in British pay. The actors and lines became quite
familiar.[87] Shippen took the Opposition lead. By 1739
he started off: 'I rise to make my annual speech against a
standing army. I have already delivered twenty-one such
speeches.' France kept an army of some 100,000 men, but
the English Opposition affected to see peace and liberty
menaced by ten or twenty thousand British soldiers. This,
to Their Majesties, seemed absurd. The Queen thought
such poses mistaken when nations behaved like chess
players, plastering the European board with their own
bishops and pawns and kings, but she refrained from exposing her opinion to Opposition mockery.[88] Let the
Opposition speak its lines so long as Walpole took up his
right cue. Her martial monarch found restraint impossible. Soldiers and money were topics unfit for jest. They
supported the grandeur of country and prince. His blockhead subjects sniggered that he loved merely to review the
one and count the other. This year Shippen shocked the
House by saying that seventeen thousand land troops boded
army rule after the German pattern. 'In England a King
who should propose to govern by an army was a tyrant.'[89]
Walpole retorted that such words so shocked members
'that he could find nothing wiser than go to the question
immediately'. His wisdom reaped a majority of 125 in
favour of keeping the seventeen thousand. He also won

over retaining the Hessian troops, who were not 'singly to defend Hanover' (the Opposition's rude thrust) but 'to guard one part of Europe from the ambitious views of another'. His trouble for the session ended with an anxious day spent satisfying Opposition curiosity over Dunkirk harbour, which the French were obliged by treaty to demolish, a thing which they showed reluctance to do.

The Queen knew that personal jealousies and political differences had split the old firm of Walpole and Townshend. Once she had acted peacemaker when Townshend flared up over a lewd but unmalicious jest of Walpole's.[90] Now matters were past jesting. Instead of soothing the Emperor over his exclusion from the treaty-making at Seville, Townshend, who saw no profit in Austrian friendship, squared up to him. Walpole and the Cabinet had not made peace with Spain to begin war against Austria, but Townshend resented criticism. Presently he talked of retiring, though in his own good time. The Queen wished him gone because his policy was troublesome and his temper uncertain.[91] When Townshend told the King of his vague intention to retire, Walpole acted swiftly. Lord Harrington was appointed Secretary of State almost before Townshend realized that he had ended his active career. He accepted the situation honourably, and spent his remaining eight years of life experimenting upon his Norfolk estates, thus earning himself a lasting reputation amongst English farmers.

To his flares succeeded Harrington's phlegm. 'There is a heavy insipid sloth in that man that puts me out of all patience,' said the Queen, but sloth suited Walpole better than temper or ingenuity in a colleague.[92] The Opposition was now justified in calling him 'sole' Minister, though this was intended as a term of opprobrium. During crises Walpole exercised the decisive influence in foreign as well as domestic policy. Harrington desultorily objected and Newcastle fussily expostulated, to be treated like a couple of well-meaning old sheep. The Queen accepted Walpole's methods but taught him their drawbacks. She expected ceaseless efficiency and would know why if affairs went amiss. At those times when the strongest man flags for want of rest, Walpole could hand over to no trusted colleague. Then the Queen criticized the slackening, and Walpole had to pay for his pauses by redoubling his efforts.

By dismissing Lord Carteret from the Lord Lieutenancy of Ireland, Walpole beheaded the last of his tall poppies. He offered Carteret one of the customary sinecures for fallen statesmen. But Carteret had no mind to be a palace mannikin as Lord Steward.[93] Yet Walpole himself said that he ruled the country from the Palace. Carteret's easy culture and fluent German must have been balm to the Queen, surrounded by the set of bores whom Walpole chose as his subordinates. Tactically, he erred in preferring to lead the Opposition in the House of Lords. Soon he sought through others that access to the Queen which he might have had by right, but Walpole brooked no rivals. 'I had some difficulty to get him out; but he shall find much more to get in again,' and Sir Robert kept his word.[94] An effeminate-looking young man, who now entered the Palace as Vice-Chamberlain, slowly assumed the part that Carteret could have played to greater effect. Lord Hervey, married to 'beautiful Molly Lepel' of Leicester House days, had returned invigorated from a health tour in Italy. With his painted frailty went the sharpest wits in the household; sharp enough to make him pet entertainer to the royal family without letting him tilt at Walpole's supremacy.

The Queen knew that Fritz was behaving as an idle young man will. He went roving by night in St. James's Park; he paid £1,500 for the pleasure of setting up a hautboy-player's pretty daughter as his mistress, and enjoyed, besides, brief liaisons with the prima donna Bartholdi and an apothecary's daughter at Kingston. Fritz was proud of his democratic amours.[95] They were expensive, however, and his scheme of financing them out of card-winnings brought him much festivity but no cash. At court he was still popular, and people resented his small allowance, but the King had no intention of subsidizing the boy's whores and card-companions. The best way of easing the growing tension was by settling Fritz's marriage with his cousin Wilhelmine, but when politics and weddings became mixed up together the simplest plans grew confused. Lord Harrington set great value on securing a friendly Prussia. In the autumn of 1729, the Queen received a letter from her sister-in-law, Queen Sophia Dorothea, still urging only the marriage between Fritz and Wilhelmine.[96] A secret messenger from Berlin told her how much the Prussian royal family had lately suffered from King Frederick William's brutality, and urged a speedy settlement of the marriage before the King forced another suitor upon Wilhelmine. Sir Charles Hotham was accordingly chosen as special envoy, but he had to arrange the double marriage; to inform the Prussian King of his servants' treachery;* and to effect an Anglo-Prussian under-standing.[97] Unfortunately it was not clear what qualifica-tion he possessed for such a delicate mission, other than being related to Lord Chesterfield!

However, Hotham reported that King Frederick William consented to Wilhelmine's marriage, and might agree to his son the Crown Prince marrying an English Princess if the Crown Prince were appointed Regent of Hanover.[98] Hotham obtained leave to make this proposal, which attracted Frederick William until reflection showed him that it cast aspersions on his own generosity towards his son, and might involve him in a dilemma if the tension between his ally the Emperor and England resulted in war. He would only consent, he said, if England promised not to fight the Emperor in Germany and guaranteed the Prussian succession to Berg. The Crown Prince was too young to marry yet anyway. England would not agree to these requests when the second marriage was so far distant, but the Crown Prince begged Hotham to arrange his sister Wilhelmine's wedding, saying that he would know how to keep his word and marry his English cousin. His father's brutality had decided him to fly the country, a design he imparted to the new permanent English Envoy to Berlin, Captain Dickens, who hurried to London for instructions. Their Majesties sent Dickens back with their sympathy, but counselled their nephew to stay where he was. Seckendorff, meanwhile, had worked to strengthen the Prussian sovereign's natural inclination to-wards Austria. Hotham played his game for him by insisting that the King should read one of Grumbkow's

* Grumbkow and Reichenbach, the Prussian chargé d'affaires in London.

intercepted letters. His Majesty had already consented to Reichenbach's recall from London. When he saw the handwriting was Grumbkow's, he threw the letter angrily to the ground; 'j'ai eu assez de ces choses-là', he said, and left the room. Hotham considered his own King slighted. He refused Frederick William's invitation to dine, and packed his bags for England instead. The Crown Prince duly attempted flight, but was recaptured and narrowly escaped being executed, so maddened was his father. Rigorous inquiry brought to light Captain Dickens's knowledge of the Crown Prince's intention.

Queen Caroline was left to excuse Hotham's stiffness to the new Prussian ambassador, Count Degenfeld. Walpole privately deplored Hotham's conduct, but either he or Harrington should have chosen an envoy for other reasons than relationship to Lord Chesterfield.[99] More tact and less dignity would have served England better with Frederick William. Count Degenfeld had just presented his credentials to the King when he had audience with the Queen at Windsor in September 1730.[100] She returned his compliments cordially by expressing her affection for Their Prussian Majesties. She was sad, she said, to see that Frederick William had servants who wished to hinder her husband from knitting the two families together. Let her brother-in-law not draw away, because their common ties of religion, relationship, and interest made close friendship utterly desirable. Dare she beg him not to resent his son's flight so fiercely and to forgive the boy? Lord Harrington, too, soothed Degenfeld. The Prince of Wales asked the ambassador to urge his uncle not to oppose his happiness.

FREDERICK, PRINCE OF WALES AND HIS THREE ELDEST SISTERS AT KEW

(BY PHILIP MERCIER)

But Hotham's pride had given King Frederick William mortal offence. Comment from Berlin upon these interviews stated that the King felt little obliged by his cousin's intention of showing him what sort of servants he had. 'I never meddle in the domestic affairs of other rulers, therefore they should not stick their noses into mine. . . .'[101] Another dispatch declared:

As for the marriages, we hold to our intention of consenting neither to the double nor to the single marriage. We ask for no Princess of theirs for our family and will give them no daughter of ours even if the best conditions in the world were to be gained thereby,

which was conclusive. Austrian guile had triumphed over British blunders. All Queen Caroline's interviews, discussions, and letters were wasted. Wilhelmine was married to the Margrave of Bayreuth in 1731 and English Fritz had no bride.

The King, seeing him docile, ignored him. The Queen, though kindly, had much to mind. She knew that her company was not what Fritz at his age wanted most, and she could not make his sisters love him if they showed no desire for it. Of course he and Anne would always scrap. Anne was a proud young lady with lively ways and a fine complexion.[102] Long before her family rose, she was busy at her paints, her books, or her needle. She spoke several languages fluently, and her painting showed high promise. The Queen found her a splendid companion. She was a little disturbed by Anne's shrewdness over the King's failings, though he always treated Anne as the pick of his brood, but happily she was ignorant of Anne's worst comments upon Papa. 'When great points go as he would not have them he frets and is bad to himself; but when he is in his worst humours, and the devil to everybody . . . it is always because one of his pages has powdered his periwig ill, or a housemaid set a chair where it does not use to stand.'[103] Astute, but unfilial Anne!

She would have made a splendid Prince of Wales; perhaps Fritz realized it. They even quarrelled over their only mutual taste. Fritz was always happy at fiddle or 'cello; Anne played the harpsichord and sang well at sight; and Amelia sometimes completed the family trio. Trouble came over the opera.[104] Anne adored her master Handel, but Fritz, to spite his family, started a rival Italian Opera in Lincoln's Inn Fields. Rich friends financed this gay experiment in bad music sung by sensuous females, who drew all fashionable London for a time. Anne observed caustically that she soon expected to see half the House of Lords in their robes and coronets acting as the orchestra. But though Their Majesties never deserted Handel's operas, he was driven to penury by this campaign.

Caroline, the third sister, loved Anne too well to be Fritz's friend.[105] Her shyness hindered people from discovering her sweet nature, but to friends she talked well, and showed a sound judgement of character. She was happiest reading or drawing. She had a pretty skin and glossy brown hair. After Anne married, Caroline came to be their mother's constant companion. Passionately loyal, she resented slights upon either of her heroines. No greater contrast to Emily, the second sister, could be found. Emily was the family flirt, and for some years the family beauty.[106] Often her tongue outran her discretion, though she could be conciliatory when she chose. Her tastes lay in kennel, hunting-field, and the spicy personalities of gossip. Fritz thought her good company at first but ended by disliking her immensely. Brother William tagged along behind this elder part of the family, a little petted by them all. He knew how to please Papa by showing himself a bold rider to hounds. Mama took pride in his quickness. One thirtieth of January, anniversary of King Charles's execution, she chid him for clamouring for his dinner on this fast day. Did he think it right in the people to execute their King? William said he could not tell what the King's crime was until he read his history. Another time Papa jestingly asked him whether he had rather be a King or a Queen. 'Sir, I never yet tried; let me be one of them a month and I'll tell you.'[107] The Queen's babies, Mary and Louise, still kept to their nurseries.

Fritz sometimes sharpened his wits with Lord Hervey. They composed a comedy which they sent anonymously to Wilks, the actor-manager at Drury Lane. Wilks thought it poor stuff but Court interest overruled his judgement and he staged it. Despite the menaces of chuckers-out, cat-calls stopped the actors after a few minutes on the second night. A member of the audience expressed the general resentment over such threats to liberty. The people had bought the right to express their thoughts as they pleased. Let this nonsense give way to a proper play. Wilks ended an ugly situation by returning his patrons their money, and they trooped contentedly home.[108] Lord Hervey left for a round of country visits that autumn of 1731, counting himself secure in Fritz's affections. He resembled a jealous girl rather than a male equal in his fervid passion for his closest men friends, which weakness drew taunts from his enemies.[109] While away, Hervey sent the Prince scraps of doggerel, describing his visits and incidentally showing his intimacy with the royal family.

Two things happened in his absence. Fawning Bubb Dodington ousted him as Fritz's favourite, and Fritz cast a loving eye upon one of the Queen's maids of honour, Miss Vane, whose virtue had long ago proved frail. When he rendered even her courtesy title untenable, he set her up in a house of her own. Lord Hervey was back in London at Christmas. Fritz, ashamed of his fickleness, tried to hide his intimacy with Dodington from Hervey, but about Miss Vane he made no secret; ignorant, apparently, that Lord Hervey, too, had been her lover. Hervey regretted the loss, not of Miss Vane, but of Fritz's affections. He felt exasperated that this shameless miss had helped Dodington steal the Prince from him.[110] He wrote and threatened that he would punish her treachery by disclosing her promiscuity to Fritz. She sensibly took refuge in a fit, and when Fritz saw the letter he felt like killing Hervey, who found himself in general disgrace.

About this time Fritz met Lord Bolingbroke, who adroitly treated him as the rising hope to whom Bolingbroke himself played the cultured elder statesman. For the first time Fritz knew the exhilaration of contact with a brain that lightened the dark places of politics, and marshalled its theories for a perfect system of government free from the canker of corruption and party squabbles. He listened entranced, making the comparisons Bolingbroke intended he should between such ordered visions and

Walpole's squalid management. He met other young satellites imbibing the new wisdom with which to flout the old wizard. There was flattery in their friendship, but they could not be blamed, for they saw him as the spearhead of their attack against palace and minister.

VIII

PARTNERS AT WORK

COURTS adopt a routine compounded of precedent and the monarch's personal inclinations. King George II and Queen Caroline always came into residence at St. James's a few days before the King's birthday on October 31st.[1] Then loyal courtiers 'made new clothes' to congratulate His Majesty at one of the Drawing-rooms, and displayed their finery at the ball that night, receiving graceful royal compliments upon their gay outfits and good dancing.[2] Similar festivities marked March 1st, when an 'extraordinary appearance of nobility and gentry' came to wish the Queen long life. The day after the King's birthday, Walpole went off to his 'hunting congress' at Houghton, there to enjoy himself as a hearty Norfolk squire. 'His mind, His Majesty said, wanted relaxation, and his body exercise; and it was very reasonable that he should have a month in the year to look after his own private business, when all the rest of the year he was doing that of the public and his Prince.'[3] Other Court officials took his cue, without receiving the royal benediction, and London was quiet until the King opened the Parliamentary session in January.[4]

Neither of Their Majesties liked St. James's, but muddy roads through Hyde Park made Kensington an inconvenient winter residence. It was also thought to be damp. Early in his reign the King said that he would build a new London palace, so William Kent designed him a pearwood model.*[5] Intended for a site in Hyde Park, Kent's palace was an attenuated Palladian range, terminated by pavilions; the central feature conceived to display a group of statuary on the roof, and the whole bearing kinship to his work at Houghton, but royal thrift rejected it. At St. James's Court life reached its most formal. Their Majesties went in state to the Chapel Royal on Sundays, with the Great Sword carried before the King. They dined formally in public; held 'public days' several times a week, and gave court balls. They proceeded to the theatre or sat freezing loyally in Handel's empty Haymarket Opera House.

After the King closed Parliament in May, he carried off his family for a quiet month at Richmond Lodge. He had a small house for banqueting and hunting built in the Park. It has several times been enlarged and is now familiar as White Lodge. The Queen caused a private road to be made, leading from her gardens over Sheen Common into the Park, where she loved walking. That proud avenue of oaks east of White Lodge is named 'The Queen's Ride' in her honour. The King devised the bizarre pastime of hunting the wild turkeys, fattened on acorns and barley, which were kept in the Park for his pleasure. When the hounds had chased the astonished victims into trees, the King shot them, and the carnage was foul, for the largest birds weighed thirty pounds. Late in his reign they were destroyed because the keepers had been

* Now in the Victoria and Albert Museum, South Kensington.

worsted too often in their fights with poachers desiring turkeys for their dinner.[6]

Though the King affected to like retirement, he never tried it without becoming impatient for more spacious excitements, but the Queen loved Richmond Lodge as her private plaything, which she could alter or improve at fancy.[7] The summer often passed vigorously at Hampton Court, where the King stag-hunted twice a week, and despised fox-hunters for 'tormenting a poor fox that was generally a much better beast than any of those that pursued him'.[8] He told his Chamberlain, the Duke of Grafton, that he should ride or walk for his health instead, 'for with your great corps of twenty stone weight, no horse, I am sure, can carry you within hearing, much less within sight, of your hounds'. The Queen followed the sport in a chaise, as the Electress Sophia had done, with young Lord Hervey riding alongside to divert her.[9] Country subjects came to watch their sovereigns dine or walk the gardens, just as they did in 1716 when the King acted as Regent. Sometimes the holidays ended with a few weeks' shooting and more hunting at Windsor before the yearly round started at St. James's.[10]

Their Majesties liked Kensington best of their palaces. Modern, rural, spacious without being grandiose, it seemed to them a home. They spent spring days there, or summered there when the King did not fancy Hampton Court or Windsor, and the Queen always chose it as her headquarters during her regencies. Her rooms on the first floor occupied the eastern range of the palace, backing on to the Princesses' court. From the main staircase at the north end to privy chamber at the other end, they totalled 150 feet in length, and were connected with the King's suite, which faced south and east.

During crises the Queen was known to discuss business before she rose in the morning; her informant standing just outside the door which opened beside her bed, because queenly etiquette forbade admitting a man whilst she was still in it.[11] She met her eldest children at about nine o'clock for breakfast in Queen Mary's gallery, flooded by sunshine from the six great windows overlooking the gardens.[12] Left to herself afterwards, she wrote letters or gave interviews. Often before the party had finished its fruit served with sour cream or sipped up the chocolate, the King would come along to take the Queen for a walk, or to stay chatting until he had enjoyed 'the military amusement of peeping through the cane blinds of the windows to see the guard relieved' at eleven o'clock.[13] Morning did not always suit His Majesty's temper. Once he stayed about five minutes in the gallery, 'snubbed the Queen, who was drinking chocolate, for being always stuffing. . . . Emily for not hearing him. . . . Caroline for being grown fat, the Duke [William] for standing awkwardly . . . then carried the Queen to walk, and be re-snubbed in the garden'.[14]

When the King held his levée, the Queen made her toilet in readiness for the Drawing-room.[15] Rippling chatter played round her whilst her head was tired and her dress adjusted; she heard requests, settled squabbles, or dipped into new books. Once Mrs. Howard, then still a bedchamber woman, struck a jarring note.[16] 'Her fierce little eyes ablaze, her cheeks a peony plush, she refused to kneel and present the basin for the Queen to wash her hands. The Queen corrected her as she would a naughty child. ' "Yes, my dear Howard, I am sure you will; indeed you will. Go, go! fie for shame! Go, my good Howard; we will talk of this another time." ' And the rebellious lady withdrew to inquire of Lady Masham, Queen Anne's Abigail Hill, whether her revolt were justified, and found it was not. Precedents governed all such details. In Queen Anne's time, the page of the backstairs brought and set down basin and ewer upon a side table. The bedchamber woman carried it to the Queen, and knelt on the other side of the table over against the Queen. Mrs. Howard did what was required of her when next she waited, and the Queen tempered forgiveness with a rebuke. Another time the King came in, which he rarely did, and scolded the poor lady for covering the Queen's bosom with a kerchief. 'Is it because you have an ugly neck yourself that you love to hide the Queen's?'

With commendable if irreverent heed for time, morning prayers were said in the next room during these domesticities—

1st Parson (behind the scenes). From pride, vain glory, and hypocrisy, from envy, hatred, and malice, and all uncharitableness,

2nd Parson. Good Lord deliver us.

Queen. I pray, my good Lady Sundon, shut a little that door: those creatures pray so loud, one cannot bear oneself speak. (*Lady Sundon goes to shut the door.*)

So, so, not quite so much; leave it enough open for those parsons to think we may hear, and enough shut that we may not hear quite so much.*

* This and the extract below are quoted from a playlet Lord Hervey composed to divert the Queen, entitled 'The Death of Lord Hervey; or A Morning at Court. A Drama.' It is printed in the *Memoirs*, pp. 585–96.

Once Lady Sundon, or her substitute, obeyed her cue too well, and the offended parson ceased his office, for, said he, he refused to whistle the word of God through the keyhole.

Sir Robert frequently closed these sessions of gossip by wanting a business talk with the Queen. The company then withdrew, leaving the partners to concert their plans before the Queen left for the daily Drawing-room at 2.30.[17]

Queen. Adieu, my good Sir Robert, I believe it is late—I must go a moment into the drawing-room; do you know who is there?

Sir Rob. I saw the Duke of Argyll, Madam.

Queen. Oh! mon Dieu! I am so weary of that Felt Marshal, and his tottering head and his silly stories about the Bishops, that I could cry whenever I am obliged to entertain him.* And who is there more?

Sir Rob. There is my Lord President Wilmington, Madam.

Queen. Oh! that's very well; I shall talk to him about his fruit, and some silly council at the Cock-pit, and the Plantations: my Lord President loves the Plantations.†

Sir Rob. He had plantations of his own for several years together, Madam, in Leicester Fields, but your Majesty would not let them grow.‡

Queen. He was, poor man, just the reverse of those people in the Gospel who reaped where they had not sowed, for my good Lord President sowed where he did not reap. But who is there beside?

Sir Rob. There is my tottering Lord Harrington.

Queen. Oh! mon Dieu! I wish he tottered till he fell quite down, that I might not have the fatigue of being obliged to entertain him. The slowness of that drone is a fatigue to me that is inexpressible: he must have six hours in the morning for his chocolate and his

* The rank of Field-Marshal was first introduced into the British Army in 1735, when the Duke of Argyll and Lord Orkney, the two oldest Generals, received that title.

† The business of the Colonies at the Privy Council which sat at what was called the Cock-Pit.

‡ Paying court to Mrs. Howard.

toilet, and the newspapers; six hours more for his dinner; six hours more for his nasty guenipes and for supper; and six more for sleep; and there is the twenty-four very well disposed: and if ever he gives by chance six hours to his business, it is for what might be done in six minutes, and should have been done six days before.*

Sir Rob. Ha! ha! ha! Poor Harrington! I wonder he need take six hours to dress, when your Majesty shows you can dress him in six minutes, with six words.

Queen. Adieu, adieu, my good Sir Robert; I must go, though you are to-day excellent conversation.

And the Queen sailed serenely into the drawing-room where, with the King and some of her children, she greeted the assembled company ranged in a circle.[18] The Queen curtsied slightly, courtiers bowed and curtsied very low. The privileged kissed her hand, the King lightly saluted favoured ladies on one cheek. Then Their Majesties singled out friends and supporters for a short conversation. The matter of His Majesty's remarks was slight. Of one, he inquired after his health. 'His question to the Duke of Newcastle was whether the wind was fair,' to the Duke of Argyll he spoke about a cure for a cold. His Majesty knew his dignity and was 'careful of what he should not say rather than what he should'.[19] The Queen beckoned another to the intimate group. 'Come near, Mr. Speaker, I think you don't care to come up,' this last a gentle rap because the Speaker appeared seldom at court, having a coolness with Walpole. 'Madam, if my distance be a sin,' came the bold retort, 'I hope your Majesty will lay it at your own door'. The Queen had the last word: 'This is a rub for me', she thought, and replied: 'Here is the Speaker of the House of Lords, I will set him on your back"', for

* The Queen once said this to Lord Hervey, *Memoirs*, p. 346.

great as Speaker Onslow reckoned himself, Lord Chancellor Talbot was greater, and paid his respects better at Court.[20] Or the Queen held discourse with Lord Egmont on Popery; about the dispute between the Jansenists and Jesuits in France, or asked his opinion about the proper pronunciation of place names in Latin.[21] She kept her concentration by mixing genuine talk with boring civilities.

After dinner, time vanished between business and pleasure. The Queen went out to direct some garden works in progress; she might inspect an artist's studio or call upon a friend with new art treasures to show her. She held her metaphysical parties most days, and forgot politics in argument or speculation. Evening usually brought Sir Robert back with the day's news, flavoured by Lord Hervey's gossip, and twice a week another Drawing-room was held. The King's subjects grumbled because he preferred giving select parties at whim to entertaining them formally. He liked masquerades best, when he slipped amongst the crowd in disguise; then passed the evening tête-à-tête, his absence tactfully unremarked. As the Queen once watched the masked dancers from a box, just opposite it, the King kissed a pretty player from the comedy. The girl was scandalized. 'Don't be shocked and don't worry, my wife never sees what I do,' came the quick tribute to conjugal discretion.[22] The Queen preferred to make this the literal truth by staying away from such revelries. 'These masquerades are the corruption of our youth and a scandal to the nation,' sighed sober men, and the Bishops petitioned the King and preached against them, but His Majesty was stout in defence of his pleasures.[23]

On private nights the Queen relaxed in cards and conversation amongst her intimates, while the King took himself to Mrs. Howard. When repetition at length staled that pastime, he played quadrille in his daughters' apartments 'talking a little bawdy to Lady Deloraine', before he reappeared round nine o'clock to see the Queen, who often summoned Hervey to enliven the talk.[24] The Queen took up her work, while the King paced the room (for talk came easier to him in movement) questioning Hervey, breaking into German asides for the Queen's private benefit, and chatting with his cronies, Lord Lifford and his sister Lady de Roucy. These pious but needy Huguenots were always his pre-bedtime audience. He prattled to the brother about armies, to the sister of genealogies, and he 'never forgot their goodness, but never remembered their poverty'.[25] The Queen humoured him in such inoffensive but insipid company 'till from yawning she came to nodding and from nodding to snoring'. She found it exhausting to guide a husband and rule a country, keeping the husband ignorant of either process. The weary Queen slept gratefully.

If Queen Caroline had been married to an English-born King, she might have helped to restore the Court to its high place in the people's affections, but not to its lost power. National pride and activity no longer centred round the Court as in Plantagenet or Tudor times. For the Revolution Settlement had enabled the House of Commons, and to some extent the Peers, to become the new founts of patronage and honour. The powerful Whig oligarchy looked to politics and cultured private life for satisfaction. It despised the Tory squires and small landowners as narrow-minded bores, but country activities brought these men fruitful rewards and a useful share in local government. Fearing innovation, they were appeased by Walpole's legislative caution. That backbone of Whiggism, the mercantile community, by contrast applauded his financial enterprise which gave it growing prosperity. Such were the only classes who normally counted politically, because the narrow franchise denied the masses a vote. Yet the common people mocked continental despotism to rejoice in their free institutions: Parliamentary government, freedom of speech and press, a slight measure of religious toleration. Any threat to these glories roused them easily; and they were too credulous of supposed attacks upon liberty. Then they wrecked a government's policy as effectively as can the vast modern electorate. Queen Caroline experienced this fact, which explained Walpole's famous motto, 'let sleeping dogs lie'.

She first saw him shape his policy to his precept over a Church matter, in which he asked her help. The request was humorous, for about the Church they had different ideas. The Queen's taste for controversy and discussion brought friendship with the boldest metaphysical thinkers. Though she favoured deism herself, she helped men for their merits, irrespective of the views they held. She envisaged the episcopacy as a select academy whose aspirants should prove their theological distinction: piety and learning sprinkled with brilliance to hurry progress. In her opinion, Dr. Clarke's lucid quest for truth deserved a place. Tory clergy were as capable as the Whig in providing members. She judged it important to hearten them by wise promotions because they were numerically stronger, though less influential, than their Whig brethren; for parish priests traditionally professed an orderly, un-Jacobite Toryism. As Queen Anne had given effect to her High Church views in choosing her bishops, why should not Queen Caroline express her policy, in George II's name? Because her father-in-law, the late King, ignorant of Churchmen and Church practice, had let his ministers exercise his patronage in this as in most other spheres of public affairs.[26] From being the Sovereign's friends, the bishops had become the Ministers' men. As King George II hated the prating, fawning pack, he cared not a whit about the change.

Walpole used his advantage practically. In the House of Lords he wanted twenty-six safe episcopal votes which Whig-thinking bishops would provide. In the parishes he desired that the Tory clergy should feel so secure from Popery and unorthodoxy as to use their influence for him at election times. That security was synonymous with intolerance did not worry him. He chose a unique clerical adviser for his policy. Edmund Gibson, Bishop of London since 1723, combined strong Whiggism with orthodoxy so rigid as to satisfy his humble clerical followers.[27] He gave Walpole Whig bishops, and kept his episcopal flock un-sullied by dangerous thinkers.

Of course the Queen warred with Walpole's 'Pope' or 'Heir Apparent' to Canterbury, as men called Gibson.[28] They first joined battle over Dr. Clarke. Gibson won because his faculty supported him in thinking the Doctor glaringly liberal; so Clarke never became a bishop. The Queen equalized neatly by obtaining a see for her learned friend, Dr. Sherlock, whose orthodoxy was stainless, but whose Toryism Gibson feared as a source of disunity among the bishops. Sherlock liked society as much as Gibson shunned it. Thereafter the Queen and Sherlock fought together, but the Queen was handicapped by duality of purpose. Though she could afford theories over Church affairs, national and family interests allowed no political adventures. When the first involved the second, then the Whig Queen triumphed over the liberal thinker.

The Queen deemed it reasonable that the Dissenters should desire, this summer of 1732, to see the Test and Corporation Acts repealed. The Acts had been passed in Stuart times under the menace of Papist domination, to exclude Roman Catholics from public influence, by making it incumbent on public officials to receive the Anglican sacrament. The Dissenters had accepted the disability, for the safety of the Protestant cause, and later been allowed to keep the letter of the law by receiving the sacrament once upon obtaining any public office. As good Whigs and sturdy traders, they now expected a Whig parliament to reward their loyalty. Yet they placed Walpole and Gibson in a dilemma.[29] Effective religious toleration still lay in the womb of time. Church and public felt stupidly nervous of any liberty that might revive Popery. Gibson, the good shepherd, feared for his flock's safety if these 'necessary safeguards' were removed. Walpole, the wary politician, feared for his majority in the general election of 1734 if he either disobliged the Dissenters or roused the nervous Tory clergy. Therefore the Dissenters must be persuaded to choose a more convenient season for their request.

Only Hoadly, Bishop of Salisbury, could so persuade them because his sympathy for the Dissenters made them trust him. Walpole had disobliged Hoadly; but the Bishop attended the Queen's discussion circle. Would she help? Walpole asked her. She agreed to preach on his text for two reasons: the coming elections and the rising clamour over a fiscal reform which Walpole meditated. To present the Opposition with two such stirring parrot cries as 'the Church in danger' and 'general excise' was to court defeat.

After praising Hoadly's past services and continued loyalty to the King, the Queen made inexpediency the motive of her request.[30] 'All times were not proper even to do proper things, so it was impossible for the Dissenters, either for their own or for the Whig interest, to choose one more improper than the present to try their strength and their friends on this favourite point.' Already the Whigs were split into ministerial and anti-ministerial parts. A third class would sprout up over this debate; Church Whigs, as stubborn against the repeal as the High Church Tories. Then the Dissenters could not hope for a majority. Strife would spread outside Parliament. Parish clergy, at present soothed by the promise of immutability, would set all turbulent spirits against the Government were this pledge to be broken, preventing another Whig Parliament from being elected. If the Dissenters chose another time, their political friends would not be hindered from supporting them through fear of losing their seats at the general election.

Hoadly expressed his unchanged conviction that the Dissenters' plea was reasonable, but said that if inquiries showed him that its present discussion in Parliament would hurt the Whigs without helping the Dissenters, he would urge its postponement.[31] Gossip destroyed the Queen's good work and Hoadly's influence by asserting that she

SIR ROBERT WALPOLE

(*By* J. B. VAN LOO)

had undermined his sympathy for the Dissenters. Other people's bad faith produced a coolness between them. However, Walpole's good luck held. The sanguine Dissenters entrusted their interests to a central committee in London. Alas, its members were all prosperous city men dependent upon Sir Robert's good will for their business prosperity. They acted as his puppets, but with the utmost respect for appearances. Committee met ministers, to hear from Walpole that their petition had no hope of present success. Other Ministers looked wise, took snuff and kept silent, but Newcastle and the Lord Chancellor added their superfluous say. The committee told a general assembly of Dissenters that patience would bring its sure reward. It did, in the following century.

It was New Year, 1733, by the time the Dissenters heard about the virtues of patience. Public attention fixed on Walpole's fiscal plan.[32] The Queen hoped that its good potentialities would still the murmurs against it. Walpole planned to abolish the existing customs duties on tobacco and wine, and substitute a lower rate of excise duty. The excise would gain the public revenue half a million pounds by foiling cheats in the assessment and collection of customs dues, and let Walpole abolish the land tax of 1s. in the £. Landowners and country gentlemen, mostly Tories, would thank him because they had long been taxed while traders escaped direct taxation. This purpose appealed to the Queen's idea for conciliating the unpolitical Tories, whose friendliness would give the Government broader support.

The King thought that such generosity would make his reign the most glorious since the Revolution.[33] Abroad, his prudence settled the peace of Europe; at home every man would be his friend. 'George the Wise', they might call him. And, happy thought, his income would grow, since one-sixth of the tobacco and wine duties passed to the Civil List funds. He played the indulgent godparent to the scheme and its sponsor, 'that brave fellow Walpole'. Thus the Queen's quiet counsels had erased his prejudices. Of his own former favourites, Wilmington had lost his confidence and Townshend left his service. Walpole basked in royal beams. If His Majesty had any affection to spare from himself and the Queen, he gave it to *ce gros homme* Sir Robert.

Walpole's excellent plan only entailed an addition of 125 officials to the existent excise staff in cities, towns, and villages. But a tactical error already imperilled its success. During the past session he innocently hinted at his intention. The fatal words 'general excise' passed his lips; fatal because they spelt tyranny to the public mind. The Civil War, the impecunious later Stuarts, and the war against Louis XIV, all needed a heavy excise to help defray their burdens. The Opposition placed the most odious meaning upon Walpole's chance remark. It was their pious duty. A whirlwind campaign incited the populace to believe that Walpole planned a tax on everything. Clothes, food, and drink would all cost more; swarms of excise officials would violate the Englishman's sacred privacy, seeing that no article escaped the tax; and vast revenues would let the Crown rule without Parliament.

Though Walpole was horrified when he heard of the grisly intentions attributed to him, the modesty of his true plan made him misjudge the potency of the clamour. He had pamphlets sent all over the country exposing the lies,

and explaining that he proposed no more than an alteration
in the method of collecting the two existing duties on
tobacco and wine, which by its simple efficiency would foil
the smugglers and illicit dealers to the public's gain.[34] He
thought any hint of retraction would invite similar obstruc-
tion to his measures in the future, and relied, for the rest,
on his own sanity to exorcise the madness, but he was
handicapped before the Parliamentary struggle began by
discontented colleagues. Certain lords, who publicly supported him, secretly resented his pre-eminence and had no
mind to share his unpopularity.[35] Their dissatisfaction did
not long remain hidden, and added fuel to Opposition fires
of criticism, which burnt merrily despite the Government
pamphlets; truth was too late and too drab to extinguish
such a promising conflagration.

One day during the clamour the Queen received a
request for an audience from Lord Stair.[36] She wondered
what this experienced blusterer wanted with her. A man
to make women quail was my Lord Stair. At once he
boomed against Walpole and his Excise: a ravaging
French tirade. This dangerous, ill-conceived, hasty scheme
would ruin the nation or chase her family from the throne
by its unpopularity. Only Sir Robert's wanton pride and
boundless egoism made him prefer to risk his master's
Crown rather than submit to reason. The Queen was
silent. Of course my Lord sympathized with Her Majesty.
She could know nothing of this man except what he or his
toadies told her. Madam, he was the most hated man in
the kingdom. Alas! some of the dislike attached to her.
Still the Queen kept silence. Then Stair warmed to home
truths. That Walpole governed Her Majesty nobody

doubted. The King was simply the engine of his Minister's ambition. What other man, Madam, could have made you love a Campbell? Yet Lord Islay, who once courted Mrs. Howard, managed all Walpole's Scotch business; a worthless rascal too. Here the Queen quietly observed that Lord Stair was speaking of the King's servant to the King's wife. Stair proceeded, thrilled by his indictment and the Queen's quietness. The defection among the Lords over this Bill would startle Their Majesties and Walpole. Only corruption could force it through the Commons. Therefore conscience alone made Stair oppose it.

'Ah, my Lord! ne me parlez point de conscience; vous me faîtes évanouir.' The Queen reminded Lord Stair that his tender conscience had not stopped him voting for the Peerage Bill, which also curtailed liberty. She then re-sumed silence to hear his bullying conclusion. Stair was pleased by his diatribe so thoughtfully received, but the Queen found that silence paid with his masterful type. She thought, while her lecturer exhausted his arguments in one harangue. Stair's over-emphasis held a bitter kernel of truth. Walpole and his Excise were hated. To the lords like Stair would presently be added other timid Whigs. New confidence and unity marked the Opposition. How simple for the Crown to stop the Excise or drop Sir Robert! The crowds would cheer outside St. James's as they had not done since the accession. But no—Stair's onslaught was a greater tribute to the Queen's influence than to his perspicacity. It might have frightened the King. His Majesty, so warlike in battle, was no political hero. Boldly the Queen counterthrust.

'Surely, my Lord, you think you are either talking to a child or

one that dotes; for supposing this Bill to be everything which you
have described it to be, do you imagine I should be weak enough to
believe that you would oppose it for the reasons you have given?
. . . Do you my Lord, pretend to talk of the opinion of the electors
having any influence on the elected? . . . Remember the Peerage
Bill, my Lord. Who then betrayed the interests of their constituents? . . . Who deprived their constituents of all chance of ever
taking turn with those whom they sent to Parliament?* To talk,
therefore, in this patriot strain . . . can move me . . . to nothing
but laughter. Where you get your lesson from I do not want to
know. Your system of politics you collect from the *Craftsman*;
your sentiments . . . from my Lord Bolingbroke and my Lord
Carteret . . . two as worthless men of parts as any in this country.
. . . For the rest . . . the best advice I can give you, if you are a
friend to the King, is to detach yourself from his enemies; . . . if
you are a friend to honesty, not to herd with those who disclaim
it; and if you are a friend to our family, never to cabal with those
who look on ours and the Jacobites' cause as things . . . to be
espoused or combated in no other view, and on no other motive,
than as this or that may least or most conduce to the wanting or
gratifying their own private avarice and ambition.'

'Madame, vous êtes trompée, et le Roi est trahi,' uttered Stair
pompously, and retired amazed.

On the day of the first reading, tension at Court was
unbearable. Extra constables and magistrates were on duty
at Westminster to tackle the expected mob; the Guards
were ready to march at need. The King had ordered his
Vice-Chamberlain, Lord Hervey, to send him news from
the House. At five o'clock the letter came. Crowds, great
but orderly, hissed the Court party. Walpole spoke
cogently, but the Opposition was out for his downfall.

* This referred to Stair as a Scotch Peer. The Peerage Bill would have
included 25 hereditary Scotch Peers in the House of Lords, instead of the
16 elected by their fellow peers for the duration of each Parliament.

After one o'clock next morning, a famished Hervey returned to St. James's. The King carried him off to the Queen's bedchamber, where they plied him with ten thousand questions but no food. The Government had secured a majority of sixty-one. By the end of this impromptu session, their Majesties knew how each speaker had looked and acted, as well as his words.

Three dispiriting weeks ensued. The Government majority sank to a handful over minor divisions, but their Majesties stood firm in their encouragement to Walpole. Lord Hervey and Mr. Pelham reported to them every day.[37] The King, cheeks aflush, praised Walpole's stand. 'He is a brave fellow; he has more spirit than any man I ever knew.' He had hearkened to the Queen's coaching in constitutional principles. No longer did His Majesty wish to play the despot directing his minions, but pronounced that[38]

'A prince who will be well served in this country must free his minister from all apprehensions at Court, that the minister may give all attention to the affairs of his master.'

Parliament and City bragged of that Minister's speedy ruin. Society ladies driving through the City were rudely stopped.

'We know this coach, it comes from St. James's end of the town knock the coachman down.'

A quick-witted lady saved her servant:

'Though we live at St. James's end, we are as much against Excise as you.' 'Are you so? Then God bless you. Coachman, drive on!'[39]

The Queen had no delusions about the public temper. Lord Scarbrough, His Majesty's Master of the Horse, and personal friend these many years, had told her: 'Madam, I will answer for my regiment against the Pretender, but not against the excise'. Rumour ran that the King had taken it not unkindly when some of his great officials, like Scarbrough, told him that they must vote against the Bill. The Queen was arbiter of Walpole's fate a second time.

Two days before the second reading was due, he came to her weary and unnerved by the stupid frenzy.[40] He would drop the Bill. If Her Majesty deemed it in the King's interest to shed such an unpopular villain as himself, he would yield up his office too. That way lay a quick end to her troubles. The Queen chid him roughly. Did he think her a poltroon, to make such an offer, or an idiot perhaps who judged his scheme rotten because fools obstructed it? No, as long as she lived he had her support. The King joined their pre-Drawing-room conference and echoed the Queen's remarks. They decided, however, that after the rejection of the City's petition against the Bill, due next day, the measure should be dropped. None of them wanted to do good at the expense of bloodshed. So they came to the evening Drawing-room with Walpole newly sustained, but the Queen's vitality had ebbed in the process. She broke up her quadrille party early, pleading headaches and vapours, and retired to hear Lord Hervey's latest town talk.[41] In his dual part of Vice-Chamberlain and Member of Parliament, Hervey made himself their private reporter, and his usefulness erased the bad impression left by his quarrel with Fritz two years ago. His duties kept him always at hand; his lodgings in St. James's lay at the foot of the Queen's back staircase. The Princesses found him good company and the Queen came to treat him with easy familiarity as she would any young friend of the family.

Next night Hervey had gloomy news. Though the City's petition was insolent and unusual, the Government only scraped a majority of seventeen to reject it. 'It is over, we must give way; but pray tell me a little how it passed,' said the Queen.[42] As Lord Hervey named the latest deserters, the King's explosive comments saved her tears that were near. The Cavendish brothers, one 'a fool', the other 'half mad'; Sir William Lowther, 'a whimsical fellow'; Sir Thomas Prendergast, 'an Irish blockhead' and Lord Tyrconnel, 'a puppy' that never voted twice the same way. At the second reading, Sir Robert moved the Bill's postponement. He left the House, jostled and hooted by an abusive mob. Three of his friends were hurt in escorting him out. That night the City rang its joy bells and burnt effigies of a fat man and a fat woman—Walpole and the Queen—in roaring bonfires. Newspaper rejoicings lasted a fortnight. Grateful letters poured in from country voters at this defeat of a tyrannical measure and minister. The Queen knew that good faith and good intentions sometimes have to be their own reward.

She counted her trust repaid by Walpole's renewed vigour. Once the Bill was dropped his force returned. In the eight remaining weeks of the session he regained his mastery of the Commons, saved by the members knowing that he enjoyed Their Majesties' full confidence. By virtue of it he controlled the many place-holders under the Crown, and secured other members through indirect patronage. Let them doubt his favour in the Palace, and at once their support cooled off so that his downfall should not end their employment. The prospect of sharing such odium as his Excise scheme aroused had shaken his following, who returned to duty eager to make amends for their timidity by obedient votes. With the Commons docile again, Walpole tackled the mutinous clique in the House of Lords. The Queen agreed that discipline was as necessary in an administration as in an army.[43] These Lords could not enjoy the King's money and vote against his measures. Chesterfield was amongst them, long convinced that his brilliance lowered itself by serving under Walpole; while the older mutineers resented the Minister's engrossing the royal confidence. When these Lords were dismissed their public or military employments, they found puerile satisfaction in forming a 'Rump Steak Club'.[44] The entrance rule laid down that the King must have 'turned his rump' to each member. Lord Clinton, no longer Lord of the Bedchamber, threw off his Bath ribbon, saying that it was unfit for a gentleman to wear.[45]

Walpole dispensed a sharp rap to fractious members of both Houses through the King's dissolution speech in June:

My Lords and Gentlemen,—I cannot pass by unobserved the wicked endeavours that have lately been made use of to inflame the minds of the people, and by the most unjust representations to raise tumults and disorders that almost threatened the peace of the kingdom; but I depend upon the force of truth to remove the groundless jealousies that have been raised of designs carrying on against the liberties of my people, and upon your known fidelity to defeat and frustrate the expectations of such as delight in confusion. . . .

Walpole had cause to be thankful for the Queen's loyalty during the slipperiest session of their co-operation.

Yet, unluckier than he, she faced a new problem. Fritz had expressed no opinion about the Excise Bill in public, but his private actions betrayed that he, like Lord Stair, took his politics from Bolingbroke. His adviser, Mr. Dodington, never spoke for the Excise, though holding a place in the Treasury, and Mr. Townshend, Fritz's Groom of the Bedchamber, voted against the Bill.[46] In flaunting his friendship for the 'Rump Steak' lords, Fritz sailed near mutiny himself, and courted cheap favour by tacitly censuring his parents' support for a just measure. To avoid giving Fritz an imaginary but hopeful grievance, Walpole refrained from dismissing Mr. Dodington from office, but by the end of the year Fritz felt enough confidence in his new politics to criticize Walpole openly.[47]

IX

'THE SOLE MOVER'

'Madam, I can do nothing without you. Whatever my industry and watchfulness for your interest and welfare suggest, it is you must execute. You, Madam, are the sole mover of this Court. . . .'
Walpole to Queen Caroline, Hervey, *Memoirs*, p. 375.

HIS prestige and Protestantism made it hard for the King to marry his children suitably. Most of his brother monarchs were Roman Catholics. The handful of German princelings who might have mated with the Elector of Hanover's children were too unimportant for the King of England's daughters, though perhaps one of their sisters could share Fritz's life. Even if King Frederick William of Prussia had not taken the huff, he had no son old enough for Anne. So it was a feat to find her one possible suitor, especially with the name of Orange, which was music to English ears. William IV, Count of Nassau, Stadtholder of Friesland, Groningen, and Guelderland, was the same age as Anne. Nobody pretended that he was an eligible party, but royal princesses were reared to take a prosaic view of marriage. The English Government had only hopes rather than expectations from this match, though William's family associations with England assured him warm greeting. The Whig system was based on alliance with the maritime Dutch Republic, which had been so torn by domestic strife since the Treaty of Utrecht, as to make it a feeble partner. The honour done the Republic by this marriage might persuade first the most powerful State, Holland, to elect William its Stadtholder, then the remaining States to follow suit. Thus he could give the Republic a sorely needed unity, to make it a powerful ally once more.[1]

'The devil take politics', when they threatened her Anne's happiness, the Queen felt like saying. She minded not a whit sacrificing herself to necessity, but she hated to think of Anne's being thwarted. The politicians had hopes, she had only fears about the match. William's good stock scarcely atoned for his poverty and worldly insignificance. He was almost a hunchback. If his character was of purest gold, the Queen doubted its ability to triumph over such misfortunes. Neither she nor the King glossed over these drawbacks to Anne.[2] Since William was first mentioned as a possible husband six years before, Their Majesties left her freedom to say no. But Anne said a quick, decisive yes and kept to it. Her character preferred a certain husband and possible scope for her talents, to future frustration when Fritz became King. She knew Papa thought it a proper match, provided she could bear William's person. 'If it was a monkey, she would marry him,' said she resolutely, and seemed much happier than the Queen. Negotiations were tedious because Holland resented the part arranged for it by the English Government.[3]

However, near the end of the Excise session of Parliament, the King was able to mitigate his unpopularity by announcing to both Houses the intended marriage of Anne to William, Prince of Orange. Government spokesmen lauded the historical connexions between Orange and

England, and praised the added security the marriage would give the Protestant succession.[4] In theory the match appeared a blessing! A neat fortune from the sale of colonial Crown Lands lay idle in the Exchequer, so Parliament made Anne a wedding present of £80,000. Like the King's Civil List and the Queen's jointure, this amount was nearly double what a marrying Princess had received before.[5] Though the King deemed William a nobody until marriage should make him the King of England's son-in-law, His Majesty's fondness for Anne supplemented the Parliamentary gift by promising her £5,000 a year to make her income nearly equal to William's £12,000. St. James's prepared its wedding finery. A covered wooden gallery to seat 4,000 was built to lead the processions from the Palace to the adjoining French chapel destined for the ceremony. Old Sarah Marlborough, who saw it from her neighbouring windows, called it the King's 'orange chest'.

William would have preferred a marriage by proxy instead of exposing his ugliness to ridicule, but the King's hauteur made him come in person to England, where he arrived early in November.[6] The King behaved in conformity with his thoughts by letting but a single Lord and coach meet William, and grew peevish at being made to send Lord Hervey with his compliments to Somerset House that evening. Anne passed the day practising at the harpsichord with some of the Opera people, as easy as she had ever been. The Queen admired her calmness but could not emulate it. She ordered a report from Hervey the instant he returned. She must know 'without disguise what sort of hideous animal she was to prepare herself to

see'. Hervey brought back some comfort. Certainly
Orange was hideous, but his sensible address and engaging
manners conveyed the impression that he had forgotten
his deformities, which made his companions overlook
them too. This was solid praise, coming from hypercritical
Hervey. Orange drove to court next morning, welcomed
for his name by cheering crowds and a throng of nobility in
the Palace. The Queen saw that Hervey was right, but her
motherly concern could not ignore his disastrous appearance. Anne's greeting to her bridegroom was so natural
that it might have been bestowed upon an Adonis. He
showed equal good breeding by feigning not to notice the
King's casual treatment. Compunction at seeing Anne
marry some one so ugly probably caused the rudeness, for,
after William's arrival, the King gave her a superb pair of
ear-rings, 'a great ornament to the person, but poor consolation to the heart'.[7]

The day before the wedding, a Sunday, William went to
the Dutch Church, which was packed with curious spectators. Coming from the overheated atmosphere straight
into the winter air, he caught pneumonia, so that the wedding had to be postponed.[8] Though he long lay ill, the
King forbade any member of the Royal family to visit him
and never proffered hospitality for the expensive extension
of a visit, which needed convalescence at Kensington and
Bath before he was strong enough for the ceremony on
March 14th, 1734.[9] It took place about seven in the
evening. Anne wore her groom's lavish present of jewel-
lery. The diamonds in the necklace were so large that
twenty-two circled her neck. William's retinue appeared
as splendid 'as gold and silver varied in brocade and lace

and embroidery could make them'; a gentle rebuke to his father-in-law's condescension. A flowing peruke hid his round back. His finery and his ease impressed everyone except the Queen, who showed maternal woe at losing her dearest Anne. The Court saw the young couple to bed; then poor Orange could use no discreet disguises. Next morning the Queen described her anguish:

'Ah! mon Dieu! quand je voyais entrer ce monstre, pour coucher avec ma fille, j'ai pensé m'évanouir; je chancelais auparavant, mais ce coup là m'a assommée . . . c'est trop sot en moi, mais j'en pleure encore.'

'Lord! Madam, in half a year all persons seem alike,' Hervey soothed her prosaically.

A mother's softness perhaps, but still the Queen pitied her Anne those six months.

Their parting was not yet. While Horatio Walpole busied himself cajoling Holland's rulers to forget their jealousy of William, and receive him with dignity, the bridal pair spent six gay weeks in London.[10] Anne courted her 'Pepin', as she called him, prodigiously, so did the public. Fritz thought himself the people's idol, but only a little clapping saluted him at the Opera. 'The moment the Prince of Orange appeared the whole house rang with peals and huzzas.' This enthusiasm irritated the King too, but he gave Orange the Garter, and Parliament made him a British subject.[11] Complimentary addresses upon the marriage dwelt too lovingly upon England's past debts to the House of Orange, to please the reigning monarch from Hanover.[12] For the Excise had left a legacy of dislike to Their Majesties no less than to their Minister.

At the end of April Anne left a mournful family, except

for Fritz, who excused himself from saying good-bye for fear they might both be too affected. His ingenuity did him credit. The King showered kisses upon Anne. Even the thought of seeing her again soon, during Pepin's planned absence from the States, could not stem the Queen's tears. She seldom exposed her tenderness, but to Anne she was always the doting mother. She wrote the day Anne sailed:

Dear Heart, My sadness is indescribable, I never had any sorrows over you, Anne, this is the first, a cruel one. Caroline behaves so well but our conversations always finish on the same sad note. The King, who sends you affectionate greetings, is worse than us all. To change the conversation I was forced to talk about Griff.* Orange is a good man and will ever be a great favourite of mine . . . love me always as tenderly as the most affectionate mother flatters herself that you do.[13]

Thereafter the Queen always wrote kindly about her son-in-law William, resolved only to remember his good sense. The day that Anne left, the Royal family moved to Richmond Lodge for their quiet holiday.[14]

As a means of taking her mind off Anne, the Queen found the General Election almost a blessing. At last it was upon them, this election to which the Dissenters had been sacrificed, only for Walpole to incur greater hatred over the Excise Bill. His personal efforts in the Norfolk county elections did not prevent Tory victory. Other Whigs who lost their seats all blamed the same cause. That strong Tory, Bishop Sherlock, came often to Richmond, exulting over his party's triumphant mood. He unnerved the Queen enough to make her grumble to Lord Hervey about the

* The family nickname for Fritz.

Whigs' disunity, which she considered responsible for their defeats. The Tories kept firmly together in spite of receiving constant discouragement at Court.[15] Whereupon Lord Hervey privately urged Walpole to leave his fascinating mistress, Miss Skerrit, and return to defend his interests. Thus were the inconveniences of being 'sole minister' apparent. Walpole could not take a deserved respite without the wrong people profiting by it.

In forecasting the election results, Bishop, Queen, and Opposition reckoned without two factors. To bring them victory, the Tories put their faith in past Whig misdeeds, rather than in a future programme of their own. The electorate on the whole disliked Walpole, but his pledge never to revive Excise lulled it back again into an apathy which was unfavourable to the Tory tactics of fanning old indignation. Then there was Newcastle, whose busy, devious methods, plain only to himself, achieved sweeping success for the Whigs. Walpole tolerated the Duke's Parliamentary ineptitude in return for this vote-catching ability. Lord Islay, Walpole's Scotch manager, had an equal though cruder knack of gaining Whig ends. Though the Opposition made headway and gained some brilliant recruits like Pitt and Lyttelton, the Queen was easy about Whig victory when the Court moved to Kensington for the summer.

The Queen welcomed Anne back, delighted at her hopes of becoming a mother. Anne kept silence about them in Holland lest they should prevent her visit, which heartened the Queen during the summer, filled with family and foreign incident. First there was Fritz, whose behaviour over the Excise indicated a new phase. The Queen believed him to be good-hearted, but what weakness he showed in letting his fine friends of the *Craftsman* dictate his behaviour and policy! Though he thought himself so independent, he danced to their direction in quarrelling with Anne the past summer for 'daring to be married before him'. Her wedding present of £80,000 irked him most, and made him consider raising a Parliamentary discussion about his own income.[16]   As if any one but the Opposition would profit by such lack of pride! Its members made open glee when Fritz sulked away from Court during the following months, then put him up to a childish trick to score off the King.[17]   He appeared at the King's New Year levee in 1734, hoping to be qualified for the 'Rump Steak' club, and thus win easy sympathy. Forewarned, the King spoke pleasantly to him, and defeated that scheme.

Lord Hervey dared the Queen's wrath by telling her that many of her friends thought that Fritz had too little money, to which she replied sharply:[18]

'My God! that people will always be judging and deciding upon what they know nothing of! . . . Pray . . . tell them that the Prince costs the King £50,000 a year, which, till he is married, I believe any reasonable body will think a sufficient allowance for him. But, poor creature, with not a bad heart, he is induced by knaves and fools that blow him up to do things that are as unlike an honest man as a wise one.'

Hervey pointed out the flaw in her reasonable defence. Why would His Majesty not let the Prince keep his own table and settle the £50,000 on him as a fixed yearly allowance? At present people credited the King with giving his son only half that sum, but the suggested plan would quiet their criticism. The Queen could not answer Hervey's pertinent query satisfactorily because it involved the King's pride. Perhaps the King's original economy deserved the blame. When subsequent events caused mutual bad feeling, the King grew more averse to making an arrangement which his son's friends would construe as an admission of former meanness. Rather than risk their triumph, he made private terms with his conscience and let the imbecile public say what it liked.

It is inconceivable how much the town resents the King's usage of the Prince with respect to money matters; the enemies of the Government are loud against it, because they are glad of any handle to make a noise, and the friends are deeply concerned for the reflection it draws on the King. . . .[19]

was a sample of what it had long been saying, but each new incident naturally stiffened the King's resolution.

Before Anne's marriage, Fritz openly disparaged both her and the Queen.[20] He only spoke to the latter in public, for form's sake, and made himself obnoxious to his sister. This heavy displeasure was due, they understood, to their both being so worthless as to make trust in them impossible. The Queen always had with her that fellow Hervey whom she knew Fritz hated. His sisters laughed at him for presuming to choose his mother's companions as a condition of behaving decently to her.[21] Did she like his precious friends or his *Craftsman* politics any better? There was Chesterfield, known to have mocked the Queen, and dismissed the Court for intriguing against Walpole. The two new Paliamentary hopes of the Opposition, Pitt and Lyttelton, both hovered round the Prince.

Now the latest ruse. About the end of June, Fritz suddenly requested an audience of the King. As time approached for that day's Drawing-room, an appointment was made for next morning and the news spread immediately. Walpole and the Queen both urged the King only to keep his temper. Some definite motive lay behind this request. Probably the same question would be raised in Parliament, with greater effect if the King refused it out of hand. Fritz's speech made their advice easy to follow. He desired the King to find him a wife and wondered how he had incurred the parental reserve. The King replied that Fritz knew as well as he did of the efforts to marry him. Their failure was not the King's fault. Fritz's general behaviour was silly, but his offensive conduct towards the Queen displeased His Majesty most of all.[22] The Queen avoided Fritz until she had heard the King's report.

When Fritz came to her the following day, she counselled clear thoughts and steady actions.[23]

'But what concerns me most is to see you can be so weak as to listen to people who are trying to make a fool of you, who think of nothing but distressing the King at any rate. . . .'

Fritz had better go warily because the King had a short temper and power to make it felt. She worked potently upon his natural timidity to produce at least the temporary resolve to mend his ways, and an apologetic letter for her to give the King. She thought Dodington had written it, but Hervey favoured Chesterfield as author of scheme and letter. Whatever the plan behind the feint, the Queen's firmness checked it, for all was quiet in her son's camp. But it was not such victory she had desired when she looked forward to Fritz 'making the chief happiness of her life'. Presently she heard that he had discarded Mr. Dodington,

Hervey's supplanter, for being too 'trimming' an adviser to such a bold spirit. He closed the connexion by borrowing £6,000 off Dodington to pay for Carlton House, sold him by Lord Chesterfield, and bragged of his smartness:

> I have wheedled him out of a sum of money for the payment of which he has no security if I die, and which, God knows, he may wait long enough for if I live.[24]

Upon retiring four years previously, Fritz's old tutor spoke out to the Queen about her son's vices being not those of a gentleman 'but the mean base tricks of a knavish footman' which had resisted correction. Bitter was the day that brought such a judgement back to her mind.[25]

A tussle faced the Queen wherever she turned. She and Walpole disagreed radically over the European War which broke out in September 1733 about the succession to the Polish Crown. Louis XV began it by replacing his father-in-law, Stanislaus Leczinski, on the elective throne of Poland.[26] His minister, Cardinal Fleury, deplored this sentimental action because Russia, Austria, and the German princes backed the Saxon elector, Augustus III, who was anxious to succeed his late father as King of Poland. Unable to avert war, Fleury used it to serve French interests more vital than a Polish crown. When Russian troops, by threatening Warsaw, chased Stanislaus to be besieged in Danzig, and made Augustus King, Fleury declared war, not on distant Russia, but on Austria, using the familiar excuse of creating a diversion as the best method of helping beleaguered Stanislaus. The Emperor Charles VI backed Augustus, but wanted war much less than Fleury did. He had taken no military action, but he had encouraged the Russian mobilization and allowed Saxon troops the use of his territory. Hopelessly unprepared as usual, he faced a campaign on the Rhine, and found his Italian territories overrun by France, Spain, and Sardinia. Their territorial lust had made it simple for France to secure these two as allies in plundering Austria. Indeed, to oust the Habsburgs from Italy, and to ensure Bourbon hegemony on the Peninsula, thus reversing the principles of the Utrecht settlement, was the prime object of French policy in this misnamed War of Polish Succession.

For the Emperor, the outcome of such a war was easy to foresee. Two years ago the Dutch and the English had promised by the Treaty of Vienna to defend him against unprovoked aggression. When he asked them to implement their pledge, they argued about the legal interpretation of 'unprovoked aggression', for Fleury had already secured Dutch neutrality by promising not to attack Belgium. Anne's William of Orange was still too uninfluential to reshape Dutch policy. And what was England thinking?

The British public considered the war a distasteful and irrelevant subject. What possible concern could it have with squabbles about a Polish King? Trade was brisk, finances sound, and the Excise bogy laid. Surely statesmen could settle treaty obligations without disrupting this halcyon scene. The Opposition trumpeted loyalty to Austria in hopes of dislodging Walpole. The real battle raged in Palace and Cabinet: Walpole versus the rest.

When war broke out he assumed direction of foreign policy.[27] Harrington and Newcastle pestered and hindered, but their counter-activities proved ineffective. At a series of Hampton Court Cabinet meetings held after the outbreak of war, Walpole successfully urged English neutrality against the wishes of the King and many of his colleagues, but the dispute was only in its infancy.[28] The Queen championed intervention because she thought Walpole obsessed by expediency. War would be unpopular, expensive, and probably fatal to his supremacy. They met for regular Monday evening conferences during the summer of 1734, besides having frequent other discussions.[29] The Queen held the Emperor to be justified in claiming British assistance. Walpole thought England bound only to act in concert with the Dutch, whose neutrality absolved his country from heroism. The Emperor's attitude towards Russian mobilization and Saxon troops scarcely made the French attack an 'unprovoked aggression'. Idealism should not be allowed to lead to war. Peace was in the best interest of the country and the Queen's family as long as a Stuart lived to threaten them both.

The shrewdness of that thrust did not blind the Queen to his flimsy defence over the question of England's good faith. Still, allowing the plausibility of his arguments on that score, surely he saw the danger of letting France and Spain weaken Austria sufficiently to wreck that essential Balance of Power, for which England under Queen Anne had poured out her best treasure? English policy had always sought to resist Franco-Spanish collaboration, as menacing to the retention of Gibraltar and Minorca and to British trade in Old World and New. Walpole pressed two main lines of counter-attack. He extolled neutrality as a means of securing the friendship of both sides, and favoured English mediation as the best way to ensure a quick peace favourable to national interests. Meanwhile the country grew wealthy in peace. 'Madam, there are fifty thousand men slain this year in Europe and not one Englishman,' he exclaimed dramatically.[30]

He hinted, like every one else, that her German birth and upbringing produced this sympathy with the Emperor.[31] Naturally she found it exasperating to sit idle while France weakened Austria and Bourbon downed Habsburg, but she considered that Walpole showed equally blind partiality to England's immediate interests. 'Whatever motives of partiality sway me ought they not naturally with double weight to bias you, who have so much more at stake?' he said, invoking 'the shadow of the Pretender' whenever his arguments were weakest.[32] The Queen's desire to preserve the Balance of Power increased as Austria fared worse in the campaign. The Emperor sent a special envoy to confer with Sir Robert, who could not be budged from his attitude, and a second emissary discredited himself by intriguing with the Opposition.[33]

And so Queen and Minister hammered at each other. Their rival policies still stir the embers of discussion.[34] Less than five years later England fought a colonial war with Spain. She had disobliged her allies and let her enemies gain strategical advantages. Then the nation blamed the Government for sacrificing everything to achieve neutrality in this Polish war. But that time was not yet. The scales of argument were unevenly weighted between the Queen and Walpole. The majority that supported her opinions lacked quality. If the Queen dropped her pilot, Walpole, neither Newcastle nor Harrington could efficiently replace him. The Opposition would come gleefully, but Walpole had public opinion, or rather, public apathy, on his side. Unwilling intervention would produce the disasters he so glibly prophesied. Only by making Walpole war-minded could the Queen's policy be successful. Since she could not achieve that temperamental change in his solid, peace-loving character, she preferred to shelve the conflict between her theories, to which time lent weight, and his expediency, seemingly justified by the immediate trend of events. An unconvinced Queen worked upon His Majesty's martial sentiments, slowly stemming them, but secretly amused that Walpole should meanwhile feel their surge.

For once the King almost liked those twin blockheads, his Secretaries of State, my Lords Newcastle and Harrington. The two chamberlains, Grafton and Grantham, took the same view as himself, though limited understanding confined Grantham's support to the friendly but asinine remark: 'I hate the French, I hope as we shall beat the French.'[35] William's governor, Mr. Poyntz, and the Queen's clever Hattorf both thought Walpole wrong.[36] Well, His Majesty would tell him so. When Walpole carried into the royal closet his daily sheaf of notes, containing the business of twenty different people and a hundred domestic concerns, the King waved such trivialities aside. Here he was, he told Sir Robert, 'growing old in peace . . . rusting in the cabinet whilst other princes were shining in the field'.[37] His military capacity fitted him to beat the French instead of concocting silly treaties, letters, and dispatches while his 'booby brother', the Prussian King, lived in camps, timid of exposing his show giants to real warfare. Sir Robert retired discomfited to pacify the teasers whose business remained undone. These explosions lost intensity as the summer proceeded because the Queen was at work. By the time the Court moved to St. James's for the King's birthday, Walpole had been ungraciously permitted to carry out the necessary plans for keeping England neutral. France he threatened with military action, championing the Austrian point of view; Austria he lectured for indiscretion grave enough to forfeit English support, hoping thereby to make both nations desire his good offices. The Emperor denounced him for evading his treaty obligations but Cardinal Fleury simulated an interest in mediation, and so Walpole set in train intense diplomatic activity.

A week before the Court moved to London, Anne made ready to return to her Pepin and prepare for their child's birth.[38] Pepin sent word that he would be back from his campaign with Prince Eugene's Rhine Army, to meet her at The Hague. Parents consulted midwives, doctors, and admirals to decide that she could cross most safely from Harwich to Helvoetsluys, and so once more she left her family, as loath to go as they were to lose her. The Queen ailed severely but was content for people to suppose it a disorder caused by Anne's going. Lord Hervey found her and Princess Caroline in the gallery, drowning their sorrows in chocolate and sighs. Next morning the door of the room where the Queen was opened to admit Anne, presumed to be at sea, who had returned on receiving news that Pepin would arrive at The Hague a few days later than he expected. Though Anne was imprudent in doubling the journey's fatigue and risking offence to her husband and the Dutch people, a sick Queen could not always be preaching discretion. She re-

ceived Anne 'with a thousand kisses and tears of joy' and
the King smiled upon her.[39] Some five weeks later Anne
reached Holland by way of Calais, having unsuccessfully
pleaded fears of miscarriage to prolong her stay in England.[40] The King, teased out of his fondness by this
trickery, which put him to great expense in the change of
route involved, snapped up any one who breathed Anne's
name. The Queen could not excuse her conduct, but
repined at it rather than censured it.

Her cough and fever had not yielded to the stock
remedy of being blooded. However, rather than annoy
the King by confessing to her illness, she dragged herself
the night she came from Kensington to St. James's to the
opening of the Opera season, and next day endured the
crowded birthday ceremonies; their heat and fatigue being
almost unbearable to her aching body.[41] The King thought
that it behoved royalty, like deity, to possess unflagging
health. Sooner than lower himself by admitting to
common afflictions, he would stagger from his bed with
a sore throat or fever, dress, hold his levée, and retire
content until the 'same ridiculous farce of health' was to
be presented next day. His affection for the Queen did
not let her avoid the duties of her station. By artifice or
by drastic expedients she schooled her gout, and her internal disorders, to simulate this desirable robustness. Their
family followed suit. Thus William had to be twice
blooded after a toss out hunting, but 'came as usually to
His Majesty . . . knowing the King does not love that any
about him should complain of being ill'.[42]

This time the Queen's constitution rebelled against pretence. It forced her to revel in the luxury of truth by

forgoing public duties and keeping to her room for a month.[43] Sir Robert, himself chivied by flying gout, came up to her on the birthday night, before leaving for his Norfolk holiday next morning.[44] He exercised an old friend's privilege of lecturing her gently upon the stupidity of self-neglect:

'Madam, your life is of such consequence to your husband, to your children, to this country . . . that any neglect of your health is really the greatest immorality you can be guilty of. When one says these sort of things in general to princes, I know, Madam, they must sound like flattery; but consider your particular circumstances . . . Your Majesty knows that this country is entirely in your hands, that the fondness the King has for you, the opinion he has of your affection, and the regard he has for your judgement, are the only reins by which it is possible to restrain the natural violences of his temper, or to guide him through any part he is wanted to go. Should any accident happen to Your Majesty, who can tell into what hands he would fall? . . . Some woman . . . would govern him, for the company of men he cannot bear. . . . She might be avaricious; she might be profuse; she might be ambitious. . . .'

Walpole indicated the disasters that such a schemer could effect, for long co-operation in a common cause made frankness easy between him and the Queen.

His note of gruff concern was new to her; his tribute caused a tired woman's tears to flow. Loyalty to King and minister shone from her reply:

'Your partiality to me, my good Sir Robert, makes you see many more advantages in having me, and apprehend many greater dangers from losing me, than are indeed the effects of the one, or than would be the consequences of the other. That the King would marry again if I died, I believe is sure, and I have often advised him so to do; but his good sense, and his affection for his family, would put a stop to any such attempts as you speak of in a second wife . . .

As for his political government, he has now such a love for you, so just a value for your services, as well as such an opinion of your abilities, that, were I removed, everything would go on just as it does. You have saved us from many errors, and this very year have forced us into safety whether we would or no, against our own opinion and against our inclination. The King sees this and I own it. . . .'

Walpole thanked her, but rebuked the self-belittlement:

'You know, Madam, I can do nothing without you. Whatever my industry and watchfulness for your interest and welfare suggest, it is you must execute. You, Madam, are the sole mover of this Court. . . . If I can boast of any success, I am very free to own, I never could have it but for the mediation of Your Majesty; for if I have the merit of giving any good advice to the King, all the merit of making him take it, Madam, is entirely your own; and so much so that I not only never did anything without you, but I know I never could. . . .'

The Queen insisted on his leaving for his holiday, though he was loath to do so. If generous recognition of her work could have cured bodily infirmities, she was well already; but a neglected hernia, incurred by the birth of her last child, exacted greater propitiation with each passing year. The discussion just ended had more than an academic value.

Change rules immutably in life, so now it made the King its subject. As a habit, Lady Suffolk had staled, though the King, being a creature of routine, took nearly eight years before the realization smote him. A mistress of 53 no longer proved his niceness; a deaf woman who constantly contradicted him was a nuisance.[45] Lady Suffolk kept friendly with little Mr. Pope, with that monster Bolingbroke, impertinent Chesterfield, and all those rogues whose smart criticism blew up His Majesty to a peevish froth. The King curtailed his evening visits. At cards or in private conversation they behaved like spouses dismayed by the doom of lifelong sentence ahead. Lady Suffolk, suddenly aware of how stupid this was, did what she had not done for twenty years—her term in the Queen's household. She took a holiday. The newspapers chronicled her unusual break with custom, which had 'occasioned as much speculation in the Kensington family as the removal of two or three minor ministers would have done'.[46] For six weeks Lady Suffolk enjoyed her freedom and her friends, the Opposition crew, before returning to London for the King's birthday, to receive barely one civil word from him in public, and not a single private visit.[47] As her husband had died a year back, she no longer needed the Court as a haven. She decided to resign, wrote the King two letters, unnecessarily tragic in tone, considering that he as well as she welcomed approaching freedom, and then requested an interview with—the Queen.[48]

The truth of Walpole's words, 'You, Madam, are the sole mover of this Court', thereby received fresh confirmation; for a Queen who closed an old chapter in her husband's love-affairs was truly indispensable. Six printed pages were filled by the record of their interview, which need only have announced Lady Suffolk's resignation as Mistress of the Robes.[49] What could the lady say? 'Madam, your husband not being so kind as he used to be, I cannot serve you any longer.'[50] Such brevity would have been merciful, and perhaps attainable but for the Queen's resolve to play the realist, in order to prevent people saying that she had turned Lady Suffolk out upon the first pretext. A lady with such long service to her credit deserved consideration!

'My good Lady Suffolk, you are the best servant in the world, and as I should be extremely sorry to lose you, pray take a week to consider of this business, and give me your word not to read any romances in that time.'[51]

Lady Suffolk, sure that the end of an episode had come, took the week but let her decision stand. After mid-November, one whose 'nominal favour and enervate reign' made her a curiosity among the European galaxy of charmers, was seen no more at Court. Home, friends, and a continued pension from the King assured her ease. No one regretted her decision.

The Queen's 'pride was glad to have even this ghost of a rival removed', though the King monopolized extra hours which might have been more profitably spent.[52] Her family was glad with her, but Anne pungently pitied her the strain of entertaining Papa. 'I wish with all my heart he would take somebody else, that Mama might be a little relieved from the ennui of seeing him for ever in her room.' The King's enemies gossiped joyfully of his ingratitude in casting off a faithful friend, just as if he had forsaken a loving wife for a dissolute paramour. They hoped to reap political harvest from the event. Outside the Court it was said that Walpole had manœuvred the disgrace, to close up this Opposition approach to the King's ear, but his master's weariness of Lady Suffolk made any help unnecessary. In a fortnight the breeze had passed.

By the end of the year the Queen had resumed her work. Talking to Lord Egmont at the Drawing-room on New

Year's eve, she inquired how his collection of portrait engravings progressed. He told her it had reached 1660.[53]

'Then you are come down to the fine gravers Nanteuil, Masson, &c. Well, it is a great curiosity that, your collection, and very useful too in calling to mind all the great people of past time: those gravers lived in Louis XIV's time and he was a great encourager of arts.' They discussed Louis's ministers, and so came to talk of flattery, which somehow led to a conversation on gardening. These discursive talks once made Lord Egmont tell her pleasantly that 'persons of general knowledge were curious in everything', but the Queen shook her head to intimate that she did not deserve his compliment, 'which yet she really does, for she reads and converses on a multitude of things, more than our sex generally does'.

X

'BORN TO ENCOURAGE'

'This Princess . . . was born to encourage the whole circle of arts,
and to do good to mankind. She appears as an amiable philosopher
on the throne, having never let slip one opportunity of improving
the great talents she received from nature, nor of exerting her
beneficence.' Voltaire, *Letters concerning the English Nation*, p. 61.

LORD EGMONT spoke the truth. The Queen at 51 kept
her zest for her catholic tastes: metaphysical disputes,
a swift tour of artists' studios, a gardening interlude at
Richmond, literature, and fine furniture, these she enjoyed
as much as ever. By a triumph of mental vigour she
seemed physically robust, brisk, busy, and alert; but really
her health was poor. She would not admit how much
trouble the hernia gave her, for she fancied that her husband's contempt for sickness in others would estrange him
from her. And nothing cured her gout. The late Elector
of Saxony, immoral but kind Augustus II, whom she
knew in her youth, gave her a novel wheeled chair, which
William guided adeptly, when she used it at the Drawing-
rooms.[1] Since she never touched alcohol, and her parents
had been abstemious, she must have expiated some for-
bear's conviviality. She and her favourite Bishop, Sherlock, commiserated with each other, and once the Queen
gave him a remedy for driving gout from the stomach
into the feet.[2] But gouty feet needed painful applications
of cold water to avoid missing the morning walk with His

Majesty. Or other tortures: 'I took the trouble to get my feet into a fit state for walking . . . and could not sleep all night for pain,' she confided to Anne the previous summer. However, Bishop and Queen seldom grumbled about their ailments.

Walpole was jealous of their friendship because dissimilar politics but comparable talents bred hostility between the two men. The Queen admired Sherlock for leavening his orthodoxy with political interests and wide culture. He was the legal expert on the episcopal bench, who spoke cogently in the House of Lords and produced forceful pamphlets at need. The Queen found his comments on current affairs the spicier for their Tory point of view, which otherwise she only heard distorted by the acrimony of debate and the weekly *Craftsman*. So she flirted with his Toryism although dynastic expediency always reminded her that she was married to the Whigs. Sherlock would have made a splendid Lord Chancellor of the Tudor pattern. He looked the part too, being no spare ascetic like his friend Bishop Hare or the French Cardinal Fleury, but a hearty, big fellow in Walpole's mould.

The Queen's old friend Dr. Clarke died in 1729. At Kensington Palace she hung his portrait with a commemorative inscription beneath it.[3] Though she favoured his deistical theories she disliked tame acquiescence from the men attending her circle, preferring that a good brain and skill in argument should be the only attributes they shared. Hoadly the radical, orthodox Hare, Sherlock himself, scholarly Potter, Secker, Pearce, and many other bishops met her regularly for discussions which roused her after the bores she was constrained to suffer patiently. For Walpole isolated her from the cleverest laymen by antagonizing them piecemeal, but he could not forbid her the consolation of their spiritual lordships! Talk was not the only amusement she offered them. One story, probably partly apocryphal, related that during the court masques so dear to the King she held private frolics and music for the grave prelates in her own rooms, being the only person who could make them dance 'as if bitten by the polka'.[4] In summer she asked them out to Richmond.

In 1736 the Queen added the greatest theological mind of his age to her circle. Talking to the Archbishop of York one day, she mentioned Joseph Butler, whose Fifteen Sermons preached the Christian life so eloquently, asking whether he was not dead. 'Madam, he is not dead, but buried,' came the pointed reply, so she made Butler her private chaplain and every day he attended her from seven till nine. On her deathbed she commended him to the Primate's care. Early in the reign she pleased Bishop Gibson by requesting a list of Whig clergy suitable for bishoprics.[5] Soon he learnt that Sherlock had given her a similar list of Tory candidates, so their battles began, but sometimes they agreed, as for instance when Gibson made Berkeley, the author of the Principles of Human Knowledge, a bishop as reward for his pioneering work in Georgia. Though Gibson prevented the Queen from being the sole distributor of patronage, her concern for men like Sherlock, Butler, and Berkeley showed that reverence for spiritual values guided her theological interests.

Her detractors sneered that she affected a curiosity in metaphysics and theology. 'God has given you the gift of sight and good books for your instruction,' she once told Anne, herself enjoying these gifts to the full. Could pretence prompt any one to master the flow of solid treatises on these subjects? Not only did she read Hoadly's book on the Sacrament the summer it appeared, but also the critical refutation of its principles.[6] During the disputes over the Quakers' Tithes Bill, she sided with the Quakers until Sherlock's pamphlet showed that the clergymen had good arguments against the Bill. To Lord Egmont she censured an Italian Count's *Philosophical Discourse upon Death*, which 'embraces the atheism of Spinoza and afterwards draws conclusions from his doctrines that destroy all society and virtue'. These two often discussed the beliefs and works of Egmont's friend, Dr. de Courayer, who had fled 'out of Paris to refuge himself in England', because his orthodoxy was doubted.[7] The Queen pensioned him with £200 a year for writing 'in defence of our English ordinations' though he was 'a learned Papist', and bade him translate Thuanus' Latin history of his own times. Admiration for this history led to her successful search for its expurgated portions and made her buy 'papers six foot high from the ground' concerned with another translation prohibited by Cardinal Fleury. To a Queen involved in the heat of politics, impersonal interests were no pose but a tranquillizing experience.

Politics alienated from the Court all the eminent men of letters because Walpole, sharing his sovereign's contempt for them, denied them patronage or employment. Reports from his gamekeeper were his favourite reading, it is said, and the King boasted that he not only disliked bookwork but actually despised it. For the Queen, a voracious reader with a superb memory, this was tragic.

Only in the Leicester House days could she meet the famous authors and poets who were her contemporaries. Afterwards Pope pilloried her in his caustic couplets; Swift hated her for letting him die an Irish dean, and Bolingbroke wrote *The Idea of a Patriot King* for Frederick's inspiration. Accordingly she helped the humbler practitioners, but her charity did not imply any lack of critical faculty; rather it anticipated the practice of giving deserving authors pensions from the Civil List. Steele, when crippled, asked her help; Milton's granddaughter she found impoverished and pensioned her. To the luckless Richard Savage, whose biographer was Dr. Johnson, she brought not only reprieve from a sentence of death incurred for murder in a drunken fray but a pension of £50 for his terse, effective poem, *The Bastard*. William Somerville, the fox-hunting squire from Warwickshire, gained her notice with *The Chase*, a didactic poem on the art of his favourite sport. The thresher poet, Stephen Duck, she took from Wiltshire to be her custodian of Merlin's Cave at Richmond, giving him £200 a year and leisure to compose.

For the same reason the Queen, at her accession, offered John Gay a sinecure at court, but absurdly he fancied himself insulted and a year later produced *The Beggar's Opera*.[8] With its satire upon the Government and catchy songs set to familiar airs, it 'made Gay rich and Rich [the producer] gay' by running for a record of sixty-two consecutive nights; it brought Lavinia Fenton, the bewitching Polly, a ducal coronet, and poked witty fun at Walpole. Much encouraged, Gay wrote *Polly* as a sequel, openly attacking Walpole, who declined to be represented as a robber in a second play, so the Lord Chamberlain banned it. Gay's lively patroness, the Duchess of Queensberry, solicited subscriptions in the King's presence for a published edition of *Polly*, and being forbidden the Court, expressed surprise and pleasure 'at so agreeable a command'. Like most banned works, *Polly* became a best-seller, bringing its author nearly £3,000. As Walpole's unpopularity grew, abusive political medleys were staged frequently, especially at the Haymarket theatre, which was nicknamed 'Mr. Fielding's Scandal Shop'.[9] At last, in 1737, a Licensing Act put all companies of actors under the Lord Chamberlain's supervision. Though Lord Chesterfield objected with polished sarcasm, the wonder was that Walpole had not acted sooner.

Although politics intruded everywhere they brought their own absorption to the Queen, who had studied the European chess-board since she was a young bride. Her foreign policy belonged to the Whig vintage of King William's time. As a German, her suspicion of renewed French hegemony made her less susceptible than Walpole to Cardinal Fleury's friendly wiles and more alive to the rivalry likely between countries both seeking fresh trading pastures. Unerringly she recognized the cause of England's greatness, 'this liberty'; sometimes indeed, 'this troublesome liberty'. But without it 'Who the devil would take you all? . . . your island might be a very pretty thing in that case for Bridgeman and Kent to cut out into gardens', she once observed to Lord Hervey.[10] The Queen accepted the innovation of government by one party but resented it as a curb upon the Crown's authority. Impartiality and love of power disposed her to wish the Sovereign were free to take his advisers for their capacity to do his business and not because they carried the correct political tag. The King, who often unconsciously repeated her ideas, talked in this strain upon his accession, making it absurd by his patent lack of the necessary perception and detachment. Though the Queen had lectured the late monarch for letting the Whigs monopolize him, she had come to realize that her dynastic interests were safest in Walpole's Whig hands. Desiring conciliatory treatment for the non-political Tories, she favoured the Excise Bill to please the country gentlemen and would have cheered the Tory clergy with discreet promotions, but suspicion and intolerance frustrated these mild impartialities.

She felt like a motherly hen towards Walpole's brood of brainless Whig chickens, whose failings were so plain to her. Harrington was lazy; Horatio Walpole *opiniâtre* just because he had some experience of foreign affairs; Newcastle so flustered 'between his objections to some things and incapacity in others that he never did anything'.[11] If they squabbled amongst themselves, she scolded them. Thus Newcastle satisfied a private dislike by criticizing Lord Islay over Scottish affairs, and heard from the Queen: 'the business of Princes is to make the whole go on, not to . . . suffer little, silly, impertinent piques between their servants to hinder the business of the Government being done'. She ignored her own pique against Lord Islay for courting Mrs. Howard, because he managed the Scottish elections for Walpole. 'I have not loved Lord Islay much but I value his ability.'[12] She considered Sir Robert himself the only character amongst his brood. 'What are you all but a rope of sand that would crumble away in little grains one after another if it was not for him?' she once asked his brother Horatio.[13]

Her patience vanished when she contemplated the Opposition, which had not transmuted itself from a shrill opposition to His Majesty to the dignified status of His Majesty's Opposition. It jibed at the Crown and ensnared Frederick, and its weekly journal pricked knavishly. For the Queen realized that the *Craftsman*'s band of stylists, Bolingbroke, Pulteney, Gay, Swift, Arbuthnot, and Pope showed up the Government writers as hirelings and gained the paper a circulation irrespective of the politics it preached. The Opposition Whigs angered her most. She thought the Tories' opposition was prompted by the harsh treatment the party had received since 1714. The King had but to beckon and the Tories would come running to do his business, but Whig disunity discredited the whole party. 'This is always the way of your nasty Whigs . . . they think that everything must be done for them and that they are obliged to do nothing themselves in return. Out of place they are always ready to fall upon the Crown and think in place they have merit enough if they do not join in distressing it,'[14] she told Lord Hervey, feeling better for the outburst. Statesmen could take holidays and had their periods out of office; the Opposition thrived on the luxuries of criticism; but the Queen remained a constant target for their shies and faced without break the anxiety for the 'good of the whole'.

She let that thought direct her dealings with the people as much as she could in a materialistic age which ignored social legislation. From humble poor and wretched debtors to famous men in need, or public institutions, none sought her practical sympathy in vain. She gave as long as her money held out, and preferred to keep her gifts secret, though newspapers heard of stray donations. A brief list indicates their variety.[15]

	£	s.	d.
Huguenots lately escaped from French prisons .	1,000	0	0
Sufferers from fires at Gravesend and St. Martin's Lane	552	10	0
A Woolwich drummer's wife who produced triplets	52	10	0
A healthy centenarian in Bushey Park .	'a purse of gold'		
Poor haymakers along the Hammersmith Road .	10	10	0
The projected Foundling Hospital . . .	5,000	0	0
A projected infirmary in Westminster . .	100	0	0
St. George's, 'the hospital near Hyde Park Corner'	100	0	0

Such items were only samples of her steady generosity. Her chamberlain, Lord Grantham, told Lord Egmont that she was 'inconceivably generous and charitable and it would amaze me to know how much she gave away and those large sums that nobody knew of'.[16] She was reckoned to spend £21,000 in salaries, make £19,000 pay for clothes, pocket expenses, building and gardening, and devote £10,000, a fifth of her income, to charities 'known only to particulars'. This reticence in one usually so forthright tempted her omniscient young friend, Lord Hervey, into commenting that giving was not her 'most glaring merit'. As Lord Egmont observed, he deplored ostentation in any one, 'but for example's sake a Queen's charity should be like a lighted candle, not set under a bushel'.

But the public knew about one liberal benefaction which she bestowed on Oxford, Tory stronghold though it was.

Following the custom of all English Queens since Philippa founded Queen's College, she became its patroness. The college was nearing the end of its rebuilding, which has given it a classical harmony unique in Oxford, when Dr. Joseph Smith was elected Provost in 1730, and at once sought funds to complete the front quadrangle.[17] Having been a chaplain to Caroline when Princess of Wales, he petitioned her, who, 'out of Her Royal Bounty and tender regard' for the college, responded with £1,000 paid in four instalments between 1733 and 1735; intending to add another £1,000 had she not died before she could afford it. The gift was applied to finishing the cloisters and gateway facing the High Street. Above the gateway stands the open temple designed by Hawksmoor but altered by Townshend to display a marble statue of 'the best of Queens', presented by the grateful Provost. From there the statue has surveyed the succeeding generations of students passing by, until at last women came to be among their number, and, final triumph that would have pleased her well, the University admitted them to its senior membership. Was it in anticipation of this that the statue 'thrice danced a courant' the year it was set up?

With a modern desire to encourage the home textile industries she had the whole of Anne's trousseau made in England and exhibited at Hampton Court before the wedding.[18] Once lacemakers came from the Midlands to show her their lovely work, of which she bought liberally, inspiring her ladies to heed her example. An ingenious musical clock so fascinated her when demonstrated by its inventor that she gave fifty guineas to his lottery to dispose of it profitably. Alive to the value of the young colony,

Georgia, she accepted a length of silk produced there to be made up into 'a suit of clothes', expressing delight at the quality of the material, which was designed to compete with silk from Piedmont.[19] When some Indians from the colony, headed by their king, adventured to England in 1734, the Queen received them at St. James's, and after the audience was ended, drew aside the king's nephew. She 'stroked his face and told him he must come again to see her, for she had a present for him', to be answered in good English by the little fellow, who was 'forward in his learning' and could repeat the Lord's Prayer, the Creed, and the Ten Commandments.[20]

When the Court was not in residence, the Queen admitted the public to her gardens at Kensington and Richmond 'to the great advantage of the town and neighbourhood'. At Hampton Court she moved easily amongst them, and humble folk who met her either there or at special audiences went away charmed by her affability; but their number was small. If she had followed up her successful idea of dining in public by persuading the King to go amongst his people she would have made him liked. Presumably his thrift and indifference to the nation, abetted by ministerial anxiety to avoid incidents, prevented the fruition of ideas which must have occurred to the Queen, who realized the importance of the people seeing their King. The nation could not be expected to appreciate his unshowy virtues—honesty and respect for the Constitution—when his failings were so easy to ridicule. It mocked his militarism and parsimony, his vanity and love for Hanover. As companion to this strutting figure, it visualized his partner as a female tyrant, resolved to keep every one in place: maids to wear badges of their servitude and receive only £10 in wages, excise to whittle down the public rights. The Queen despised their credulity but cared not a fig for their insults.

In her spare time the Queen visited 'Persons of Taste' to see their art treasures. Such people accepted certain rules for the correct execution and appreciation of art, and any work that neglected the formulae forfeited praise.[21] Form and proportion were the twin deities, Italy and France their shrine. Taught these rules at Charlottenburg and Herrenhausen, the Queen's appreciation was valued by the connoisseurs. Lady Berkeley heard with pleasure that the Queen 'intends me the honour of seeing my house and drinking a dish of coffee with me'. Lord Tankerville invited the Queen to appraise his staircase, decorated by Giacomo Amiconi, the fashionable Italian painter of historical scenes.[22] History painting had a great vogue because it communicated those ideas 'of a lofty, noble and tragic character' which the current taste judged more elevated than landscapes with their reproduction of crude nature. A Person of Taste only bought a landscape painted by some foreign master long dead, for then it had an antiquarian value which excused its subject matter. After seeing the staircase the Queen visited Mr. Wootton's studio to look at his equestrian pictures. English artists, it was understood, only painted dogs and horses well. She saw a picture of the King astride a grey charger. Charles Jervas, the Crown Painter, had done the face, which confirmed the Queen's bad opinion of his work. Earlier that day she had reviewed his command portraits of the King and herself—and passed them by in silence. Jervas, however, had a rich wife, many friends, and a superb picture collection to console him for this frigid verdict.

Dr. Mead owned the best private collection, for which he begged a portrait of the Queen painted by Amiconi.[23] Though she relished seeing such treasures as his, she found her visits expensive, feeling obliged to tip the servants liberally. The King told her to stay at home, for 'you do not see me running into every puppy's house to see his new chairs and stools', he bantered her.[24] But a chair was simply a useful object to him, just as pictures conventionally decorated walls; one became accustomed to them and disliked newcomers. Once when he had gone to Hanover, the Queen removed the deplorable pictures from the great drawing-room at Kensington and hung others including two by Vandyck of King Charles I on his horse, and with his family.[25] Home again, the King missed seeing his familiar fat Venus, a picture that George I, equally inartistic, had bought as part of a lot. Now this was the sort of trifle which, as Anne once said, 'made him the devil to everybody'. Peremptorily he ordered his Vice-Chamberlain to restore the old horrors before next morning. 'Would Your Majesty have the gigantic fat Venus restored too?' asked Lord Hervey aghast. 'Yes, my Lord, I am not so nice as your Lordship. I like my fat Venus better than anything you have given me instead of her. . . . I suppose you assisted the Queen with your fine advice when she was pulling my house to pieces and spoiling my furniture.' The Queen never again tried to improve his taste.

The only artist who secured his approval was Frederick Zincke, a miniaturist from Berlin 'for that his portraits were beautiful and like'.[26] This enthusiasm had an explanation. When Zincke first came to draw pictures of the whole royal family, the Queen took him aside and advised him 'to make the King's picture young, not above 25'. Presently His Majesty whispered to him to make the Queen look about 28. Zincke took the hints so deftly that the King bade him 'employ all your time in pictures for me, for I will take them all'. But the Queen saw merit in other artists too. She allowed the great Sir Godfrey Kneller, famous long before she arrived in England, to include her in his picture gallery of monarchs. They numbered eleven, including Louis XIV, Peter the Great, and every English sovereign from Charles II to her own George. She noted that German artists like Kneller and Zincke could be popular in England while at Hanover the best commissions went to Italians and Frenchmen. For cultured men in both countries returned from their classical tour scornful of their countrymen's work. English architects were excepted from the censure; Inigo Jones and Christopher Wren reproduced the new ideas with genius. Hawksmoor, Gibbs, Vanbrugh, Talman, and Kent each made his distinctive contribution. Their work stimulated pleasure in those splendid tomes of architectural drawings and designs for furniture, which captured the spaciousness of the age to perfection.

The Queen was amongst several members of her family who sat to John Vanderbank, a painter of natural talent gradually wrecked by dissolute habits. She granted patronage to Isaac Gossett, a Huguenot, who modelled portraits in wax so ingeniously as to make them indistinguishable from miniatures painted on ivory. William Kent, as Master Mason to the Office of Works, had full scope for his versatility in the royal households.* At Kensington he designed and decorated a suite of rooms; their effect was pronounced by George Vertue, the most celebrated antiquary and engraver of this period,to be 'poor stuff . . . a terrible glaring show'.[27] His restorations of mural paintings at Windsor earned him £750 one year; at Hampton Court he was furniture designer and architect.[28] When the King talked about a new palace, Kent submitted a model, and when the Prince of Wales wanted a new State barge, Kent designed him one. The Queen found him an eager collaborator in her 'new tact of gardening' at Kensington, where he perpetrated an absurdity which has never been forgotten. To follow Nature faithfully he planted dead trees 'but was soon laughed out of the excess'.[29]

Greatly discerning, the Queen would have patronized the rebel William Hogarth, but for Kent's jealousy of his official prerogatives.[30] Hogarth's biting originality was deemed bad taste and, like many underrated artists, he retaliated by making out that every one save himself was a fool. The Queen commanded him to paint a conversation piece of the royal family, and gave him permission to make sketches of Anne's wedding to William of Orange, from which he proposed publishing engravings. But Kent had the same intention and when Hogarth began to sketch, he was made to desist. He appealed to the Queen, who admitted that she had acted without reflection, or the wish to interfere with Kent. The incident ended Hogarth's royal connexions. Since he had lately diverted London

* He also succeeded Charles Jervas as principal Crown Painter (1739–48). The barge he designed for Frederick, Prince of Wales, is in the Victoria and Albert Museum, South Kensington.

with caricatures of Kent, the latter's action was excusable.

The Queen's allowance met so many other calls that she felt like a pauper compared with her rich dilettante friends, my Lords Burlington and Pembroke, Dr. Mead and Sir Andrew Fountain, for of course the King would not waste his money on fiddle-faddle pictures. Sometimes she added a choice miniature to her group, which included the work of such masters as the Cooper brothers, but her praise and her time were all that she could usually bestow on artists. An occasional extravagance made restraint easier for her. She heard the sculptor, Mr. Rysbrack, highly praised. In the gardens at Richmond she was building a Hermitage, for which she wanted busts of her favourite mentors. Signor Guelphi had finished Dr. Clarke's bust and then left England. At Rysbrack's studio the Queen saw a bold equestrian statue of King William III, commissioned by Bristol, and at once she gave him her own commission.

Thus Bacon and Boyle, Sir Isaac Newton, Locke and Wollaston employ the hand of Rysbrack. . . . It hath been allowed in his praise, that he never undertook any great work but with an industry which far exceeded his reward, and always showed he wrought more for reputation than any other recompense.

The Queen had chosen one of the three greatest sculptors of her century. George Vertue endorsed Voltaire's tribute to her:

It is to the honour of the British Court that the Queen who now adorns it . . . hath taken Statuary into her protection.[31]

Lack of money prevented her being an extensive collector, but she had enthusiasm and discrimination and she encouraged many painters; unfortunately their lustre was insufficient to save her artistic reputation from being dimmed by the notorious philistinism of the first two Georges. Reynolds, Romney, Gainsborough, and Richard Wilson all shone after her time.

The Queen's zeal was rewarded by rediscovering the choicest treasures for the Royal Collection of drawings, which ranks amongst the best in Europe.[32] Rummaging through an old bureau, long unopened, she found it stuffed with prints, drawings, and old medals. Further examination showed twenty-seven separate lots of drawings; some on loose vellum, others pasted in albums, drawings by Italian masters, curious Indian sketches, prints from Wenzel Hollar. Best of all were two books of drawings by Leonardo da Vinci and about a hundred sketches by Holbein. Exquisitely drawn on flesh-coloured paper, these sketches of celebrities at the Court of Henry VIII had been used by Holbein for his oil portraits. 'This is the greatest treasure of its kind now in England', rejoiced Vertue, who considered that only the Raphael cartoons at Hampton Court surpassed them.

It was presumed that these things had been hastily thrust into the bureau when the fire broke out in Whitehall in 1698, and forgotten in the calamity of the Palace being burnt. Before that the Holbeins had had a chequered career. Edward VI either sold or gave them to the Earl of Arundel, whose son-in-law, Lord Lumley, inherited them from him. Henry, Prince of Wales, probably bought them with Arundel's library. At any rate his brother, Charles I, exchanged them for a picture belonging to the Earl of Pembroke, who was Inigo Jones's patron. From Pembroke they passed again into the Arundel family and wandered back for the third time into the Royal collection during Charles II's reign. And then all was silence until the Queen found them in 1728.

She had them framed and hung at Richmond, later bringing them to her closet at Kensington.* Thereafter she bore her comparative penury serenely, a jealous foster-mother to the Holbeins. Her friend, Lord Egmont, suggested that they should be engraved, but the Queen replied that 'we had no good gravers, and besides they might be spoilt'. Happily her admirer George Vertue did not hear of that remark.

The Queen used this closet or dressing-room in which the Holbeins hung as a private sitting-room, where at night the King, Lord Hervey, and the Liffords came for their final chat.[33] She made it her picture gallery too; almost from floor to ceiling she crowded her treasures, over the doors, between windows, over the fireplace. It was a motley collection. Inartistic potraits of obscure relatives sandwiched between exquisite miniatures by Peter Oliver or Cooper; Dolci's devotional picture of the Madonna and Christ contemplating two delicious mice by Raphael in a tiny black frame; Maria van Osterwyck's flower studies besides limnings, wax portraits, and models. Boit, the famous enameller of Queen Anne's reign, contributed a large plate depicting that Queen and her solid Danish spouse. Two hundred and seventeen separate frames hung in this room, twenty-three feet by twelve, and what space remained the Queen devoted to a collection of lovely Japan ware presented to her by the East India Company.

* They are now at Windsor with the rest of the Royal Collection of drawings, which was augmented and rearranged by the Prince Consort.

Gardening was her outdoor hobby. When she came to England, Addison and Steele had been grumbling gently at the fashion of losing Nature in art, as the Queen described the formal style.[34] In 1718, a famous practical gardener, Stephen Switzer, advocated laying out gardens informally, and Charles Bridgeman and Vanbrugh were the first designers to follow his ideas. Conceived to present a natural but stimulating prospect wherever one looked, the new romantic or informal style created conventions and artifices of its own. Stiff parterres and prim topiary gardens gave place to simple grass swards, groves of trees and wildernesses; formal walks and straight canals, to winding paths and meandering streams. Archly informal grottoes enhanced the distant view. Ranked as the chief contribution to garden design, the romantic in its various phases dominated garden planning for the rest of the century, giving rise to several Jardins Anglais and Englische Gärten on the Continent.

The Queen's contemporaries praised her ingenuity in 'helping nature', as she aptly termed the new ideas, but posterity has often overlooked her part in popularizing them. At Richmond, with Bridgeman to help, she laid out informal gardens on either side of the great avenue (a wise concession to formality) leading from the south front of the Lodge down to the riverside terrace; joining Kew to the west[35] 'Through several fine walks and agreeable labyrinths', amidst trees she set Merlin's Cave, 'a thatched edifice and very Gothic', containing a waxwork show of which Merlin, musing at his table, was the central figure. A few volumes bound in chaste white vellum graced each end of the room, and Mrs. Duck, the thresher-poet's wife, did the honours to visitors. This peepshow probably deserved the *Craftsman's* scorn. Past the river terrace, beyond alleys with clipped hedges, which also kept allegiance to the old style, stood the Hermitage. It, too, looked 'very Gothic, being a heap of stones thrown into a very artful disorder and curiously embellished with moss and shrubs to represent rude nature'; a description applicable to the artfully disordered caves as prescribed by romanticism in many other gardens. Such features proved that the designer knew the rules, but Richmond abounded in glorious trees, peaceful walks, glades and parkland. A farm and a demure dairy house proved the Queen's practical nature, and like all keen gardeners she was busy altering and improving the grounds to the end of her days.

Kensington, where alterations were in progress when George I died, gave the Queen a second opportunity for landscape gardening. An area known as the Upper Paddock was being laid out as parklands for deer to roam at liberty.[36] The parterres to the north and east of the Palace laid out in Queen Anne's time were swept away. By replanning this Paddock, the Queen created the garden's most famous features; the Broad Walk, the little stream taught to meander as the River Serpentine, and in the midst of a huge lawn, the Round Pond, which figured in the plans as the Great Basin, 2,216 feet in circumference. Gravel came from the pits in Hyde Park to make the new walks traversing the grounds, turf was taken from such places as 'lye out of sight' there for the verges and lawns, and presently the ubiquitous Kent helped with the landscaping. As the gardens lay thick under dust from the coaches bowling from Hyde Park corner to Kensington, the Queen, in 1735, had a new road made outside the Boundary Wall. Years later when the trees matured, which she unselfishly planted for posterity, a lady traveller wrote that her 'whole soul was gladdened by the beauty and peace she found there'.[37]

Bridgeman, gardener to the two previous sovereigns, was retained by Queen Caroline.[38] Paid at the rate of £15 an acre, he earned £2,220 for tending all the royal gardens. Out of this sum he provided the tools, seeds, labour, and the new forest and fruit trees; and he enjoyed all the emoluments, perquisites and privileges pertaining to the gardens. The King paid for structural repairs, the tubs and shrubs or trees that grew in them, all greenhouse plants and the carriage of the produce. Between 1728 and 1731 Bridgeman received £5,000 for the new works at Kensington. He died soon after the Queen, whose gardens at Richmond then came under the King's care. Her hobby had added 188 acres to the royal gardens, more than doubling the cost of their maintenance and necessitating separate gardeners for Richmond, Hampton Court, Windsor and Newmarket together, Kensington, and the acre and a half at St. James's. The new contracts drawn up in August 1738 might have made the King fume had he not been still grief-stricken over losing his best companion.[39]

For somehow the Queen daily spared hours to be with him, weaving hints and amusement so deftly into the conversational strands that by the end of their session he said or promised exactly what she wanted. He imagined besides that the initiative had been his, though his talk consisted chiefly of expletives and ejaculations mingled with bald assertions he dared anyone to deny. She won her influence by feigning a bland indifference to his unfaithfulness.

Too stupid for clever men and too dull for the rakes, His Majesty found the ladies a more tolerant audience for his harmless posturings. The Queen, however, disliked the insipidity of most women though she always put her own ladies at their ease. A young maid of honour, after her first interview, described how 'the Princess sent for me in immediately; and though I was in a prodigious fright . . . the Princess was so mighty good to me that it lessened it very much'[40]. The Queen had no intimate women friends in England. Lady Sundon she perhaps knew best, though she did not feel sufficiently familiar with her to discuss the King's private affairs, as she had to with Walpole, when they obtruded upon politics by keeping the King overlong at Hanover. The unbroken collaboration between Queen and Minister, and especially their parting, witnessed to their intimacy. Leibniz, Sherlock, Clarke, she was proud to call her friends. She treated Hervey with maternal indulgence, convinced that his constant care for her ease and entertainment betokened reciprocal affection, yet he saw no disloyalty in perpetuating words and scenes best forgotten. Of the Queen's family, Caroline was her comfort, William her chief hope, and Anne her tenderest joy. To them she spoke French, which she also preferred for correspondence. With the King she often talked German, and her English was a bold hybrid of the three languages. If her speech was often coarse, so was everyone else's, and her frequent invocation of the Deity was a German habit which still persists. In public her aptitude for the pleasant remark, the obliging gesture and the friendly aside, never failed her.

Her presence at a Drawing-room sent a shock of vitality coursing through the company; everyone talked a shade faster and a shade better than usual. 'This Princess was born to encourage,' wrote Voltaire. 'Comme elle soutenait sa dignité avec grâce, avec politesse, avec douceur,' murmured her husband.[41]

XI

THE KING PLAYS TRUANT

Lady Suffolk's retirement ended a phase in the Queen's private life just as the failure of the Excise Bill closed the most exhilarating chapter of her collaboration with Walpole. Hitherto, the King had been tolerably content with life in England, spiced by Hanoverian interludes. But in need of fresh thrills after discarding Lady Suffolk, he found them at Hanover, and became impossible at home. Fretful, huffy, and blustering by turns, he demanded all the Queen's patience and tact to soothe him. His intractability acted like a speck of grit impeding the wheels and cogs of government, already suffering from want of skilled labour to tend them. For Walpole, intent upon personal supremacy, had ranged against himself every politician of brain or promise, and they gave him no peace. Gone were the precision and ebullient self-confidence that marked his former triumphs. Too much devolved upon him. Increasingly pre-occupied with keeping his weak Ministry intact, he had little time to plan ahead.

Soon after the new Parliament met in January 1735, the Queen was aware that his mastery was weakening. Each general election produced many disputed returns, upon which decisions were given, not by a judicial tribunal as to-day, but by the whole House in a partisan spirit. A strong government contrived that its supporters should not be unseated. Consequently the Queen was vexed to find that this time only two amongst the bevy of Walpole's followers whose returns had been questioned kept their seats. She was only partially mollified when Lord Hervey explained that Walpole was distracted by the critical illness of his mistress, Miss Skerrit. His enemies should not be able to score every time he relaxed his attention.

The King felt jaded after being denied the fillip of a holiday abroad for three years. Despite the continental war, he asserted that he would visit Hanover when Parliament rose in May. Aware of the objections to it, but in need of quiet herself, the Queen left Walpole to do what he could. 'Pooh and stuff,' snorted His Majesty in reply to Walpole's excellent arguments against the trip, 'you think to get the better of me but you shall not'. And at five in the morning of May 17th he sped over Blackheath to join his yacht at Gravesend.

Poor Anne, disappointed in her hopes of a baby this winter, had suggested that she might spend the summer in England, because her husband would be away with the Imperial army on the Rhine.[1] But her expensive change of plans the previous autumn still rankled in her father's mind, and he squashed the Queen's tentative approach for permission. Anne hoped to see him when he landed in Holland, to point out how cheaply she could slip across the North Sea in his returning yacht; but divining her plan, the King forbade her to meet him, and raced on to Hanover.

The Queen and Walpole were left to concentrate on a second attempt at mediation to end the Polish War.[2] The first Anglo-Dutch peace plan, published in February 1735, had been rejected by both the Emperor and the French, though Fleury intimated readiness to consider fresh proposals. In October, however, he suavely informed the mediators that he no longer needed their aid, for he had signed preliminaries of peace with the Emperor, whose losses made pride impossible once France wanted peace. Thus Fleury snatched from Walpole the laurels of a peacemaker, wherewith to crown France's martial triumphs. In the treaty that followed, he allowed the Emperor to gaze at France's signature to the Pragmatic Sanction as consolation for territory lost in Italy and fortresses captured on the Rhine. Walpole had kept England out of a war that apparently infringed her interests nowhere. But the abstention, as the Queen foresaw, made France the arbiter of Europe once more, puffed up Spanish pride to thwart English trade expansion in the New World, and so weakened Austria as to invite the spoliation which befell her. Fleury, not Walpole, was the dominant diplomatist of these years.

Meanwhile the King revelled in his holiday.[3] The electoral army camped near Hanover awaiting his inspection, which took place in a downpour and ended with a march past and a three-salvoed salute. The ladies begged for one more salvo, to which the gallant King assented, but his unprepared troops disgraced themselves. The ladies quarrelled for his company at meals or out walking, and he asked his favourites to secret parties, pretending to the world that he had retired to rest. He raved to the Queen at indecent length over Madame Walmoden, the young charmer who was making him so happy. For his Caroline of course understood him and behaved sensibly about his affairs. He loved her none the less, oh dear no!—how often he said so amidst babbling of his new passion!

Though the Queen accepted his new folly with her usual philosophy, her dignity suffered by gossip about Madame Walmoden. When the courier brought the King's belated order to send his yacht to Helvoetsluys for his return home, the Queen became so gay that it was evident her calm had been mainly on the surface.[4] Once resolved to quit Hanover for his 'mean dull island', the King returned with such imprudent haste that he succumbed to fever and piles. Though such mundane ailments were kept secret, no one escaped their shocking effect upon his temper. He carped incessantly about all things English, snubbed the Queen almost whenever she opened her mouth, and spent his mornings scribbling budgets to Madame Walmoden. Even his jovial interludes were hard for the Queen to bear. He decorated her dressing-room with pictures com-memorating his bawdy revels at Hanover. On nights when he felt mellow he toured the room, candle in hand, stop-ping before each picture for reminiscences.

Walpole compiled an astute Speech from the Throne to open the Parliamentary session in January 1736. He claimed more than his due of merit for the pacification of Europe and disarmed criticism by promising reductions of the armed forces. The Queen distrusted this sop to the public, because the treaty was still to make, and Spain would give trouble by claiming a disproportionate share of loot. Walpole took that risk, but he appreciated her reasoning and lectured Hervey for dismissing it too lightly.

Since Pulteney was ill and Bolingbroke had retreated to France when the Government discovered him to be in

French pay, both the Opposition in Parliament and the *Craftsman* lacked sting. Together the members enjoyed the sport of baiting the Church. The increasing secularization of the State, the growth of Nonconformity and dislike of evils like pluralism and nepotism within the Church, had bred contempt for it. First Walpole pleased the clergy by rebuffing the Dissenters, who had tired of patience and unsuccessfully tried to secure the repeal of the Test and Corporation Acts. Then, without warning his satisfied Bishops, he permitted the Commons to pass with 'very hard as well as very popular slaps' at them the Mortmain and Quakers' Tithe Bills.[5] By supporting these Bills, which did not undermine the Church's authority, Walpole hoped to exhaust the laymen's spleen without offending the clergy immoderately. The first Bill prohibited a dying man from bequeathing all his property to a charitable institution, thus leaving his heirs penniless. Only the two Universities secured exemptions from its provisions, though many worthy societies petitioned against it.

Because Quakers refused to pay tithes for the support of the established Church, the clergy sued them, often in central or ecclesiastical courts which mulcted the Quakers. The Tithe Bill was designed to make quicker and cheaper the process of recovering tithes from these loyal adherents of Walpole. But he never told Bishop Gibson, his clerical adviser, that the Bill was to be brought in. He thought his rebuff to the Dissenters entitled him to the bishops' support in this matter, and was enraged to find them hostile.

For they fought the Bill hard, maintaining that it deprived them of ancient rights. Bishop Sherlock stated their arguments in a lucid pamphlet which was commended by the Queen, though she deplored the opposition to the Bill. Knowing, however, that the Government could not afford to antagonize twenty-six bishops, she and a furious Walpole decided at the last minute that the Bill should not pass the House of Lords. The law lords accordingly gave a lead by opposing it, but the mortified bishops were shown how unpopular they were for procuring its defeat. They made their peace with the Court amidst mutual recriminations.

The episode decided Bishop Gibson to sever his connexion with Walpole, thereby forfeiting his certainty of presently becoming Primate. Hervey advised Walpole to choose instead some learned figurehead with less will of his own. And Walpole censured Sherlock's conduct to prevent the Queen from thinking that she could make him Archbishop in Gibson's place when the time came. The Queen, a little exasperated with Church affairs, and a little impressed by Walpole's words, dismissed Sherlock to his diocese to live down the effects of his successful campaign against the Tithe Bill.

Directly the King had prorogued his prating Parliament in May 1736, he hurried off to Hanover again, to the dismay of the Queen and his advisers. She spent her summer at Kensington, going out to Richmond every Saturday to garden. Business between London and Hanover proceeded smoothly because Horatio Walpole had gone with the King instead of Lord Harrington, who was by no means Sir Robert's most zealous colleague. Soon a puzzled King regaled the Queen with an intricate story about a ladder being found against Madame Walmoden's bedroom window and a suspicious gallant lurking in the grounds. He bade her 'consult the fat man' (Sir Robert), whose experience in such matters might be a help, and in the end the affair was explained to his satisfaction. Lord Hervey diverted the Queen with verse and a playlet which dissected the inmates of the Court so amusingly that she forgave him her inclusion amongst the specimens. In fact, she bubbled with health and good spirits; more the reward for past trials, she supposed, than the result of the present state of her private or public affairs.

For the nation was in turbulent mood. There were corn riots in the West Country, and at Spitalfields the weavers rose and slew some of the Irishmen who were undercutting them. A mad non-juring parson upset the dignity of the law by contriving an explosion in Westminster Hall whilst the courts were sitting. The whole country resented the approaching attempt to stop their gin-drinking orgies by imposing a £1-a-gallon tax on all spirits, and a charge of £50 for a retail licence. One autumn day the Queen was driving back to Kensington from London when a gin-frantic mob held up her coach, yelling, 'No gin, no King'. Calmly she showed herself and told them to be patient until the next session when they should have both back again.[6] The severity of the new Gin Act was multiplying abuses and it had to be modified later.

The Queen was angriest over Edinburgh's misconduct, vividly described in *The Heart of Midlothian*. At the execution of a smuggler who had helped his companion to escape, sympathetic spectators pelted the Town Guard with stones, whereupon the Captain ordered his men to fire amongst them, killing eight people.[7] For this Captain Porteous himself was sentenced to death. As the verdict seemed to slight justice in order to pander to the mob,

258

LORD HERVEY

(*Studio of* J. B. VAN LOO)

the Queen reprieved Porteous pending further inquiry into his trial, but the rabble circumvented her clemency by hanging him with such disciplined dispatch as to suggest either complicity or negligence on the part of the City authorities. Popular tradition related that when she heard the news, the Queen told the Duke of Argyll that sooner than submit to the insult she would make Scotland a hunting-ground. 'In that case, Madam, I will take leave of your Majesty and go down to my country to get my hounds ready,' he replied significantly. Certainly she expected effective penalties for Edinburgh when the matter came to be discussed during the session of 1736. But Walpole, disturbed by the dissensions in his Cabinet, abandoned justice to patch up peace as speedily as possible.

Taking the lead from his brother Argyll, Lord Islay, who managed the elections in Walpole's favour, resisted punishment as a slur upon Scotland. He averred that it would make the country impossible to govern peacefully. Walpole was impressed—by the thought of losing supporters. Hervey sided with them to spite Newcastle and Hardwicke, who urged an inquiry into Scottish judicial methods. The Opposition made the same demand and so the inquiry had to be shelved. Amidst heated polemics the proposed penalties were whittled down until Parliament, after discussing the matter for five months, merely disabled the Provost of Edinburgh from holding office again and fined the city £2,000 for the cook-maid widow of Porteous, making her bless his death 'with most unconjugal joy'. Personal feuds had obscured the wider issues and so confused the Queen that she admitted ruefully, 'I am like that judge, Gripus I think you call him, that, after one side had spoke, begged t'other might hold their tongue, for fear of puzzling what was clear to him . . . and since the more I hear the more I am puzzled, I am resolved I will hear no more about it.' Walpole's expediency did him no good. Before the next General Election he had antagonized Argyll with the result that, out of sixty-six Scottish members, only five supported him.[8]

When autumn 1736 came without bringing back the King, his subjects grumbled that they had not provided him with a huge civil list to defray travelling expenses and enrich his German whores. Tradesmen complained of slack business and scurrilous jests multiplied daily. Out of the last two years the King had spent fifteen months in Hanover, which gave point to the acid note pinned up on the Royal Exchange:[9]

It is reported that His Hanoverian Majesty designs to visit his British dominions for three months in the Spring.

Some scoundrel affixed a grosser satire to the very gates of St. James's:

Lost or strayed out of this house, a man who has left a wife and six children on the parish; whoever will give any tidings of him to the churchwardens of St. James's Parish, so as he may be got again, shall receive four shillings and sixpence reward.

N.B.—This reward will not be increased, nobody judging him to be worth a Crown.

Indeed, the King had achieved the miracle of uniting the nation against him.

Even the Queen's patience dwindled. She used to acquiesce in his flirtatious holidays, sure that he would return to conjugality once he came home. But his rudeness last year plus the humiliation of his spending his birthday away were new experiences. His absurd joy in partnering Madame Walmoden had evidently obscured what was seemly for a monarch of 53. The Queen's copious screeds shrank to perfunctory scrawls. Almost more trying than abuse of the King was the pity loyal subjects gave her, 'railing at His Majesty for using so good a wife, who had brought him so many fine children, so abominably ill'.

In his usual bluff way Walpole told the Queen that she could no longer hope to influence the King by 'her person' but her brain could outwit the Walmoden's any day.[10] Get the lady to England, and assuredly in three months she would be all that Lady Suffolk had been, except deaf. The Queen checked him with effusive thanks, disliking his familiarity upon that topic, but to herself he admitted him right. Lure home the King somehow, she must. So she wrote him the tenderest of letters, telling him to bring Madame Walmoden back with him if he wished. The wayward little monarch was touched. For months he had thought very little about his wife or his country but how like dear Caroline to make such an offer—so generous, so sensible. He grovelled his thanks; how unworthy he was of her. And Madame Walmoden? Well, perhaps she would stay in Hanover after all.

Considerately he begged the Queen to move to St. James's because Kensington was so inconvenient and damp in winter. Correctly divining that her informal life there pleased him best, she declined to leave, driving up to London on December 7th, the day before he left Hanover alone. The people's sullen mien showed that they would not forgive their sovereign as quickly as she had done. But she felt too relieved over Madame Walmoden's remaining behind to be depressed. On December 11th the King arrived at Helvoetsluys to wait for the right wind.[11]

Treacherous mid-winter was no season for him to cross the North Sea, hazarding a convoy because he would not leave Hanover betimes. Twice a favourable east wind rose, to be followed each time by deadly westerly gales. Twice the nation assumed that the King had put to sea in the fine interval, and assuredly been drowned, twice the Queen's suspense lasted all but a week. Her miseries were stressed by Fritz's ill-concealed relish at the thought of becoming King and by the nation's callous indifference to George II's fate. At the same time Anne's life was imperilled by a complicated labour, enough to distract the Queen normally, but in her greater anxiety for the King she forgot that 'any such body' as Anne existed.

Finally the news of his safety came to cheer her. His yacht had regained Helvoetsluys harbour after thirty ghastly hours in a gale which took heavy toll of his convoy. Anne, too, was safe, but her babe had been stillborn. Walpole celebrated the double relief by getting drunk, and the Queen wrote joyfully to Anne that night:[12]

Words are unnecessary, dear Anne, to tell how I have suffered and my joy at receiving you back from God, whom I thank with all my soul. I have you and that is enough. May He grant you renewed strength and make you a happy mother of a family. . . look after your Prince . . . and your health, upon which our tranquillity depends . . . and be certain that you will have happier and easier labours in the future. . . . And so to-day's courier has made me perfectly content. I have had the most miserable time since Friday. Your sisters have been a great comfort to me though heavy-hearted themselves. . . . I am assured that I have recovered my usual beauty to-day. May God give you every blessing and you will not lack it,

mein liebes Kind, if you submit yourself entirely to His Will. I
insist that you do not write to me; your dear Prince will willingly
act as your secretary until the end of the month. God bless you.

Though the Queen affected to believe her husband's
own account of his patience in the face of delay and his
heroism in danger, very different stories were circulated.
The King had ordered Admiral Wager to sail against his
better judgement, swearing that he would sooner spend
twelve hours in a storm than another day at Helvoetsluys.
'Well, Sir, you can make me go, but I can make you
come back again,' retorted Wager, but he was almost
unable to keep his word. In a frenzied attempt to lighten
ship, the sailors had demolished the King's suite on the
quarter-deck, pitched the furniture overboard, and sacrificed every inessential to ride those Alp-like waves. Prostrated by sickness, the King had been indifferent to his
peril. With harbour regained, Admiral Wager inquired
whether his curiosity about storms was satisfied. 'So
thoroughly satisfied that I do not ever desire to see another,'
murmured His Majesty.

If the Queen heard these tales she held her peace and
sent the King her felicitations upon his happy escape. He
replied that he would suffer such horrors repeatedly to
procure her affection. Little as he deserved her toleration
and goodness, he could never forget them; how impatient
he felt for their meeting! To disprove Sir Robert's theories
about 'her person' the Queen showed him the letter:

Do not think because I show you this that I am an old fool and
vain of my person and charms at this time of day. I am reasonably
pleased with it, but I am not unreasonably proud of it.

Sir Robert and Lord Hervey privately agreed that no man

wrote a love-letter better than their Sovereign. Pity it is that his correspondence with Caroline has been destroyed, or at least so deeply immured within some archives as to have eluded discovery. Some day, perhaps, like George I's last testament, it will come to light.

Until mid-January 1737 the King was pent up at Helvoetsluys. 'How is the wind for the King?' men asked each other. 'Like the nation, against him,' came the reply pat. Finally the wind blew fair, and after nine months' absence a chastened monarch drove through London noting ruefully that nobody uncovered for him and hisses punctuated his passage through Stocksmarket.[13] How sweet the balm to be greeted in the Palace courtyard as the noblest of sovereigns and best of husbands! He showed his gratitude with warm kisses for the Queen and smiles for the courtiers.

No sooner home than he fell ill again; it was becoming a habit after his Hanoverian holidays. Because he went to bed and did no business people thought he must be dying. Though he had fever and piles, nervous strain was the real trouble and rest the cure. For nine months he had gallivanted with a lady twenty years his junior, then almost been drowned at sea, and ended with a reception icy enough to chill even his vanity. His docility showed the measure of his exhaustion. He only sulked when a Lord-in-waiting forgot to ignore his illness and asked how he felt. That lord was relieved of his week in waiting.

Walpole annoyed the Queen by disbelieving her bulletins on the King's health, and making tactless suggestions as to its cause. He could never perceive that she was fond of her wayward husband despite his follies. When the

King was obstinate or aggressive, then Walpole and the Queen combined to manage him, but in his rare phases of benignity, Walpole was superfluous. Because the Queen possessed qualities considered commoner in the male, Walpole forgot that she also felt as a woman and a wife. His stable metaphors enlivened business but became offensive when applied to the royal relationship. Lord Hervey's instinct for psychology gained and kept him the Queen's intimacy. He perceived when a dig at His Majesty would not come amiss and he always paid the Queen a subtle, affectionate deference. Consequently no topic was debarred him, though some should have been had the Queen guessed that his tact outweighed his loyalty and discretion. He was seldom away from her. When the other ministers had taken their holidays during the past autumn, she bade him stay and save her the tedium of domesticity. 'If I were younger they would talk of me for this man,' she laughed, describing him another day as 'one of the greatest pleasures of my life'. At times Walpole resented their intimacy, but he had only himself to blame. Had he not antagonized the best writers, talkers, and politicians, the Queen would not have been dependent exclusively upon Hervey to amuse her and polish her wits. Walpole and the Queen disagreed over the successor to Archbishop Wake, who died in January 1736. She still wanted to advance Bishop Sherlock, but Walpole favoured his former tutor, Francis Hare. Finally they compromised by appointing John Potter of Oxford, who made a Primate wise enough to have been preferred on his own merits.

XII

THE PRINCE MARRIES

W<small>HEN</small> the Prince had interviewed his father in 1734 he had asked that a wife should be found him. The quest for a bride had suggested Princesses of Holstein, Nassau, Saxe-Eisenach, and an ill-favoured Danish Princess as candidates, without concluding the marriage.[1] Hearing of his debts, Sarah Marlborough had proposed settling £100,000 on her granddaughter, Lady Diana Spenser, if he married her secretly. Walpole found out in time to prevent the match, which might have been most suitable and popular had it not been intended as a snub to Their Majesties. For fiery Sarah added the Queen to her capacious black list for supporting Walpole, who, in preserving the Tory alliance with France, seemed to Sarah to have betrayed Marlborough's lifework. Besides, it would at that time have appeared as a flouting of precedent and rank had the Heir Apparent married a commoner.

While the King was at Herrenhausen in 1735 enjoying Madame Walmoden's company for the first time, he sent home word that he had met sixteen-year-old Princess Augusta of Saxe-Gotha, whom he considered a suitable bride. Fritz was allowed to dispatch a trusted valet to see the girl, and after receiving this man's report he agreed to the marriage.[2] The Queen advised him to part from Miss Vane, and he complied readily because his transient affections rested on Lady Archibald Hamilton. Although the pair displayed the usual symptoms of an affair, their liaison has been questioned because Lady Archibald was six or seven years older than the Prince. But his record made him unlikely to desire only a platonic friendship and the gossip was such that the Queen refused to allow the lady a place in Augusta's household.

The Queen leisurely assembled her wedding finery and arranged about her future daughter-in-law's accommodation, ignoring the mockers who doubted that the marriage would take place. The winter of 1735 passed without advancing matters. Then, in the spring, the King, who was impatient for Hanover, ordered full speed ahead. A deputation of the Cabinet Council formally conveyed to the Prince the King's offer of marrying him to Augusta. Though he accepted it respectfully, he did not scruple to tell the Prussian envoy at a masked ball that he was being forced to marry against his will.[3] He ended their secret conversation by condemning England's policy towards Prussia, which may have been diplomatic but was certainly dishonourable.

Now Walpole had continued his predecessors' dubious but useful habit of opening foreign correspondence. Since 1718 a special department, staffed by four decipherers and five clerks, had existed at the Post Office for this purpose.[4] The Crown defrayed its expenses, amounting to £3,500 a year by 1742. The fruits of its labours have survived in the form of a hundred volumes of *Intercepted Correspondence* at the Public Record Office, consisting of extracts, copies, and translations from the original dispatches of the resident foreign ministers. By this simple means, then, Walpole learnt about the Prince's talk with von Borcke, which produced in his parents' minds an unfortunate impression of duplicity.

Lord De la Warr, a plain and proper person, was sent over as escort for the young Princess, whose comparatively humble rank disappointed the English public. One story related how he had wandered all over Germany without finding Gotha. At last a trusty guide from Hanover took him there only to experience great difficulty in discovering the Duke's (her brother's) house.[5] Lord De la Warr was nervous lest Augusta's governess, who dominated her and spoke only German, should accompany her to England.[6] After some scenes the lady was left behind, but Augusta's first request to Fritz was to have her sent over. He assented gallantly, and repented at leisure, finally packing the officious creature back to Gotha.

Before Augusta arrived he was more concerned with his finances than his bride. He grumbled to the Queen that his debts equalled the £50,000 to which the King proposed raising his allowance on marriage, giving him some £63,000 with the duchy revenues.[7] He spoke glibly of obliging moneylenders, whose help his parents resented because they were promised repayment of their loans upon the King's demise. Perhaps the King would give him one extra £50,000 to discharge the debts? Though the Queen recognized the ultimatum she knew that she would never coax the money out of the King. His thrifty nature despised profligacy and justly considered that £50,000 was enough to be wasted on the pleasures that had so far swallowed most of his son's money. Of course, he should have settled a jointure on Augusta, but he was too moonstruck over Madame Walmoden to concentrate on a prosaic item like that. It was deferred until the harm had been done. The Queen procured Fritz £6,000, for which he never said thank you. Her mediation between father and son always provoked their ingratitude. The King snapped her up for extenuating Fritz's conduct, while Fritz never acknowledged her help. This time he made a virtue of buying nothing for his household and enjoyed the sympathy over the King's withholding the £100,000, which most people thought was his due as a married man.

When Augusta arrived in April he found her so much to his liking that he told the Queen 'if he had been himself to look all Europe over he should have pitched his choice on' Augusta, for whose sake the Queen felt extremely relieved.[8] Poor girl, her position was bleak enough without incurring Fritz's dislike. She spoke no English, because her mother supposed that the Court would all prattle German after twenty years under the Hanoverian dynasty. Since her English ladies-in-waiting could produce only halting French, dumb show filled the gaps.

Two days after her arrival, Their Majesties amidst their Court waited to receive her in the great drawing-room at St. James's. The King fussed because the appointment was not kept to the minute. In fact an hour passed before the doors were thrown open and the Queen saw Fritz lead in a short, flushed girl who preserved her composure under the battery of critical eyes trained on her. She swept her lowest curtsy to Their Majesties, earning favour by her tact. That night the Queen mothered her through the marriage service, for which Handel composed an anthem, which was spoilt by bad singing. The Court observed its privilege of seeing the bridal couple to bed and the Queen described her new daughter-in-law and the wedding to Anne, with details that had eluded even Hervey's vigilance.[9]

Heaven be praised, everything passed off wonderfully well, my dear Anne. The King behaved like an angel. Your sisters will tell you about Griff's silliness and the sweetness of his wife, who, far from being beautiful, has a wretched figure . . . pretty eyes and a good mouth. She is as anxious as a good child to please. Her blond hair is almost the same shade as the duchess of Diswoncher [Devonshire?] but rather more of a sheep's colour. I felt excessively sorry for her in the chapel, which was beautifully decorated. I told her to take off her gloves and she wanted to give me them to hold. Though I would have taken them willingly I feared the King and her amiable husband for different reasons so I made her hand them to Lord Effingham. I told her to look at me and I would make a sign when she ought to kneel. She clutched my skirt and said 'For Heaven's sake, please don't leave me', but Griff bawled in her ear, making her repeat the marriage sentences. She did not want to let go of my skirt. After the service, she and her husband knelt to ask the King's and my blessing, which the King bestowed most benignly, and she poor creature, just as one has seen in plays—she was sick . . . so I let her withdraw. . . . Her undress was so miserable that it made me go quite gray, and as she felt ill, she looked like——*in bed. The bridegroom arrived in a grenadier's bonnet and knelt before the King. She is the best creature in the world, one puts up with her insipidity because of her goodness. As far as one can judge her husband is perfectly pleased with and likes her. . . . I could scold the old duchess of Gotha for not having given the poor good child a better education. . . . I have written you quite enough but if only I could have the joy of seeing you our conversations would never end. There are no bounds to my affection and love for my more than dearest Anne.

The Queen expressed the general verdict on Augusta, whose docility suited Fritz admirably. Always genial with the public, he gained popularity at his father's expense, an

* This significant word is undecipherable in the Queen's writing.

easy matter but fatal because it fortified him in his insolence
to his parents. This year, for instance, appeared *L'Histoire
du Prince Titi*, either written or sponsored by him. Under
the flimsy guise of a fairy tale it libelled the King, Queen,
and Walpole, making the wronged but winsome Titi, alias
Fritz, its hero. To prevent its circulation, all copies were
bought from the booksellers upon publication.[10] Congratu-
lating the King on Fritz's marriage, the Prince's Parliamentary friends untruthfully maintained that Fritz had forced
the King to arrange the happy union. For this imperti-
nence, one of them, Mr. Pitt, received advertisement by
being dismissed his cornetcy of horse.

Indeed, the Prince's marriage had widened the breach in
the royal family by reopening the question of his allowance
and by inflating him with his own importance. For
instance, he resented not being appointed Regent when the
King went to Hanover just after the wedding in 1736, and
he resolved on a campaign of pinpricks against his mother's
authority. She wished he could see what a bore he made
himself in trying to force a quarrel by manœuvres which
would not deceive a simpleton. Certainly they never upset
her serenity.

His friends, who were Walpole's enemies, of course
abetted him. They were hatching a scheme to make party
capital out of his curtailed allowance. For a few days,
when the King was thought to have been drowned, it
seemed that power was theirs without strife. To their
chagrin the buoyant sovereign survived. But the episode
showed them the extent of his unpopularity, and his illness
revived their hopes of his demise. Had not the psychological moment for their project come? On with the fight!

XIII

FAMILY HISTORY REPEATS ITSELF

THE scheme of Fritz's friends had a simple maleficence which proclaimed its paternity as Bolingbroke's.[1] He fashioned this triple-barbed shaft some years before to embroil Walpole with Their Majesties, to enrage the King and to wreck the Queen's influence. The Opposition brought a motion in Parliament asking the King to grant the Prince £100,000 out of the Civil List and to settle a jointure on Augusta: most plausible requests. The King had enjoyed that income when Prince of Wales, and his wife had had her jointure. That Prince Frederick had never discussed his grievances with his father was considered irrelevant: they might have been settled privately. Whereas, if this motion triumphed, it took no acumen to see that the King would dismiss Walpole, and if it were narrowly defeated he might do likewise for Walpole's failure to prevent Parliament discussing his private affairs.

In pious whispers the Prince spread it abroad that as the King had ordered him to prefer any request through the Queen, he had often asked her help over the £100,000. For part of the scheme to discredit her with the King was to reveal to him his silken leading strings. Then 'dapper George' would strut no more, but in a fury send Walpole to the Tower and his Queen to—Coventry. The Prince could not really have deemed himself more filial in attack-

272

ing his father publicly than in disobeying his command and requesting an audience. At least he might have left the choice to the King.

The Queen flatly denied her son's statement, and she had every right to be believed when it was her word against his.[2] It was neither her inclination nor her interest to alienate him from the King. Indeed, she had so often excused his conduct that the King presented her with a typical testimonial to that effect, convincing because he did not give it specifically as a result of Frederick's charge. 'I have scolded the Queen oftener for taking that rascal's part,' he told Hervey, 'and have had more quarrels with her when she has been making silly excuses for his silly conduct, than ever I had with her on all subjects put together'.[3] Those words bore the authentic stamp, and in truth the King's honesty, like his parsimony, has become proverbial.

Though Walpole exposed the motion as an attack on the King's prerogative (once Parliament had voted the King a Civil List it could not dictate how he should spend the money), he would have been defeated had not his old enemies, the Tories, shared this view. Resenting interference with the King's rights as highly democratic and dangerous, all 45 of them abstained from voting. Walpole scraped a majority of 30 and the House of Lords in their turn defeated the motion by 103 votes to 40.

How could Frederick have won his £100,000? By asking the King for it. If he had met with a refusal then he could have regretted that necessity compelled him to ask Parliament for a grant out of the *national revenues*; a perfectly constitutional procedure. His old friend Dodington suggested this course.[4] 'I would rather beg my bread from door to door than be a further charge upon the nation,' he replied. A worthy sentiment, but was he so obtuse that he could not see what must have happened? Faced with his legitimate intention, Walpole and the Queen must have forced the King to pay him out of the Civil List. Forewarned, they could never have allowed the Opposition to abuse His Majesty for an old miser, and to point out that Parliament had already voted a Civil List sufficient for normal calls upon it. The matter must have been settled privately, and if Frederick had not gained £100,000 at once, he might have been given £75,000, with the rest to follow when he had a family.

Provoked beyond bearing, Their Majesties wanted to expel the Prince from the Palace, expressing their disgust in regrettable terms. Walpole, however, persuaded them against a public break, so the Prince came to Court; but the King ignored him and the Queen 'gave him her hand on all these public occasions' without vouchsafing him a word. Walpole also prevailed upon the King to implement the offer made to the Prince in hopes of staving off the Parliamentary attack. The Prince's £50,000 was settled on him independently instead of being doled out by instalments, and Augusta received a jointure of £50,000. Then the sordid affair was dropped but not forgotten.

How nearly the Opposition succeeded in getting Walpole dismissed appeared from the Queen's fury with Pulteney's section of Whigs for supporting her 'rascally puppy of a son', as the King called him.[5] Since 1714 the Whig party had monopolized the fruits of office, which should have kept them all loyal to the King. With better excuse to vote against the Government, the Tories had refrained sooner than attack the monarch. So the Queen listened favourably when Bishop Sherlock and Lady Sundon descanted on their readiness to serve the King. These two also championed Carteret, feebly excusing his support of the Opposition's motion by saying that he had disapproved of it. At heart the Queen shared her family's attraction to Carteret, a statesman in the grand manner, cultured, suave, and a brilliant linguist. How much preferable to see him daily rather than Newcastle, for example, always preaching concessions to Fritz. She considered Carteret's either replacing one of Walpole's dunderheads or leading a new ministry.

For she and Walpole, after six years of smooth co-operation, had lost their rhythm. First they faltered over the Excise Bill, then they fell out about the Polish War. Thereafter Walpole became an apostle of safety first, taking 'Thou shalt compromise' as his eleventh commandment. All this was at a time when the Queen needed vigorous support over family trials and public disorders, and lacking it she began at last to consider dropping her old pilot.

Walpole grasped the nettle of her discontent.[6] To change the ministry at this juncture was an admission of defeat, he said, while for him to work with Carteret was impossible. Impertinent as this statement sounded, he felt it more honest to make it and let the Queen choose between them. It was noteworthy that he recognized that she, not the King, made or dismissed ministries. How right was her desire to strengthen the Government appeared from Walpole's private confession to Lord Hervey that he had grown 'too old to form new schemes', preferring to rub along until his ministry disintegrated, when he would throw in his hand. But Walpole's arguments convinced the Queen that she must find a better moment to make the change.

Several times during the following months her thoughts strayed towards Carteret. Had he been in the Palace as Lord Steward pressing his claims, Walpole's spell of power might have been considerably shortened, with benefit to his reputation. After the Queen's death he clung over-tenaciously to office, uncertain of his fate when ousted.

When Parliament rose the Court went to Richmond, and the Prince to Kew. All was peace. The Queen heard her husband mention neither Hanover nor Madame Walmoden, but in return for this pleasant surprise, listened resignedly to his amatory tales about his latest love, Lady Deloraine. He salved his conscience over the Hanover lady by sending her £1,000 worth of lottery tickets. Walpole felt nervous about the mischief Lady Deloraine's malicious tongue might cause, but Lord Hervey reassured him: 'If she got the ear of anybody that had power, it might be of very bad consequence, but since 'tis only the King, I think it is of no great signification', and they both enjoyed the satire.

The Prussian ambassador, Count von Borcke, departed for Berlin in June.[7] The King had had him recalled because he hunted for giant grenadiers in England. So ceased the 'Anecdotes Secrètes' with which the Count had plied his sovereign since 1733, composing this court gossip in the form of letters from an anonymous correspondent to himself. Bolingbroke, Carteret, and Chesterfield were reported to be writing the history of their times.[8] Carteret told his friend Lady Sundon, 'Madam, if you dare own at Court you talk to so obnoxious a man as I am, you may tell the Queen I have been giving her fame this morning'. Related to the Queen, it provoked an amusing discussion between Their Majesties. 'Yes, I dare say he will paint you in fine colours, that dirty liar', commented the King. 'Why not! Good things come out of dirt sometimes,' the Queen replied. His Majesty thought that all three histories would have about as much truth in them as the *Arabian Nights*, but they agreed that Bolingbroke's style would make his version the best reading.

Early in June the Queen received a letter from Fritz announcing his wife's pregnancy. This was the first intimation given Their Majesties, though Augusta's ladies had known since March, when she was reckoned to be in her fourth month.[9] The Queen duly congratulated her and put some natural questions, to be answered each time with a parrot-like 'I don't know'. Such a doltish reply made the Queen wonder what information was being hidden. Was Fritz planning to thrust a spurious child on them? Last summer he hinted often that Augusta was pregnant but no child arrived. The Queen remembered the pathetic hints he dropped soon after his marriage, which, combined with the glandular troubles of his adolescence, made her question his ability for fatherhood.[10] Very unwisely, she had communicated her doubts to Hervey. 'At her labour I positively will be,' declared the Queen, as she pressed Walpole to send Fritz the King's intended command that Augusta should be confined at Hampton Court, where Their Majesties would be resident. For it was common knowledge that Fritz wanted the child born in London, though his mother had a right and a duty to be present at the birth of an heir to the throne. Walpole told the Queen there was time enough for the message, since apparently the child was not expected till October.[11]

Their Majesties, the Prince and Augusta moved to Hampton Court during July. On the last day of the month, a Sunday, they dined together in public as usual, but apart from these ceremonial occasions they rarely met. That evening the King played his game of commerce, the Queen her quadrille, and they retired to bed about eleven o'clock.[12] All of a sudden someone was trying to wake them. Was the Palace on fire? queried the Queen as she roused up. No, replied Mrs. Titchburne, but the Princess was in labour. 'My God! my nightgown. I'll go to her this moment.' 'Your nightgown, Madam, and your coaches too; the Princess is at St. James's.' 'Are you mad, or are you asleep, my good Titchburne? You dream.' It was no dream, as Mrs. Titchburne rapidly explained. Whereupon, the King, caught asleep for the second time at a crucial moment in his life, blustered in German: 'You see, now, with all your wisdom how they have outwitted you. This is all your fault. There is a false child will be put upon you, and how will you answer it to all your children?' Ignoring him, the Queen dressed hurriedly. Within an hour of being called, she had collected Emily and Caroline, the Duke of Grafton, Lords Hervey and Essex, and the party was jolting urgently to St. James's. They arrived at about four o'clock as summer dawn was breaking upon the sleeping city. The Queen hurried up to her son's apartments.

Clad in nightgown and cap he met her with the news that his daughter had been born at 10.45 on the Sunday night. The Queen exlaimed that it was curious the news had not reached Hampton Court before she left, since the journey only took an hour and a half. But she accepted his glib explanations, resolved to make no comments for him to misconstrue later. She wished Augusta joy and congratulated her on withstanding her double ordeal. Then the babe was brought; the littlest mite, swathed in a red mantle and some napkins. At least this tiny she-mouse was no spurious child, thought the Queen, taking it in her arms. 'The good God bless you, poor little mite, you have arrived in a disagreeable world,' she told it.

From Fritz's lips tumbled the tale of that night's mad proceedings. Without a word to any one, he had driven Augusta, far advanced in labour, at full gallop to St. James's. Nothing was ready for them, but all the essentials were hurriedly borrowed from neighbours whilst the Princess was put to bed between tablecloths, giving birth to her child three-quarters of an hour after her arrival. The Queen heard out this recital of folly in silence, observed that it was a miracle for the babe to have been born alive, and then went to say good-bye to Augusta. If there was anything she wanted, the Queen promised it should be done. Presently the Prince repeated his account to Walpole and Harrington, whom the King had sent post haste to witness the birth for which, of course, they were too late. He added that he had driven Augusta to London twice during the previous week upon her complaining of pains. As the pains had gone off, the pair had returned to Hampton Court. His story proved this latest escapade to be no flustered improvisation of an overwrought young husband. Later it was established that Augusta, too, had wanted the child to be born away from Their Majesties' surveillance.[13] But any mother knows that whatever she said beforehand, she must have begged for peace once her pains engulfed her. The thought of her agonies inside the coach, as admitted by Fritz, roused resentment against the fool who endangered two lives and insulted his parents to gratify a whim.

'My God,' inveighed the Queen afterwards, 'there is no human patience that can bear such treatment.' Scoundrel, puppy, knave, fool, stormed the King when he heard what had passed. He refused to see his son, who should be thoroughly chastened, as Walpole admitted, unwilling though he had previously been to countenance an open breach in the royal family. The Queen wrote Anne the tale as Fritz told it her and Hervey related it in his memoirs.[14]

Fritz's counsellors were so aghast at his conduct that he never disclosed how he had vitiated defence by telling three people the damning truth.[15] Naturally they advised him to plead his distraught state in extenuation of his behaviour and obviously this fiction increased his parents' fury. Taxed later with his damaging admissions, Fritz denied them and retorted that the Queen had incensed the King against him. When writing to her he omitted to style her 'Majesty'. The Queen told Hervey how Fritz had once explained that his rank was superior to hers. Laughingly she admitted herself unable to accept his reasoning, 'Since, believe me, my dear Fritz, let your quality be ever so great, the King, if I was to die, would never marry you'.

Nine days after the child's birth, the Queen drove up to

inquire after Augusta. This time her sullen son vouchsafed her neither greetings nor thanks during the hour she spent at St. James's. He led her to the coach in silence, but on seeing a crowd gathered round it, he knelt in the mud to kiss her hand, and in that posture she saw him for the last time.

The formal break followed quickly. The King ordered his son to leave St. James's. His guards were removed, foreign ministers were notified of his disgrace, and people who visited him were forbidden to appear at Court. With the kindly difference that the new-born infant was left to her parents' care, the bad old precedent of 1718 was followed. Yet the King had no other way of meeting insults which demanded penalization. Unruly heirs to other thrones could be summarily punished, but English laws bound even English Kings. 'The King, my Lords . . . must stand the battle and must conquer, and those who advise him to decline the battle must advise him to show he thinks himself in the wrong or the weakest. When he has conquered, he may forgive,' Walpole told the Cabinet Council; but unfortunately the King lacked weapons for a victory. The advantage passed to the Prince directly he was expelled. Though his counsellors knew that he had behaved badly, they were not less anxious to oust Walpole. To keep the Prince as their figurehead was essential to their purpose. It baited the King and showed Walpole what to expect from Frederick. The King might have foreseen this from his own experience of Opposition at Leicester House, but his ablest supporter, Walpole, had deserted to George I. Walpole in his prime stood no baiting. Now he had become the ageing pack leader whose predatory rivals no longer feared him. By Walpole's help, George I had conquered and forgiven after a fashion, whereas poor George II never conquered and never forgave.

However, he and the Queen were at least delighted to be rid of their son. 'I hope in God I shall never see him again,' the Queen wished, and it came true.[16] 'Thank God, to-morrow night the puppy will be out of my house,' the King echoed. '...I can never forgive his behaviour to you. I must say you have been an excellent mother to all your children, and if any of them behave ill to you they deserve to be hanged. I never loved the puppy well enough to have him ungrateful to me, but to you he is a monster and the greatest villain that was ever born.'[17] That the Queen agreed appeared from what she said about her son. Once dearer to her than all her children, he was now become hateful, and the mere sight of him made her redden with rage.

There was no woman less quarrelsome than the Queen by nature, yet few Queens were so cursed with internecine disputes. Life at Hanover had been a perpetual skirmish with her father-in-law. No sooner was he King than he flared up over a fancied insult to one of his servants, declaring an uneasy truce during his last years. He wronged Caroline most by keeping Frederick at Hanover, so that when he came to England he was a stranger. At once the Opposition saw that his curtailed allowance was a grievance which could be used to dissatisfy Their Majesties with Walpole and with each other. The campaign against the Queen was likewise a party project shaped to the same ends. In their first object the Opposition nearly succeeded, but in their second and baser object they failed utterly.

Hervey's tedious account of the family quarrel made it seem abnormal, but it has been observed that every Hanoverian Prince of Wales eventually fought with his Sovereign. Idleness drove him to it; an enforced idleness which persisted into the nineteenth century. Albert Edward, Prince of Wales, being long denied a real share in the administration, 'declined happily upon Society', and his mother was not amused. But he had his own sons trained to careers and then he let them become his trusted helpers. During the eighteenth century, while an Heir Apparent remained friendly with the King, he counted for nothing. Though this also applied to Prussian Crown Princes, for instance, and often provoked feuds with their sovereign papas, they were urged to become good soldiers. But the easy-going English loathed professional soldiers; as George II and his second son, William Duke of Cumberland, had cause to know. Therefore the Prince of Wales sought self-expression in the personalities of opposition politics, which gave him a sporting chance to humiliate the King.

It was supposed that Frederick would inevitably fight again for his £100,000.[18] Rumour held him willing to waive his succession to Hanover in William's favour if given the money. Besides saving the nation from keeping his brother, he would increase his popularity by severing a connexion obnoxious to it. From what the Queen told Lord Hervey, Their Majesties had previously discussed the possibility of dissolving the Personal Union; indeed, George I's will forced them to do so. Hervey understood that there existed a plan to effect it, but he never learnt what it was. His story has been twisted to represent an attempt on Their Majesties' part to disinherit Frederick, despite Hervey's statement that whenever the matter had been discussed, the Queen had always objected that it would be unjust to deprive Frederick of his birthright. However, when she heard that he preferred £100,000 to Hanover, she was inclined to reconsider the matter. Walpole never doubted that Parliament would acclaim the separation, but told the Queen to ponder well what she wanted done and it should be so. If the bargain were struck, he added, the nation that would benefit most from it should pay Frederick the extra £50,000. Thereafter Hervey heard neither Walpole nor the Queen mention the subject again.

Had she been longing to disinherit Frederick, Walpole's tempting promise must have decided her to do it. Instead, she held to her original views, seeing that, whatever the merits or demerits of separation, they had to be weighed in a calm, judicial spirit. For the King to regard his Electorate as a cash proposition or a mere swap was fatal. So she told Lord Islay, who passed on the news to Hervey. Walpole kept his word to the Queen, and there the matter rested until after she was dead and his ministry had ended.

The archives of Hanover bear this out, for there lie the documents and memoranda concerning George I's efforts to dissolve the Personal Union by the provisions of his will. These efforts foundered on the legal rocks. Then come the papers dealing with George II's moves in the matter; the first made, not during this quarrel with Frederick, but in 1744.[19] Yielding to the clamour that England had been involved in the War of the Austrian Succession owing to the Union, the King requested the advice of his Hanoverian Privy Councillors over dissolving it. He consulted them again in 1757, six years after Frederick's death. Both times his advisers mistrusted the permanence of any solution of the constitutional problems of separation. They wanted no wars of Hanoverian Succession. Nor could they produce overwhelming political arguments in its favour, from the standpoint of Hanover, already menaced by Prussia. But George III's desire to be only an Englishman made him neglect Hanover, whose sufferings during the last decades of the Union far outweighed the blessings expected from it. This unhappy future being veiled from George II, he was too good a Hanoverian to go against his advisers. He let the matter drop. Queen Victoria's accession severed the partnership because the Salic Law obtained in Hanover, which survived for thirty years as an independent kingdom before being swallowed by Prussia.

After his expulsion from Court, the Prince held sway at Norfolk House, later moving to that 'pouting place of Princes', Leicester House. His friends, the Patriots, promised social reforms, efficiency, and economy if returned to power. For Walpole had outstayed his political vigour and men were forgetting that his genius for finance and commerce had given England economic prosperity. They pointed only to the abuses and corruptions of his system. But when in 1742 the Patriots downed him, they forgot their ideals in the scramble for office, and the Prince for some time went into the retirement which best suited his character. Although his resentment against the King had some justification, the Opposition propaganda fuddled his brain and made him act shiftily amidst the acrimony of politics. In private life he showed himself a happy father and an amiable neighbour, cultivating the artistic tastes inherited from his mother. He professed the progressive principles advocated by Bolingbroke's *Patriot King*, but never lived to be judged as King by the test of performance.

XIV

'GOD GIVE HER LIFE'

AUTUMN came before Their Majesties left Hampton Court, just in time to celebrate the King's birthday at St. James's. Sir Robert, in mourning for his wife, was absent that October 30th. The Queen was touched, however, by the rest of her friends appearing in full force, dressed sumptuously, making a record crowd to wish the King long life despite the absence of the Prince's court.[1]

She was absorbed in her new library built on the site now occupied by the London Museum.[2] An unrepentant bibliophile, she accumulated books until they overflowed into the spare lodgings at St. James's. Even if the arrangement had contented her, she could not always have the use of these lodgings, formerly occupied by Lady Suffolk, which had nearly acquired a new tenant in Madame Walmoden this winter. Besides, it is the ambition of every book collector to make a fitting temple for his treasures, so William Kent designed her a library overlooking the Green Park. She walked over there one November morning, the 9th, pleasantly pre-occupied by schemes for its interior arrangement. She promised herself splendid editions of the best European literature, for which English ambassadors abroad were already searching. She looked forward to meeting her friends there for stimulating dis-

287

cussions. The library was to be her spiritual home, insulated from politics and family troubles.

Scarcely had she begun discussing her plans this Wednesday morning when violent pain and sickness prostrated her.[3] Taken back to the Palace, she gulped down an anodyne and tried to rest in bed. At two o'clock she struggled up to appear at the Drawing-room, rather than let the King think she was shirking her duty. Seeing her ashen face, Lord Hervey implored her 'For God's sake, Madam, go to your own room. What have you to do here?' She did not heed him, though presently she admitted, 'I am no longer able to entertain people', and waited quietly until the King left the circle. As he passed her on his way out, he said that she had overlooked the Duchess of Norfolk. The Queen made graceful amends, sending her Grace contented home. Then she collapsed into bed but humoured the King in his belief that her ailment was slight, so he went off to his evening game of cards, leaving her in charge of Caroline and her German doctor. By night she could no longer hide her intense pain. Now thoroughly alarmed, the King summoned a second doctor. Assuming that she had a bad colic, they dosed her with numerous strong purges, but she retained none of them. Their only effect was to throw her into a high fever, whereupon the doctors ordered her to be bled twelve ounces. The King packed Caroline protesting to bed at two o'clock, showing his own devotion by lying on the Queen's bed, effectually banishing sleep for both of them.

All Thursday and Friday she suffered pitifully, murmuring to Caroline and Lord Hervey, 'I have an ill which nobody knows of', which they simply took to mean that

QUEEN CAROLINE, 1736

(*By* J. VANDERBANK; *from an engraving by* J. FABER)

her pain was inexpressible. Her physicians, then increased
to four, continued their relentless clysters and purges,
cuppings and blisters, though her exhausted body longed
only for peace. The King had had his bedding laid on
the floor of a little room opening out of her dressing-room.
Emily sat up in a big chair in her mother's apartment at
night, whilst Lord Hervey and Caroline dozed fitfully in
the anteroom.

The Queen's illness could no longer be kept from the
world. The Prince sent to inquire if he might see her but
his father returned him an angry refusal.

'This,' he raged, 'is like one of the scoundrel's tricks; it is just of a
piece with his kneeling down in the dirt before the mob to kiss her
hand at the coach door when she came from Hampton Court to see
the Princess, though he had not spoken one word to her the whole
visit. . . . No, no! he shall not come and act any of his silly plays
here',

and the King forbade further messages. Ignorant of this
incident, the Queen wondered that same afternoon that
her son had not asked to see her yet. When the King told
her what had happened she acquiesced in his decision, but
later sent a private message of forgiveness to her son
through Walpole.[4] If the King's attitude seemed harsh,
his son's behaviour justified it. Even his friends admitted
that he sent often to St. James's saying, 'Well, well, we
must have some good news soon. . . . I think I am a very
good son, I wish her out of her pain.' Why, indeed, should
he have intruded upon real grief and suffering nobly
borne, to justify himself with the mob?

Before dawn on Saturday the Queen was so racked with
pain that the doctor on duty summoned the King from

his improvised bed. Urgently His Majesty whispered to her that he must tell the surgeon what he feared was causing her illness but she implored him not to. She had neglected the hernia so long already, fourteen years now, deeming it a shameful complaint, that she desired her secret might die with her, but her husband salved his conscience by ignoring her pleas. She knew it was too late. Presently the surgeon found out her secret, and she who had endured her suffering dry eyed, turned her head away to hide the furtive tears. Fearful of his responsibility, Ranby summoned two colleagues. On Saturday morning they operated, pessimistic about the result.

The Queen thought her release approached when, before daybreak next morning, they perceived in her wound the symptoms they dreaded. Sadly her family came round her. She spoke to the children, commending her two younger girls to faithful Caroline's care, telling William that she reposed her chief hope in him as his father's mainstay, bidding him mortify his brother in 'no way but by showing superior merit'. To the King she said she had always imparted her thoughts as they arose, which made final requests superfluous. She handed him her keys, and taking off the ruby ring he gave her on their Coronation day, she placed it on his finger.

This is the last thing I have to give you—naked I came to you, naked I go from you. I had everything I ever possessed from you, and to you, whatever I have I return.[5]

The King and his children sobbed, but her own eyes remained dry as she advised him to marry again, knowing his need for feminine sympathy. Choked by his emotion, he spluttered, 'Non—j'aurai des maîtresses.' 'Ah! Mon Dieu! cela n'empêche pas,' was all she replied.

She was weary now and would rest. 'She said she fancied she could sleep. . . . The King . . . kissed her face and her hands a hundred times.' She fell into a doze. The King, close beside her, kept whispering to the watchers that she would pass away in her sleep. But she was denied that mercy for which all sufferers pray. She woke again feeling refreshed, yet knowing it was only a short reprieve, she regretted it. 'I wish it was at an end; for I cannot recover; but my nasty heart will not break yet.' When next they examined her wound, the surgeons found that the mortification had not spread, so they pared away what was necessary and declared she might survive. Thereafter she was tortured daily—often twice a day—by the agonies of surgery without anaesthetics. Before each probing she asked the King whether he approved the operation. Upon his replying that it was necessary, she submitted patiently though she yearned to be let alone. If an involuntary groan escaped her, she bade the surgeons proceed, contrite at 'interrupting them with her silly complaints when she knew they were doing all they could to help her'.

Sir Robert, summoned by express messenger from Norfolk, arrived on the Monday, when she had been ill five days. 'How is the Queen?' he inquired, kneeling awkwardly to kiss His Majesty's hand. 'Come and see yourself, my good Sir Robert,' and the King led him to her bedside.

'My good Sir Robert,' she said quietly, 'you see me in a very indifferent situation. I have nothing to say to you but to recommend the King, my children, and the kingdom to your care.'

Flattered but sad he left her—to toil alone after their partnership of ten years. 'If ever I heard a corpse speak, it was just now in that room,' he told Hervey. 'Oh! My Lord, if this woman should die, what a scene of confusion will be here! Who can tell into what hands the King will fall? Or who will have the management of him?' Everyone asked themselves the same questions.

Garrulous with grief, the poor King chattered perpetually of his dear Caroline. Praise that would have warmed her living tumbled forth as she lay dying. The best wife, mother, friend that ever lived, he called her. All her time she devoted to helping and amusing him; though they passed more hours with each other than any two people ever spent together, by God! he had never been bored one minute. What a wonderful woman to win his love, he whom all women adored. Ah yes, had she not been his wife, he would sooner have had her for his mistress than any woman he knew. What more could he say? He would run in to see her, order her to eat and drink, else how the devil could she expect to live? To please him she swallowed whatever he prescribed, knowing it would lie burning inside her and be rejected. Tears in his eyes, he kissed and thanked her. 'It is the last service I can do you,' she replied.

And in a second he would scold her for tossing about the whole time, but finding her once lying motionless, gazing into space, he burst out in fright: '*Mon Dieu*, what are you looking at? How can you stare like that? You look like a calf that has just had its throat cut.' His daughters persuaded the doctors to add a caution to their written prescription that the Queen should be spoken to little, and always in a low voice. Before pinning it on to her bedside curtain, they showed the paper to the King as usual, but the hint never impinged on his distraught mind. Anxiety made silence impossible for him. Far into one night, nightcap perched on his head, he kept up Emily and Lord Hervey to hear about his courage in the great storm. 'What, are you frightened?' he had laughed to his pale, cowering page. 'Yes, sir,' whimpered the lad, 'truly I believe Your Majesty is the only man on board who is not.' Oh yes, in the great storm he had been as brave as his poor Caroline suffering in there; and off he rambled, her kind heart, her brains, his intrepidity. . . . Those were ghastly times.

So passed a week. All Wednesday the King was distracted because she had fancied she might die that day. She had been born, married, crowned on Wednesdays, and given birth to her first child on a Wednesday. A coincidence less remarkable than that would have upset him. The Archbishop of Canterbury came to her:

He expressed his sorrow to see her so ill and her pains so great, but she told him though her body suffered, she had a good conscience which spoke inexpressible comfort to her and supported her in the midst of all her torments.[6]

Thereafter he visited her on the few remaining days, telling one of her ladies that he had never seen 'a behaviour equally glorious and christian to hers and that all she had said deserved to be printed'.[7] She asked him to look after Joseph Butler, the Clerk of her Closet, who was the only one of her servants she mentioned by name during her illness.

Those who watched believed she might rally, having

survived so much. 'God give her life to make us go through this world easily,' prayed her daughter Emily. The second Sunday of her illness faded into evening; heavy curtains drawn across the windows isolated the chamber of suffering from the outer world. Silence fell on the outer rooms as the last sad inquirers left. Firelight and candles flickered amongst the shadows in the sombre bedchamber. The Queen lay wondering how long she must live. Through her suffering came the doctor's voice, 'I think that your Majesty will soon be at rest.' '*Tant mieux,*' she whispered, beckoning William close. The boy looked weary with watching by her. To-night he must sleep. Softly she blessed him and bade him go to bed. He went weeping away. The Queen lay silent awhile. Presently she asked for something to raise her spirits so they brought her palsy drops in madeira wine, but swallowing it started her coughing. It grew late. She murmured good-bye to Emily and Caroline, then thanked the King so gently for his kindness that they all fell sobbing again. 'My poor servants are under the utmost affliction. Give me leave, Sir, to recommend them to your protection.' She asked for the candles by her bed to be removed. The King inquired whether they hurt her eyes. 'No, but I would spare you the affliction of seeing me die,' she said.[8] As the seconds ticked by in silence, sounds of breathing still came from the great bed. Then she spoke to the watchers in the shadows, bidding them pray for her, and read aloud that she might hear. She held the King's hand; the voices grew fainter. 'Pray,' she said, and peace came to her.

· · · · · ·

One night a month later they laid her to rest in Henry VII's chapel in Westminster Abbey. Choir boys of the Chapel Royal chanted Handel's beautiful tribute to his Queen, but the King could not face those last obsequies. He stayed sorrowing at home, utterly lonely. The only people he could tolerate were his daughters and Lord Hervey, who had shared his sad vigil. Still he talked of no one but her, recalling their life together, their first meeting, her smallpox, incidents at Hanover. Forced to see Sir Robert or any minister on business, he cried without restraint. Waking early one morning, he summoned one of his Hanoverian gentlemen. 'I hear you have a picture of the Queen, which she gave you, and that it is a better likeness than any in my possession. Bring it to me here.' When he saw the portrait, the King burst into tears, saying it was exactly like the Queen. 'Put it on that chair at the foot of my bed, and leave me until I ring the bell.' Two hours later he rang. 'Take the picture away, I never yet saw a woman worthy to buckle her shoe,' he observed.[9]

To all her servants from the highest to the lowest he promised their salaries for life.[10] After discovering that she had distributed pensions amounting to £13,000, he confirmed them, commanding her ladies also to give him the names of those they helped intermittently at her behest. 'And this is the King whom men called avaricious,' wrote one, marvelling greatly. Dr. Courayer, her learned French friend, was amongst the first to be summoned to an audience, when the King said that he desired no one save himself to be a loser by her death.[11] He kept her room exactly as she had left it, so that Horace Walpole, going over the

Palace twenty-one years later, saw it as it was the day she died.[12]

Months passed before the King could compose himself in public. Forcing himself to appear at a Drawing-room early in the New Year, 'he stayed not two minutes out and had grief still fixed on his face'.[13] Opening Parliament at the end of January, he took his speech in his hand, but paused a long time whilst he struggled to master his voice. 'He often put his hand to his forehead and had tears in his eyes.'[14] Seeing him so desolate, men sympathized with their King, speaking better of him than they had done for years.

The happiest years of his reign had ended. He faced conflicting counsels and the consequences of his blunders. He saw his country beset by rebels at home and attacked by victorious armies abroad. He enjoyed a brief triumph when he unsheathed his rusting sword to win glory at Dettingen, but his soldiers were fighting on three continents as his life drew to its close. Before they succeeded he was dead, and buried beside his dear Caroline, a side removed from each of their coffins to symbolize their eternal reunion.

Jan. 7. 1940.

APPENDIX

THE Queen's Letter describing Frederick and Augusta's flight
from Hampton Court is worth reproducing for the first time,
as sample of her execrable French and as proof that she did not
embroider the tale. An occasional comma was her only attempt
at punctuation, so full stops and semicolons have been inserted to
make the sense clearer.

hamthancour le 13/2 d'out. 1737.

Je vais ma chere anne vous faire le recit juste et sur lequelle vous
pouvie despantre mon cher coeur, de la nessance de lapetitte fille qui
vien de n'estre dimanche a 11 du soir, vous vous souvienderais ma
chere anne, que se ne faut que le 5 du mois passes, que votre frere
ainé mescrit la grossesse de la Prs.* vous vous souvienderais ausy des
reponces que cette peauves creature feut obligé de me faire.* dimanche elle dina avec le Roy, je minformes de sa santes. elle massure
quelle esttes tout a fait bien asteur [à cette heure]. je vais vous dire
mot pour mot, ce que fritz me dit la nuit du dimanche au lundy, que
le lundy auparavean elle avée desja eu des doulleur ce qui lavie fait
aller a londes [à Londres] avec elle pour demander ala sage feme,
et au docteur ce qu'il panses si c'esttes des aproché de son travaille.
hollings luy avee assuré que si n'estte que des doulleur du desvoiment,
ce qui lavée fait ramener isy, quelle avée ressandy les même doul-
leurs vandrty [vendredi]; qu'on luy avée prandre de la Rubarbe et
qu'il avée ramene a londes; mais que hollings lavée assure que se
n'esttes rien; que le dimanche elle avée eu des vomissement, qu'apres
le dine lau [l'eau] c'esttes rompu; qu'il lavée hattes de se mestre
an carosse; qu'a toute pritte il lavée ramene en ville ou il avee
envoiye che les lords wilminthon [Wilmington] et godolphin;
qu'en de mis heur apres la Prs. avée estes deslivery; que larcheveque
esttes venu trop tar, lord pressistenth [president], et privicelle [Privy

* Cf. Hervey, pp. 749, 750.

297

Seal] avée esttes au coty de Mrs. cannon la sage femme qu'an [quand] lanfean feu nes. je me tourne ver lady archibald,† qui avee cestte peauves petitte creature dans ces bras, 'je mestonne que vous qui avée eu plusieurs enfeans ayée hassardy lavie de cestte peauves creature et de sa mere. votre tettes et tous ceu qui ont eu a faire a la ramener de hamthan cour en, reponderon s'il ariveé du malle a la mere ou a lanfean'—elle se tourna ver luy et luy dit, 'vous voigè Msr.' je revien a ce qui se passa isy. nous ne sume pas un mot que lon avée entrenè c'estte peauves creature par force disy, ny qu'il esttes party, a 1 heur du madin Titzchborne antré dans la chambes en nous evellian avec une lettre de thaunsenth [Townshend]† a lord chersey [Jersey], pour lui dire que la Prs. esttes en travaille d'anfean a londes. le Roy fort encollere me fit lever au plus tost et fit apeller tous les conseillies privée dans un moment, nous eume des carosses. les duc de grafthon lord essexe lord harway esttes les seulles qui pouvée partir d'ap avec moy, les dames lady hariet cambel [Campbell] lady belle fintzche [Finch] et la titcheborne. nous arivame a 3 heur et de mis, je mis pie a terre pour ne pas faire du bruit. jantres avec vos deu soeurs ainée amalie et caroline. je ne trouve personne ala maison tous paraisces mort, je demandes apres la Prs. il me dire qu'elle dormes, et qu'elles seportes tres bien. je creu que ces douleurs c'esstes pasees, en antran dans la chambes du lit il vien dans sa villaine Robes de chambes se jestter ames genous me les cher la main, je luy demandes des nouvelles de sa femes. il me dit que le tout esttes pasees, et qu'elle avée une fille. jallais ason lit elle me resut [reçut] come je pouvais faire asteur [à cette heure]. la petite creature n'est pas plus grande que mon evantaille. je suis tres sure quelle ne poura vives et ausy sure quelle est de luy, come je crois destre sauvèe. d'ap—apres les combliment d'afectassion que je fis de bon pourtans du bon coeur a la peauves creature ma belle fille, j'allais ché lord harway. je vous diré que discy il la traine par forces lesttes pre pour sen aller quand elle crié le hau cri, il est un monstre.

† Lady Archibald Hamilton and Mr. William Townshend, M.P., Groom of the Bedchamber to the Prince, both accompanied Their Royal Highnesses to London. Lord Jersey, a Lord of the Bedchamber to him, evidently remained at Hampton Court.

le Roy luy fera dire de ne pas paraitre de vean luy qu'an il viendera isy, j'ay la tettes [tête] assy confuse que je lesay les autres circonstances avos soeurs a vous dire. mes combliment a pepin et suis tres tandrement avous

CAROLINE.

This is the last of the Queen's letters now at The Hague, but in her desk in December 1737 was found a minute of a letter she wrote to Anne just before her fatal illness, in which she expressed the presentiment 'd'une mort très prochain, dans des termes extrêment remarquables et très touchant'. (Berlin, Rep. XI. 73 conv. 61.)

Bruford, W. H., *Germany in the Eighteenth Century*. 1935.

Calendar of Treasury Books and Papers, 1729–30, ed. W. A. Shaw. 1897.

Carlyle, T., *Frederick the Great*. 5 vols. 1903.

Carpenter, *Sherlock* = Carpenter, E., *Thomas Sherlock*. 1936.

Cibber, C., *Life*. 2nd edition, 1740.

Chance, J. F., and Firth, C. H., *Notes on the Diplomatic Relations of England and Germany*. 1907.

Chancellor, E. B., *The Private Palaces of London*. 1908.

Colman, B., *A Narrative of the Method and Success of Inoculating the Small Pox in New England*.

Cobbett, W., *Parliamentary History*, vols. VIII, IX.

Collenette, C. L., *A History of Richmond Park*. London, 1938.

Connell, Neville, *Anne*. 1937.

Lady Cowper = *Diary of Mary Countess Cowper*. 1864.

Coxe's *Walpole* = Coxe, A. W., *Memoirs of the Life and Administration of Sir Robert Walpole*. 3 vols. 1798.

Curl, E., *Rarities of Richmond*. 1736.

Defoe, D. = *Tour Through Great Britain*. 4 vols. London, 1762. 6th edition.

Dodington, George Bubb, *Diary*. 1784.

Droysen, J. G. = *Geschichte der preussischen Politik*. 9 vols. Leipzig, 1855–68.

Dutton, R., *The English Garden*. 1937.

Erleigh, Viscount, *The South Sea Bubble*. 1933.

Esdaile, K. E., *The Art of Rysbrack in Terra-Cotta*. 1932.

Fisher, H. A. L., *History of Europe*. 3 vols. 1935. Vol. II.

Geerds, R. = *Die Mütter der Könige von Preussen und England*. Leipzig, 1913.

Gwynn, S., *Life and Friendships of Dean Swift*. 1933.

Haggard, H. W., *Devils, Doctors and Drugs*. 1937.

Hervey = *Lord Hervey's Memoirs*, ed. Romney Sedgwick. 3 vols. 1931.

Johnston, R. B., ed., *Mrs. Delany*. 1925.

Kemble, J. M. = *State Papers*, ed. J. M. Kemble. 1857.

Kielmansegge, E. Graf von, *Briefe des Herzogs Ernst August zu Braunschweig-Lüneburg an J. F. D. von Wendt*.

Klopp, Onno = *Der Fall des Hauses Stuart*. Vienna, 1875–88. 14 vols. Vol. XIV.

Künzel, C., ed., *Die Briefe der Liselotte*. Munich, 1912.

Lamberty, G. de, = *Mémoires pour servir a l'histoire du XVIIIme siècle*. 14 vols. The Hague, 1724–40. Vol. XIII.

Landau, M. = *Geschichte des Kaiser Karls VI als König von Spanien*. Stuttgart, 1889.

Laprade, W. T., *Public Opinion and Politics in Eighteenth Century England*. New York, 1936.

BIBLIOGRAPHY

I. Abbreviations used in the Notes

A.D.B.= Allgemeine Deutsche Biographie.
Add. MSS. = British Museum, Additional MSS.
Berlin = MSS. in the Preussisches Geheimes Staatsarchiv, Berlin–Dahlem.
B.P.H.A. = Letters in the Brandenburg-Preussisches Hausarchiv, Berlin–Charlottenburg.
B.M. = British Museum MSS.
C.M.H. = Cambridge Modern History, vol. VI, 1934 edition.
E.H.R. = English Historical Review.
Hague= Letters in the Koninjlik Huisarchief, The Hague.
Hanover= MSS. in the Preussisches Staatsarchiv, Hanover.
H.H.St.A. = MSS. in the Haus, Hof und Staatsarchiv, Vienna.
H.M.C. = Reports of the Royal Historical Manuscripts Commission: Carlisle; Cowper, vol. III; Egmont, 3 vols.; Laing, vol. II; Polwarth, vol. I; Portland, vol. V; Report 8, Appendix I; Report 14, Appendix 9; Stuart, vols. III–V.
Preuss. Staatsarchiv = Publicationen aus dem K. Preussischen Staatsarchiv, vols. IV, IX, XXXVII, LXXIX.
P.R.O. = Public Record Office.
T.R.H.S.= Transactions of the Royal Historical Society.
Wolfenbüttel = MSS. in the Landshauptarchiv, Wolfenbüttel.
Z.H.V.N.S. = Zeitschrift des Historisches Vereins für Niedersächsen.

II. Contemporary Newspapers from 1714

Dawks News Letter, Evening Post, Flying Post, Original Weekly Journal, Post Boy, Saturday Evening Post.

III. Printed Matter

Alvensleben, U. von, *Herrenhausen.* Berlin, 1929.
Bernbeck, Karl, *Die Denkwürdigkeiten der Markgräfin von Bayreuth und die englische-preussische Heiratsverhandlung von 1730.* Giessen, 1894.
Bibliothek des litterärischen Vereins in Stuttgart, vol. CVII.
Bodeman, E. ed., *Aus den Briefen der Herzogin Elizabeth Charlotte von Orleans.* 2 vols. Hanover, 1891.
Boyer, A. = *Political State of Great Britain, 1714–1737.*

301

Bruford, W. H., *Germany in the Eighteenth Century.* 1935.

Calendar of Treasury Books and Papers, 1729-30, ed. W. A. Shaw. 1897.

Carlyle, T., *Frederick the Great.* 5 vols. 1903.

Carpenter, *Sherlock* = Carpenter, E., *Thomas Sherlock.* 1936.

Cibber, C., *Life.* 2nd edition, 1740.

Chance, J. F., and Firth, C. H., *Notes on the Diplomatic Relations of England and Germany.* 1907.

Chancellor, E. B., *The Private Palaces of London.* 1908.

Colman, B., *A Narrative of the Method and Success of Inoculating the Small Pox in New England.*

Cobbett, W., *Parliamentary History*, vols. VIII, IX.

Collenette, C. L., *A History of Richmond Park.* London, 1938.

Connell, Neville, *Anne.* 1937.

Lady Cowper = *Diary of Mary Countess Cowper.* 1864.

Coxe's *Walpole* = Coxe, A. W., *Memoirs of the Life and Administration of Sir Robert Walpole.* 3 vols. 1798.

Curl, E., *Rarities of Richmond.* 1736.

Defoe, D. = *Tour Through Great Britain.* 4 vols. London, 1762. 6th edition.

Dodington, George Bubb, *Diary.* 1784.

Droysen, J. G. = *Geschichte der preussischen Politik.* 9 vols. Leipzig, 1855-68.

Dutton, R., *The English Garden.* 1937.

Erleigh, Viscount, *The South Sea Bubble.* 1933.

Esdaile, K. E., *The Art of Rysbrack in Terra-Cotta.* 1932.

Fisher, H. A. L., *History of Europe.* 3 vols. 1935. Vol. II.

Geerds, R. = *Die Mütter der Könige von Preussen und England.* Leipzig, 1913.

Gwynn, S., *Life and Friendships of Dean Swift.* 1933.

Haggard, H. W., *Devils, Doctors and Drugs.* 1937.

Hervey = *Lord Hervey's Memoirs*, ed. Romney Sedgwick. 3 vols. 1931.

Johnston, R. B., ed., *Mrs. Delany.* 1925.

Kemble, J. M. = *State Papers*, ed. J. M. Kemble. 1857.

Kielmansegge, E. Graf von, *Briefe des Herzogs Ernst August zu Braunschweig-Lüneburg an J. F. D. von Wendt.*

Klopp, Onno = *Der Fall des Hauses Stuart.* Vienna, 1875-88. 14 vols. Vol. XIV.

Künzel, C., ed., *Die Briefe der Liselotte.* Munich, 1912.

Lamberty, G. de, = *Mémoires pour servir a l'histoire du XVIIIme siècle.* 14 vols. The Hague, 1724-40. Vol. XIII.

Landau, M. = *Geschichte des Kaiser Karls VI als König von Spanien.* Stuttgart, 1889.

Laprade, W. T., *Public Opinion and Politics in Eighteenth Century England.* New York, 1936.

Larwood, J., *Story of the London Parks*. 2 vols. 1872.

Law, E., *Hampton Court in Orange and Guelph Times*. 1891.

Leadam, I., *Political History of England*, vol. IX, 1702–60. 1908.

Leibniz' correspondence = *La correspondence de Leibniz avec l'electrice Sophie*, publié par Onno Klopp. Hanover, 1874.

Leibniz' Werke = ed. Onno Klopp. 11 vols. Hanover, 1864–73.

Lodge, Sir R., *Great Britain and Prussia in the Eighteenth Century*. 1922.

Lysons, D., *Environs of London*. 4 vols. 1792–6.

Macpherson, J., *Secret History of Great Britain from the Restoration to the Accession of the House of Hanover*. 2 vols. 1775.

Malortie, C. E. von, *Der Hannoversche Hof unter dem Kurfürst Ernst August und der Kurfürstin Sophie*. 1847.

Malortie, Beiträge = *Beiträge zur Geschichte des Braunschweiges-Lüneburgisches Hauses und Hofes*. 1860.

Melville, Lewis, *The First George*. 2 vols. 1908.

Melville, Lewis, *Lady Suffolk and Her Circle*. 1924.

Melville, Lewis, *Maids of Honour*. 1927.

Michael, W.=*Englische Geschichte im XVIII Jahrhundert*. 4 vols. 1896–1937.

Montagu, Lady M. Wortley, *Letters*, ed. Lord Wharncliffe. 2 vols. 1893.

Morley, John, *Walpole*. London, 1921.

Nöldeke, A., *Kunstdenkmäler der Provinz Hannover*. 2 vols. Hanover, 1932.

Oliver, F. S., *The Endless Adventure*. 3 vols. 1930–5.

Overton, J. H., *A History of the English Church, 1714–1800*. Overton and Relton, 1924.

Pemberton, W. B., *Carteret*. 1936.

Ranke, L. von, *Sammtliche Werke*. 54 vols. Leipzig, 1867–90. Vols. 27, 28.

Robertson, Sir C. Grant = *England under the Hanoverians*. 9th ed., 1928.

Royal Society, *Philosophical Transactions*, vols. 32, 49.

Salomon, F. = *Geschichte des letzen Ministeriums Königin Annas*. 1894.

Schnath, G. = *Briefwechsel der Kurfürstin Sophie von Hannover mit dem Preussischen Königshause*. Berlin, 1927.

Schultz, W. E., *Gay's Beggar's Opera*. 1923.

Smith, A. Clifford, *Buckingham Palace*. Silver Jubilee edition.

Steegman, J., *The Rule of Taste*. 1936.

Suffolk Correspondence = *Letters to and from Henrietta, Countess of Suffolk, 1712–1760*. 2 vols. 1824.

Sundon, Viscountess, *Memoirs*, ed. Mrs. Thomson. 2 vols. 1847.

Sykes, N. = *Church and State in the Eighteenth Cetnury*. 1934.

Sykes, Gibson = *Edmund Gibson*. 1924.

Thompson, M., *The Secretaries of State*. 1932.

Trevelyan, G. M., *England under Queen Anne*. 3 vols. 1930–4. Blenheim, Ramillies, the Peace and the Protestant Succession.

Turberville, A., *The House of Lords in the Eighteenth Century*. 1927.

Turner, E. R., *The Cabinet Council of England in the Seventeenth and Eighteenth Centuries*. Vol. 2. 1932.

Vaucher, P. = *Robert Walpole et la Politique de Fleury*. 1924.

Vaucher, P., *La Crise du Ministère Walpole*. 1924.

Vehse, E., *Geschichte der Höfe des Hauses Sachsen*. Hamburg, 1854. 6 vols.

Vehse, E., *Geschichte der kleinen deutschen Höfe*. Hamburg, 1856–60. 13 vols.

Vogtherr, F., *Geschichte der Stadt Ansbach*. Ansbach, 1927.

Voltaire, *Letters Concerning the English Nation*. Introduction by Charles Whibley. London, 1926.

Walpole Society, *Vertue Notebooks*, 3. 1933–4.

Ward, Sir A. W. = *The Electress Sophia and the Hanoverian Succession*. 1909.

Ward, Sir A. W., *Great Britain and Hanover*. 1899.

Wentworth Papers = ed. J. J. Cartwright. 1705–39.

Whitley, J., *Artists and Their Friends in England*. 2 vols. 1928.

Wilkins, W. H. = *Caroline the Illustrious*. 2 vols. 1901.

Williams, B., *Stanhope.* 1932.

Yorke, P. C., *Life and Letters of Lord Chancellor Hardwicke*. 1913.

Young, Sir G., *Poor Fred*. 1937.

IV. ARTICLES

Arkell, R. L., 'Des Hauses Oesterreich Werben um Caroline von Ansbach, spätere Gemahlin Georgs II,' *Niedersächsisches Jahrbuch*, 1938.

Arkell, R. L., 'George I's letters to his daughter,' *English Historical Review*, vol. XLI. 1937.

Chance, J. F., 'George I and his relations with Sweden,' *English Historical Review*, vol. XVII. 1902.

Drögereit, R., 'Das Testament Königs Georgs I und die Frage des Personalunions zwischen England und Hannover,' *Niedersächsisches Jahrbuch*, 1937.

Gerig, H., 'Die Memoiren des Lord Hervey als historische Quelle,' Freiburg, 1936.

Geyl, P., 'William IV of Orange and his English Marriage,' *T.R.H.S.*, Series IV, vol. VIII.

Geyl, P., 'Engelsche Correspondentie van Prins Willem IV en Prinses Anna (1734–43),' *Bijdragen en Mededeelingen van her Historisch Genootschop*, 1924.

Lodge, Sir R., 'English Neutrality in the War of Polish Succession,' *T.R.H.S.*, vol. XIV. 1931.

Michael, W., 'Die Personalunion von England und Hannover und das Testament Georgs I,' *Archiv für Urkundenforschung*, VI. 1918.

Pauli, R., 'Aktenstücke zur Thronbesteigung des Welfenhauses in England,' *Z.H.V.N.S.* 1883.

Popham, A. E., 'Drawings in the Royal Collections,' *Burlington Magazine*. May, 1935.

Schnath, G., 'Die Königsmarck Briefwechsel, eine Falschung?' *Niedersächsisches Jahrbuch*. 1930.

Sykes, N., 'Queen Caroline and the Church,' *History*, January 1927.

Sykes, N., 'Bishop Gibson and Sir Robert Walpole,' *E.H.R.* vol. XLIV. 1929.

Terry, Sir H. I., 'An Unwanted Prince,' *Transactions of the Royal Society of Literature*, New Series, vol. XV.

Williams, B., 'The Duke of Newcastle and the Election of 1734,' *E.H.R.*, July 1897.

Williams, B., 'Foreign Policy under Walpole,' 5 parts, *E.H.R.*, vols. XIV, XV.

NOTES

I

'SHE SCORN'D AN EMPIRE'

[1] F. Vogtherr, *Geschichte der Stadt Ansbach*. Ansbach, 1927. Engravings, pp. 16, 38, 52, 64, 84.

[2] Ibid., pp. 63-5, 67, 69.

[3] *A.D.B.* XIII-XIV, pp. 384-6. J. G. Droysen, *Geschichte der Preussischen Politik*, IV, Teil 1, p. 127. Cf. P.R.O., S.P. 81/87, Stepney's dispatches of Oct. 1693-March 1694.

[4] Hanover, MS. Y. 46c, XI, f. 61.

[5] Hanover, M.S. Y. 46c, XI, f. 77. The narrative of Caroline's courtship by the King of Spain and the attempt to convert her is based on this set of MS. newly discovered in the Archives at Hanover. Cf. *Niedersächsisches Jahrbuch*, 1938: 'Des Hauses Oesterreich Werben um Caroline von Ansbach, spätere Gemahlin Georgs II,' by R. L. Arkell.

[6] E. Vehse, *Geschichte der Höfe des Hauses Sachsen*, Teil VII, p. 92 et seq.

[7] Landau, M., pp. 385-8.

[8] Cf. Neville Connell, *Anne*, pp. 135-6. 1937. G. M. Trevelyan, *Blenheim*, p. 402.

[9] Hanover, MS. Y. 46c, XI, ff. 97-8. This is implicit from a letter written by the Empress Eleanor to the Elector Palatine, her brother.

[10] *A.D.B.* XIII-XIV, pp. 314-15.

[11] Lamberty, G. de, XIII, p. 451.

[12] Hanover, MS. Y. 46c, XI, ff. 69-70.

[13] R. Geerds, *Die Mütter der Könige von Preussen und England*, p. 395. *Preuss. Staatsarchiv*, LXXIX, 59.

[14] P.R.O., S.P. 90/3, f. 153.

[15] *Leibniz' Correspondence*, III, pp. 108-9.

[16] P.R.O., S.P. 90/3, f. 157.

[17] Landau, M., p. 388.

[18] P.R.O., S.P. 90/3, Lord Raby to Robert Harley. Berlin, March-May 1705, ff. 201, 209, 213.

[19] P.R.O., S.P. 84/161. The account of the Electoral Prince's courtship is based on information given by Poley's dispatches to Harley. Hanover, June-July 1705.

[20] Hanover, K.G. Cal., Br. 24a, No. 19, f. 51.

[21] Ibid., ff. 52–3. Baron von Eltz's dispatch to the Elector describing the interview with Caroline.

[22] Hanover, MS. Y, 46c, XI, ff. 74–5.

[23] Hanover, Cal. Br. Des. 2, Dom. 132. Copy of the marriage pact between Caroline and George Augustus.

[24] P.R.O., S.P. 84/161. After Poley's dispatches.

[25] G. Schnath, Nos. 80, 85.

[26] Ibid., Nos. 83, 86, 87.

[27] P.R.O., S.P. 90/3, ff. 229, 235.

[28] Hanover, MS. Y. 46c, XI, ff. 106, 107–8, 109, 110–11.

[29] G. Schnath, No. 94.

II

ELECTORAL PRINCESS

[1] *Preuss. Staatsarchiv*, LXXIX, p. 199.

[2] Hanover, MS. Cal. Br. Des 2,132b; and K.G. Cal. Or. 2,132b.

[3] A. Nöldeke, *Kunstdenkmäler der Provinz Hannover*. Hanover, 1932. I., 263–303, is devoted to the history of the Leine Palace.

[4] The Electorate is well described in a memorandum entitled 'An Account of the Elector and Princes of Brunswick-Luneburg . . . 1705.' Copies of it are in B.M. Stowe MSS. 241, ff. 13 seqq. and in P.R.O., S.P. 81/161. Cf. *E.H.R.*, vol. 17, 1902 ; J. F. Chance, *George I and his Relations with Sweden*; L. Melville, *The First George*, I. 90–1.

[5] G. Schnath, Nos. 95, 157: 'Er geht noch immer zu keiner Ratsitzung.'

[6] B.M. Add. MSS. 7075, D'Alais–Stepney, May 6, 1706.

[7] Ibid., Jan. 7, 1706.

[8] *Preuss. Staatsarchiv*, LXXIX, pp. 200–1.

[9] G. Schnath, No. 99.

[10] B.M. Add. MSS. 7075, Howe–Stepney, Apr. 4, 1706, 'The Princess Electoral grows very big and is very well.'

[11] ed. E. Bodeman, vol. II, pp. 128, 130, 135, 138, 139.

[12] Ibid., p. 130.

[13] G. Schnath, No. 157, second paragraph.

[14] His letters are in the Brandenburg-Preussisches Hausarchiv, Berlin. *E.H.R.*, July 1937, 'George I's letters to his daughter,' R. L. Arkell.

[15] G. Schnath, No. 104.

[16] P.R.O., S.P. 81/162, f. 258. Howe–Harley, Feb. 1, 1707.

[17] Ibid., f. 282, Howe–Harley, Feb. 22.

[18] G. Schnath, No. 154.

[19] P.R.O., S.P. 81/162, f. 286. Howe–Harley, Feb. 14/25.

[20] G. Schnath, No. 374.

[21] R. Geerds, p. 385. Sir A. W. Ward, pp. 304–24. *C.M.H.*, VI, pp. 5–11.

[22] Its major provisions enacted that:

   (i) The Privy Council should not be dissolved upon the Crown's demise but should sit, and proclaim the successor.

   (ii) A Regency of Lords Justices should rule the country until the successor's arrival. It would be composed of the 7 principal officers of State and persons specially nominated by the Hanoverian heir.

   (iii) Parliament should not be dissolved upon the Crown's demise but should meet at once and sit for six months.

[23] Macpherson, II, 29–30, 37.

[24] Malortie, pp. 144–5.

[25] P.R.O., S.P. 90/162: Howe's dispatch, June 15, 1706.

[26] *Preuss. Staatsarchiv*, LXXIX, p. 206. Electress Sophia to Schütz, Oct. 29, 1706.

[27] P.R.O., S.P. 90/162, ff. 202, 221.

[28] Ibid., ff. 289–321. R. Geerds, p. 408, Electress Sophia to Leibniz, March 19, 1707.

[29] P.R.O., S.P. 90/162, f. 321.

[30] ed. Eric Graf von Kielmansegge, *Briefe des Herzogs Ernst August zu Braunschweig-Lüneburg an J. F. D. von Wendt*, p. 79.

[31] G. Schnath, Nos. 173, 174, 176.

[32] *Preuss. Staatsarchiv*, LXXIX, p. 251. Electress Sophia to Bothmer, July 22, 1707.

[33] *Briefe des Herzogs Ernst August . . .*, p. 82.

[34] Ibid., p. 85.

[35] G. Schnath, No. 178. Electress Sophia to Crown Princess Sophia Dorothea, Aug. 24, 1707.

[36] Ibid., No. 181.

[37] Macpherson, II, p. 111.

[38] G. Schnath, No. 191.

[39] *Descriptions of Herrenhausen based on U. v. Alvensleben*. Herrenhausen, Berlin, 1929.

[40] G. Schnath, Nos. 192, 200.

[41] Ibid., No. 227.

[42] Ibid., Nos. 196, 197.

[43] R. Geerds, p. 413.

[44] G. M. Trevelyan, *Ramillies*, pp. 359–60.

[45] Lady Cowper, p. 24. Congreve used this expression in a song celebrating Oudenarde,

[46] *Preuss. Staatsarchiv*, XXXVII, p. 284. Duke of Marlborough to Elector George Louis.

[47] G. M. Trevelyan, *Ramillies*, p. 386.

[48] *H.M.C.*, Report 8, Appendix I, p. 42.

[49] *Preuss. Staatsarchiv*, LXXIX, p. 266. Electress Sophia to Bothmer, Oct. 28, 1708.

[50] Ibid., p. 307. G. Schnath, No. 204.

[51] G. Schnath, Introduction, p. xxv, and Nos. 241, 308, 309.

[52] Ibid., No. 241.

[53] Leibniz *Werke*, vol. XI, pp. 5–6.

[54] Hervey, p. 262.

[55] Hanover, MS. Y. 46c, XI, ff. 113–14.

[56] Ibid., f. 116.

[57] Ibid., ff. 114–15.

III

THE CROWN COMES TO HANOVER

[1] Macpherson, II. Hanover Papers sections for 1712–14 are chiefly concerned with the Whig fears and suggestions.

[2] *Preuss. Staatsarchiv*, IX, p. 213. Michael, I, p. 328, footnote 1.

[3] G. M. Trevelyan, *Peace and the Protestant Succession*, gives a masterly account of these times.

[4] Ibid., p. 90.

[5] Ibid., p. 248.

[6] Macpherson, II, p. 482.

[7] B.M. Stowe MSS. 225, f. 140.

[8] Macpherson, II, p. 498.

[9] Michael, I, pp. 309–11.

[10] Ibid., p. 310.

[11] Ibid., I, pp. 313, 314.

[12] Klopp, XIV, pp. 510–11.

[13] Ibid., p. 513.

[14] Ibid., p. 516.

[15] Macpherson, II, p. 592. They were: Devon, Somerset, Nottingham, Argyll, Oxford, Somers, Cowper, Halifax, Wharton, and Townshend, Anglesea and Sir Thomas Hanmer, consulted later, agreed with them.

[16] Macpherson, II, p. 595.

[17] Ibid., p. 597.

[18] Memorandum and a copy of Queen Anne's answer to it are in P.R.O., S.P., 81/164, next to d'Alais' dispatch of June 15, 1714.

[19] G. Schnath, Nos. 398–9, 400, 403.

[20] Klopp, XIV, p. 568.

[21] *Z.H.V.N.S.*, 1883, R. Pauli, 'Aktenstücke zur Thronbesteigung des Welfenhauses in England' prints a memorandum by Robethon in favour of the Prince's going to England.

[22] *Leibniz' Correspondence*, III, pp. 449, 451.

[23] Salomon, p. 288.

[24] Cf. J. M. Kemble, p. 512, General Schulenberg's letter to Leibniz.

[25] G. Schnath, No. 402.

[26] Macpherson, II, p. 621; English translation of Queen Anne's letter in French to the Elector. Klopp, XIV, p. 583; German translations of the Queen's letters to the Elector and his son, and the original French letter from Queen Anne to the Electress on p. 585.

[27] J. M. Kemble, pp. 503-4.

[28] P.R.O., S.P. 81/164: D'Alais' memorandum of June 12, 1714. Malortie *Beiträge*, Heft I, pp. 7-9.

[29] G. Schnath, Introduction, p. xxiii.

[30] *Preuss. Staatsarchiv*, IV. Memoiren der Herzogin Sophie nachmals Kurfürstin von Hannover.

[31] J. M. Kemble, I, p. 512.

[32] Ibid.

[33] Macpherson, II, p. 264.

[34] P.R.O., S.P. 81/164: Clarendon's dispatches. Coxe's *Walpole*, II, pp. 41-6.

[35] G. M. Trevelyan, *Peace and the Protestant Succession*, chap. XVII and Epilogue. Grant Robertson, pp. 15-16. Leadam, pp. 221-3. *C.M.H.* VI, pp. 17-19. Michael, I, chap. IV.

[36] Klopp, XIV, p. 646.

[37] Malortie *Beiträge* . . ., Heft I, p. 56. Anne died Aug. 12, N.S.

[38] B.P.H.A., T. 14, 6. King George I to Queen Sophia Dorothea. Herrenhausen, 29 August (1714).

[39] Michael, I, p. 319. George I's will, clause III, decreed that a 'court-state' must be maintained in Hanover; clause IV, that a Regent should rule there. If possible he was to be the person next in, or close in, succession to the King-Elector. *Niedersächsisches Jahrbuch*, 1937, pp. 184-5.

[40] *Z.H.V.N.S.*, 1883, R. Pauli, 'Aktenstücke zur Thronbesteigung . . .', pp. 69-75. Malortie *Beiträge*, Heft I, pp. 57-9. These accounts disagree in minor details.

[41] Leibniz *Werke*, XI, p. 14.

[42] Ibid., XI, p. 16.

[43] *Bibliothek des litterärischen Vereins in Stuttgart*, CVII, pp. 437, 441, 448.

[44] A. Boyer, VIII, pp. 248-9. *H.M.C.*, Cowper, III, p. 114; Portland, V, pp. 492, 495; Wentworth Papers, 419; Leadam, p. 228 for King George I's reception at Greenwich and State entry into London.

[45] Larwood, *Story of the London Parks*, II, p. 47.
[46] Wentworth Papers, pp. 423, 425.
[47] Leibniz *Werke*, XI, p. 17.
[48] *Flying Post*, Oct. 12, O.S., 1714.

IV

PRINCESS OF WALES

[1] Defoe, *Tour*. 4 vols. London, 1762. 6th edition, pp. 160–1.
[2] *Flying Post*, Oct. 14, 1714.
[3] *Wentworth Papers*, p. 431.
[4] Ibid., p. 433.
[5] Michael, I, p. 442.
[6] Lady Cowper, p. 6.
[7] *Evening Post. Dawks News Letter*, Oct. 21, 1714. Lady Cowper, pp. 3–5.
[8] *Post Boy*, Nov. 2, 1714.
[9] Lady Cowper, pp. 10, 11.
[10] Ibid., p. 11.
[11] Michael, I, p. 421.
[12] Lady Cowper, p. 41.
[13] Ibid., p. 14.
[14] N. Sykes, *Church and State in the Eighteenth Century*, p. 348.
[15] Ibid., pp. 386–8.
[16] Lady Cowper, p. 17.
[17] Ibid., p. 41.
[18] Michael, I, p. 418.
[19] Ibid., I, p. 414.
[20] Lady Cowper, p. 21.
[21] Michael, I, p. 414.
[22] Lady Cowper, p. 46. *Weekly Packet*, Nov. 13, Dec. 4, 18, 1714.
[23] Michael, I, p. 414.
[24] *Evening Post*, June 5, 1716.
[25] *Dawks News Letter*, Mar. 18, 1715. A. Boyer, IX, p. 198.
[26] *Saturday Evening Post*, Sept. 14, 23, 1714.
[27] Viscount Erleigh, *The South Sea Bubble*, p. 34.
[28] Ibid., p. 35.
[29] Lady Cowper, p. 50–2.
[30] Michael, I, pp. 531–2. Lady Cowper, p. 58.
[31] Lady Cowper, pp. 67–8.
[32] Ibid., p. 72.
[33] Ibid., pp. 80–3.
[34] Michael, I, p. 602.

[35] Coxe's *Walpole*, II, p. 51. Lady Cowper, p. 84.
[36] Michael, I, p. 452. All important documents concerning *foreign affairs* were submitted to the King in French translations.
[37] Lady Cowper, p. 79.
[38] A. Turberville, *The House of Lords in the Eighteenth Century*, p. 166.
[39] Michael, I, p. 606.
[40] Lady Cowper, p. 104.
[41] Ibid., p. 79.
[42] Michael, I, pp. 615–19. Lady Cowper, pp. 107–11, 116.
[43] Coxe's *Walpole*, I, p. 54.
[44] B.M. Add. MSS. 34523, f. 377.
[45] Michael, I, p. 619.

V

STRIFE

[1] B.M. Stowe MSS. 229. Bothmer–Robethon, Aug. 3/14.
[2] Coxe's *Walpole*, II, p. 60.
[3] Ibid.
[4] E. Law, *Hampton Court in Orange and Guelph Times*, pp. 206–7.
[5] A. Boyer, XII, pp. 139–40.
[6] Ibid., p. 140.
[7] *Saturday Post*, Sept. 29, 1716.
[8] E. Law, *Hampton Court in Orange and Guelph Times*, pp. 213–14.
[9] Michael, I, p. 771.
[10] Coxe's *Walpole*, II, p. 78.
[11] Ibid., p. 64.
[12] Michael, I, p. 771.
[13] A. Boyer, XII, pp. 115, 117, 118.
[14] *H.M.C.*, Polwarth, I, p. 62.
[15] Ibid., p. 112.
[16] *Lady Montagu's Letters*, ed. Lord Wharncliffe, London, 1893, I, p. 258. *H.M.C.*, Polwarth, I, pp. 37, 38.
[17] B.M. Stowe MSS. 229, f. 46.
[18] *Memoirs of Viscountess Sundon*, I, p. 334.
[19] *H.M.C.*, Polwarth, I, p. 78.
[20] *Saturday Post*, Sept. 29. *St. James's Post*, Sept. 27–9, 1716.
[21] B.M. Stowe MSS. 229, f. 127.
[22] Lady Cowper, p. 126.
[23] Ibid., pp. 126–7. B.M. Stowe MSS. 229, ff. 246, 284. *H.M.C.*, Polwarth, I, pp. 128, 129.
[24] H. W. Haggard, *Devils, Doctors, and Drugs*, p. 43.

[25] Coxe's *Walpole*, II, pp. 92, 94, 123. B. Williams, *Stanhope*, pp. 234–52. B.M. Stowe MSS. 143, 146, 148–50. 229, ff. 276, 280, Michael, I, 747 seqq.

[26] *H.M.C.*, Polwarth, I, pp. 132, 146. A. Boyer, XII, p. 647.

[27] *H.M.C.*, Polwarth, I, p. 146.

[28] *Evening Post*, Saturday, April 27–Tuesday, April 30, 1717.

[29] *H.M.C.*, Polwarth, I, p. 145.

[30] *Original Weekly Journal*, Saturday, Jan. 26, 1717.

[31] *Original Weekly Journal*, June 15, 1717. *H.M.C.*, Stuart, IV, pp. 143, 221, 356, 533.

[32] *H.M.C.*, Polwarth, I, pp. 320–1.

[33] *H.M.C.*, Laing, II, p. 194.

[34] B. Williams, *Stanhope*, pp. 246–52.

[35] *H.M.C.*, Rep. 14, App. 9. Onslow MSS., p. 509. *C.M.H.* VI, p. 70.

[36] The account of this quarrel is based on *H.M.C.*, Portland, V, p. 536 seq. Michael, II, pp. 52–9.

[37] B.M. Egerton MSS. 921, f. 84.

[38] ed. C. Künzel, *Die Briefe der Liselotte*, p. 371.

[39] Michael, II, Appendix 1, prints the letters in their original French text. Hervey gives the English versions. The 2nd and 3rd letters are exact translations but the English version of the 1st letter omits two short paragraphs.

[40] L. Melville, *Lady Suffolk and Her Circle*, London, 1924, pp. 30–1.

[41] W. H. Wilkins, I, p. 288. L. Melville, *Lady Suffolk and Her Circle*, chap. iii.

[42] Hervey, p. 279.

[43] Michael, II, pp. 58–9.

[44] *H.M.C.*, Portland, V, p. 553. B.M. Add. MSS. 21488, ff. 91–2; 21499, ff. 10–11. The laws upholding the father's rights over his children were: Stat. 4 and 5, Phillip and Mary, cap. 8, and 12 Carolus 2, cap. 24.

[45] B.M. Stowe MSS. 231, ff. 54, 55. *H.M.C.*, Polwarth, I, pp. 438–9, 441. *H.M.C.*, Stuart, V, p. 510.

[46] *St. James's Evening Post*, May 22, 1718. A. Boyer, XVII, p. 512.

[47] Michael, II, p. 58.

[48] B.M. Egerton MSS. 1717, f. 78. *H.M.C.*, Portland, V, p. 572.

[49] This series of letters is amongst Anne, Princess of Orange's correspondence in the Koninjlik Huisarchief at The Hague. The letters are undated and generally addressed 'pour ma chere fille Anne'.

[50] This letter is among King George II's papers in the Royal Archives at Windsor.

[51] ed. C. Künzel, *Die Briefe der Liselotte*, p. 310.

[52] These spellings all occur in the letters from Caroline to Princess Anne, which are now at The Hague.

[53] *H.M.C.*, Portland, V, p. 559.

[54] *St. James's Post*, May 3, 1718.
[55] *St. James's Post*, May 20, 1718.
[56] *St. James's Evening Post*, Saturday, May 31; Aug. 23, 1718. *Weekly Journal*, Aug. 2, 1718.
[57] L. Melville, *Maids of Honour*, pp. 202–3. *Lady Suffolk and Her Circle*, p. 70.
[58] *Weekly Journal*, May 24–31, 1718.
[59] *St. James's Evening Post*, May 28, 29, 31, July 10, 1718.
[60] *Weekly Journal*, July 12, 1718.
[61] B.M. Egerton MSS. 921, f. 85.

VI

PEACE WITHOUT HONOUR

[1] W. T. Laprade, *Public Opinion and Politics in Eighteenth Century England*, p. 217.
[2] B. Williams, *Stanhope* (Oxford, 1932), pp. 403 seqq. gives detailed account of the Peerage Bill. Cf. Michael, II, pp. 572 seqq.
[3] B.M. Add. MSS. 32686, f. 156.
[4] B. Williams, *Stanhope*, p. 417.
[5] Viscount Erleigh, *The South Sea Bubble*, 'The Pipe'.
[6] W. T. Laprade, *Public Opinion . . .*, p. 230. B. Williams, *Stanhope*, pp. 420–2. Michael, II, pp. 613 seqq.
[7] Lady Cowper, p. 134. Michael, II, p. 615.
[8] Lady Cowper, p. 145.
[9] Ibid., p. 137.
[10] Ibid., p. 132.
[11] Ibid., p. 129.
[12] Ibid., p. 145.
[13] Ibid., p. 143.
[14] *Suffolk Correspondence*, I, p. 53.
[15] Lady Cowper, pp. 149–50.
[16] *E.H.R.*, July 1937, p. 497, R. L. Arkell, 'George I's Letters to his daughter'.
[17] Lady Cowper, p. 152.
[18] Ibid., p. 145. Michael, II, pp. 617–20. B. Williams, *Stanhope*, p. 424.
[19] Lady Cowper, p. 155.
[20] Ibid., p. 158.
[21] Ibid., p. 148.
[22] Ibid., p. 159.
[23] Ibid., pp. 157, 165, 175.
[24] Viscount Erleigh, *South Sea Bubble*, pp. 80, 109.

[25] Hervey, p. 41.

[26] L. Melville, *Lady Suffolk and Her Circle*, chap. vii.

[27] Berlin Rep. 81, no. 15, *Anécdotes Secrètes* 3, London, Sept. 17/28, 1734.

[28] Hervey, p. 43.

[29] Ibid., p. 600.

[30] Berlin Rep. 81, no. 15, *Anècdotes Secrètes* 3, London, Sept. 17/28, 1734.

[31] Hervey, p. 381.

[32] Hanover, Cal. Br. 24, Dom. Nr. 37. That Frederick's parents had him educated free by allowing 'common schoolmasters of the city' to compete for the honour, is false gossip. George I alone supervised his education most carefully. The King's instructions and the reports on Frederick's progress are in the Hanoverian archives.

[33] ed. Lord Wharncliffe, *The Letters and Works of Lady Mary Wortley-Montagu*, I, p. 308.

[34] Benjamin Colman, *A Narrative of the Method and Success of Inoculating the Small Pox in New England*, Introduction, p. 5.

[35] B.M. Sloane MSS. 4034, ff. 9 seqq. *Philosophical Transactions of the Royal Society*, 49, 1765–6, pp. 516–20.

[36] *Phil. Trans. Royal Soc.*, 49, p. 518.

[37] B.M. Add. MSS. 34327, f. 7. Hanover, Cal. Br. 24, Dom. Nr. 37, April 14/25, June 12/23, 1722.

[38] *Phil. Trans. Royal Soc.*, vol. 32, 1721–3, pp. 2 seqq.; 1724, pp. 12 seqq.; 1725, pp. 55 seqq.

[39] Stephen Gwynn, *Life and Friendships of Dean Swift*, p. 253.

[40] Ibid., pp. 260–1.

[41] Ibid., p. 226.

[42] W. H. Wilkins, pp. 158–60.

[43] Voltaire, *Letters Concerning the English Nation*, pp. 61–2.

[44] Michael, III, pp. 511–12. Leadam, p. 332.

VII

QUEEN CAROLINE REIGNS

[1] Description of the events of June 14–18 is based on Hervey, pp. 22–34. Cf. Leadam, pp. 334–5. Grant Robertson, pp. 57–9. Michael, III, pp. 513–15.

[2] Hervey, xxxiv–xxxvi. W. Michael, 'Die Personalunion von England und Hannover und das Testament Georgs I' in *Archiv für Urkundenforschung*, 6, 1918. W. Michael, III, pp. 518–23; IV, pp. 523–8. Dr. R. Drögereit, 'Das Testament Königs Georgs I und die Frage des Personalunions zwischen England und Hannover', *Niedersächsisches Jahrbuch*, 1937,

announces the author's discovery of all three copies of George I's will in the Hanover Archives.

³ *H.M.C.*, Report 14, Appendix 9. Onslow MSS., p. 517.

⁴ Hervey, p. 31.

⁵ Ibid., pp. 4–7. Michael, IV, pp. 46–112. Leadam, p. 335.

⁶ Hervey, p. 10.

⁷ Ibid., p. 47.

⁸ Ibid., pp. 33–5, 47–8.

⁹ Ibid., pp. 151–2.

¹⁰ Leadam, pp. 334–5. Michael, III, pp. 514–15, and Grant Robertson, p. 57. Hervey, p. 34.

¹¹ A copy of the document concerning her jointure is in the Windsor Archives. Compton, Walpole, and Sir Robert Eyre were named trustees.

¹² Hervey, p. 34.

¹³ Ibid., pp. 39–40.

¹⁴ Ibid., p. 40.

¹⁵ Ibid., pp. 43–4, 93. L.Melville, *Lady Suffolk and Her Circle*, pp. 207–11.

¹⁶ L. Melville, *Lady Suffolk and Her Circle*, p. 211.

¹⁷ Hervey, p. 44.

¹⁸ Ibid., p. 68.

¹⁹ Ibid., p. 69.

²⁰ Ibid., p. 69.

²¹ This account is based on a paper by Dr. G. Schnath, 'Die Königsmarck Briefwechsel eine Falschung?' *Niedersächsisches Jahrbuch*, 1930.

²² See Note 2 to this chapter; Dr. R. Drögereit's paper.

²³ Hanover, Cal. Br. 27. Wolfenbüttel Nr. 222. Relatio No. 4, October 6/17, 1727. Count Conrad von Dehn was sent by the Duke of Wolfenbüttel to arrange about returning the copy of George I's will and to conclude the military subsidy treaty. See p. 152.

²⁴ Berlin, Rep. XI, 73 convolut 53. Wallenrodt's dispatches, July 14/25, Aug. 1/12, 1727.

²⁵ Ibid., Wallenrodt's dispatch of August 29, 1727. Rep. XI, 73 convolut 55, Reichenbach's dispatch of Dec. 27/Jan. 7, 1729–30. Cf. Hervey, p. 342. A. W. Ward, *Great Britain and Hanover*, p. 77.

From the Hattorf family papers at Hanover it emerges that John Philip was born there between 1675 and 1680. He studied law at Helmstadt, presenting his dissertation on June 24, 1700. His father, John, was raised to the nobility in 1703 by the Emperor Leopold I. He himself was appointed a Councillor of War in 1709 and George II created him a Hanoverian Privy Councillor in 1728. Thereafter all German requests and petitions to the King went through him, and his Hanoverian colleagues constantly assured him of their loyalty, while his advice carried 'more weight with the Queen, next to Sir Robert, than any man that had access to her', in Hervey's opinion. His health gave way in 1733 and he died on September 3, 1737, and was buried in the family vault at Böhme.

[26] B.M. Add. MSS. 32686, f. 88.

[27] Berlin, Rep. XI, 73 convolut 53, Sept. 26/Oct. 7, 1727.

[28] ed. R. Brimley Johnston, *Mrs. Delany*, pp. 38–40. Hervey, p. 66.

[29] ed. R. Brimley Johnston, *Mrs. Delany*, p. 39.

[30] Berlin, Rep. XI, 73 convolut 53, Oct. 17/28, Oct. 20/31, 1727.

[31] Ibid., Rep. XI, 73 convolut 54, Oct. 15/26, 1728.

[32] *H.M.C.*, Egmont, I, p. 94, pp. 476–7; II, p. 10. Hervey, p. 804.

[33] ed. R. Brimley Johnston, *Mrs. Delany*, p. 41. Berlin, Rep. XI, 73 convolut 53, Oct. 31/Nov. 11, 1727.

[34] Michael, III, pp. 476, 500; IV, pp. 361–90. Leadam, pp. 327–30, 336–7. Hervey, pp. 76–8.

[35] Hervey, p. 79.

[36] Berlin, Rep. XI, 73 convolut 54, Aug. 27/Sept. 7, 1728.

[37] Ibid., Aug. 16/27, 1728.

[38] Ibid., Sept. 3/14, 1728. Hervey, pp. 596, 732–3.

[39] Berlin, Rep. XI, 73 convolut 54, Oct. 15/26, 1728.

[40] Ibid., convolut 53, Nov. 10/21, 1727.

[41] Ibid., convolut 54, Nov. 5/16, 1728.

[42] Wolfenbüttel, Acta betreffend Gemahlinen 14, Christine Luise No. 10. Queen Caroline's letter of June 10/30, 1727.

[43] Hague, 430; Prince Frederick to Princess Anne, Herrenhausen, June 27, 1727.

[44] Michael, III, pp. 360, 436, 453. L. von Ranke, XXVII–XXVIII, p. 91. J. G. Droysen, IV, 2, pp. 355, 381.

[45] Berlin, Rep. XI, 73 convolut 53, vol. I, Aug. 1/12, 1727. Instruction to Wallenrodt.

[46] Pollnitz's memoirs fabricated the story, copied by Coxe and many historians, that Prince Frederick (May 1728) apprised the Queen of Prussia that he would come incognito to Berlin and marry Wilhelmine. The Queen elatedly tells the English envoy, Du Bourgay. He reports it to England. Project is foiled by Frederick being ordered to England forthwith. As Carlyle stated in *Frederick the Great*: 'Nearly the whole of which on examining the documents proves to be a myth'. Cf. Du Bourgay's dispatches in the Record Office, S.P. 90/23, Berlin, May 28, June 1, 5, 8, N.S. He simply reported the *rumour* of an intended visit of Frederick to Berlin to participate in the current festivities in honour of the Elector of Saxony. He heard it from one of the Queen's household, not from the Queen, nor does he ever mention the marriage. Nine days later he notes that the rumour is dead. Frederick did not leave Hanover until *December* 1728.

[47] J. G. Droysen, IV, 2, p. 441. Sir R. Lodge, *Great Britain and Prussia*, pp. 20–1.

[48] Berlin, Rep. XI, 73 convolut 53, Sept. 22/Oct. 3, 1727.

[49] Ibid., Oct. 7/18, 1727. Instruction to Wallenrodt.

[50] Berlin, Rep. XI, 73 convolut 53, Dec. 11/22, 1727. Instruction to Reichenbach.

[51] Berlin, Rep. XI, 17 convolut 54, vol. 3, Dec. 10/21, 1728, Reichenbach to King Frederick William, who scribbled this comment in the margin of the dispatch.

[52] Ibid.

[53] Ibid. J. G. Droysen, IV, 2, p. 446; IV, 3, p. 87. L. von Ranke XXVII-XXVIII, pp. 96–7.

[54] B.M. Add. MSS. 32758, f. 427, contains a copy of Queen Sophia Dorothea's letter to Queen Caroline.

[55] B.P.H.A. 46, T. 17. Queen Caroline to Queen Sophia Dorothea, St. James's, Sept. 26, 1728.

[56] Berlin, Rep. XI, 73 convolut 54, vol. 3, Dec. 10/21. Reichenbach to Frederick William.

[57] Berlin, Rep. XI, 73 convolut 54, vol. 1, 1728. Reichenbach's dispatches all through the year discuss the topic.

[58] Dr. R. Drögereit's paper, *Niedersächsisches Jahrbuch*, 1937. See Note 2 of this chapter. Berlin, Rep. XI, 73 convolut 54, vol. 1, Jan. 12/23, 1728. Reichenbach's dispatch.

[59] Hervey, p. 485. Michael, IV, p. 501.

[60] Berlin, Rep. XI, 73 convolut 54, vol. 1. Reichenbach's dispatches, Jan. 12/23, Feb. 20/March 2, March 12/23, 1728.

[61] See Note 57 above.

[62] Hervey, p. 95. Berlin, Rep. XI, 73 convolut 54, vol. 1. Reichenbach's dispatch, Dec. 3/14, 1728.

[63] Ibid.

[64] Ibid.

[65] Ibid.

[66] H.M.C., Egmont, III, p. 327.

[67] Hervey, p. 95.

[68] Berlin, Rep. XI, 73 convolut 54, vol. 1. Reichenbach's dispatches, Dec. 2/13, Dec. 9/20, 1728, give all information contained in this paragraph.

[69] Hervey, p. 95.

[70] Ibid., p. 646.

[71] Ibid., pp. 250–1.

[72] Ibid., pp. 492–3.

[73] Ibid., p. 100.

[74] Ibid., p. 539.

[75] Michael, IV, p. 503.

[76] Hervey, p. 102.

[77] Hervey, p. 457.

[78] W. H. Wilkins, II, p. 114.

[79] P.R.O., S.P. 43, Regencies, 9 passim.

[80] Michael, IV, pp. 375–80. Grant Robertson, pp. 61–2. Leadam, pp. 337–8.

[81] Hervey, p. 291.

[82] W. H. Wilkins, II, p. 117.

[83] Lysons, Environs of London, p. 90.

[84] W. H. Wilkins, II, pp. 119–20, 125–8.

[85] Ibid., II, p. 134.

[86] H.M.C., Egmont, I, p. 2.

[87] Michael, IV, pp. 59–61.

[88] Hervey, pp. 257–8, 524–6.

[89] H.M.C., Egmont, I, pp. 11–12.

[90] Hervey, pp. 85–7.

[91] Ibid., pp. 118–19.

[92] Ibid., p. 346.

[93] W. Baring Pemberton, Carteret, pp. 116–18.

[94] Hervey, p. 410.

[95] H.M.C., Egmont, I, pp. 92, 207, 375, 390.

[96] B.M. Add. MSS. 32765, f. 355 (copy of the Prussian Queen's letter), ff. 357–60. Cf. Add. MSS. 32761, f. 469.

[97] Sir R. Lodge, Great Britain and Prussia, pp. 20–1. L. von Ranke, XXVII–XXVIII, pp. 97–109, 128–9. J. G. Droysen, IV, 3, pp. 89–107, 117.

[98] Karl Bernbeck, Die Denkwürdigkeiten der Markgräfin von Bayreuth und die englische-preussische Heiratsverhandlung von 1730, (Giessen, 1894), pp. 42 seqq.

[99] Berlin, Rep. XI, 73 convolut 56. Degenfeld's dispatch, Aug. 18, 1730.

[100] Ibid., Degenfeld's dispatch, Sept. 26, 1730.

[101] Ibid., King Frederick William's marginal comment on this dispatch.

[102] Hervey, pp. 195, 233, 276. H.M.C., Egmont, I, p. 466. Suffolk Correspondence, pp. 295–6.

[103] Hervey, pp. 196, 277–8.

[104] Ibid., pp. 273–4.

[105] Ibid., p. 276.

[106] Ibid., pp. 275, 654–5, 667. W. H. Wilkins, II, pp. 94 seqq.

[107] H.M.C., Egmont, I, p. 16.

[108] Ibid., p. 205.

[109] Hervey, Introduction, pp. xxiii–xxix.

[110] Ibid., pp. xxxix–xli.

VIII

PARTNERS AT WORK

[1] Hervey, pp. 372, 488, 608, 854.

[2] *H.M.C.*, Egmont, I, pp. 294, 404; II, p. 201; III, p. 267.

[3] Hervey, p. 493.

[4] Ibid., pp. 75, 235, 412.

[5] A. Clifford Smith, *Buckingham Palace*, pp. 32-3 and plate 21. Berlin, Rep. XI, 73 convolut 53. Reichenbach's dispatch, Nov. 10/21, 1727.

[6] C. L. Colenette, *History of Richmond Park*, pp. 40, 43-4, 67.

[7] Hervey, p. 79.

[8] Ibid., p. 494.

[9] Ibid., p. 221.

[10] Berlin, Rep. XI, 73 convolut 54, Sept. 1728; convolut 56, Sept. 1730. *H.M.C.*, Egmont, I, p. 101.

[11] Hervey, p. 435.

[12] Ibid., pp. 371, 585-7.

[13] Ibid., p. 508.

[14] Hervey, p. 490.

[15] Ibid., pp. 587-93.

[16] Ibid., p. 474. L. Melville, *Lady Suffolk and Her Circle*, pp. 208-10.

[17] Hanover, Cal. Br. 27. Wolfenbüttel No. 222. Relatio, No. 4, Oct. 6/17, 1727.

[18] Ibid. Hervey, pp. 593 seqq.

[19] *H.M.C.*, Egmont, I, p. 127.

[20] Ibid., I, pp. 205-6.

[21] Ibid., I, pp. 32-3, 92, 171, 197, 395.

[22] Berlin, Rep. 81, no. 15. *Anécdotes de la Cour Britannique*, Lettre 3, Sept. 1734.

[23] *H.M.C.*, Egmont, I, p. 10; II, p. 145.

[24] Hervey, p. 498.

[25] Ibid., p. 253.

[26] Sykes, p. 39.

[27] Sykes, *Gibson*. Michael, IV, pp. 472-3.

[28] N. Sykes, 'Queen Caroline and the Church,' *History*, January 1927.

[29] Michael, IV, pp. 475-8. Sykes, pp. 315-16. Sykes, *Gibson*, pp. 280-5, 332.

[30] Hervey, pp. 124-6.

[31] Ibid., pp. 127-31.

[32] Ibid., pp. 132 seqq. Michael, IV, pp. 127-40. Leadam, pp. 344-5. Grant Robertson, p. 68. F. S. Oliver, *The Endless Adventure*, II, pp. 245-97.

[33] Hervey, p. 149.

[34] Hervey, p. 146.
[35] Ibid., pp. 135–6.
[36] Ibid., pp. 136 seqq.
[37] Ibid., p. 150.
[38] Ibid., p. 151.
[39] *H.M.C.*, Egmont, I, p. 357.
[40] Hervey, pp. 157–8.
[41] Inid., pp. 158–9.
[42] Ibid., p. 162.
[43] Ibid., p. 162.
[44] *H.M.C.*, Egmont, II, pp. 14, 53.
[45] Ibid., II, p. 52.
[46] Hervey, p. 176.
[47] *H.M.C.*, Egmont, I, p. 459.

IX

THE SOLE MOVER

[1] Michael, IV, pp. 407–11. P. Geyl, 'William IV of Orange and his English Marriage,' T.R.H.S., Series IV, vol. VIII.
[2] Hervey, pp. 194, 231.
[3] P. Geyl, ibid.
[4] Hervey, p. 193.
[5] Ibid., p. 194.
[6] Berlin, Rep. 81, no. 15. *Anécdotes de la Cour Britannique*, Lettre 1, March 21, 1734.
[7] Ibid.
[8] Ibid.
[9] Hervey, pp. 266 seqq.
[10] Ibid., pp. 272, 283–4.
[11] Ibid., pp. 205, 286.
[12] Ibid., pp. 278–80.
[13] The Hague, Queen Caroline's letter, St. James's, April 22 [1734].
[14] Hervey, p. 291.
[15] Ibid., pp. 292 seqq. For Newcastle's part in this election, see B. Williams, 'The Duke of Newcastle and the Election of 1734,' *E.H.R.*, July 1897.
[16] Ibid., pp. 196, 273.
[17] Ibid., pp. 205, 233.
[18] Ibid., p. 234.
[19] *H.M.C.*, Egmont, I, p. 10.
[20] Hervey, pp. 233, 272.

[21] Hervey, p. 274.

[22] Ibid., pp. 298–9.

[23] Ibid., pp. 299–300.

[24] Ibid., p. 312.

[25] Ibid., p. 306.

[26] Michael, IV, chap. 12. H. A. L. Fisher, *History of Europe*, II, pp. 739–41. *C.M.H.* VI, p. 62. Vaucher, chap. 2. Sir R. Lodge, 'English Neutrality in the War of Polish Succession', T.R.H.S., vol. XIV, 1931.

[27] Michael, IV, p. 401. Sir R. Lodge, 'English Neutrality in the War of Polish Succession', pp. 155 seqq.

[28] Michael, IV, pp. 405–7.

[29] Hervey, p. 360.

[30] Ibid., p. 361.

[31] Ibid., pp. 218, 228, 342.

[32] Ibid., pp. 361–2.

[33] Michael, IV, pp. 412–16. Hervey, pp. 355–6.

[34] Cf. Richard Pares's letter to *The Times*, August 1937. Sir R. Lodge and P. Vaucher also disagree with Walpole's policy, but Grant Robertson (p. 66), Michael, Fisher, and Leadam (p. 350) support it.

[35] Hervey, p. 345.

[36] Ibid., pp. 342, 343, 345, 355.

[37] Ibid., pp. 340–1.

[38] Ibid., pp. 370–1. *H.M.C.*, Egmont, II, p. 133.

[39] Hervey, p. 372.

[40] Ibid., pp. 390–2.

[41] Ibid., pp. 372–3.

[42] *H.M.C.*, Egmont, II, p. 437.

[43] Hervey, p. 392.

[44] Ibid., pp. 373–4.

[45] Ibid., p. 382. Berlin, Rep. 81, no. 15. *Anécdotes de la Cour Britannique*, Lettre 4, December 1734.

[46] L. Melville, *Lady Suffolk and Her Circle*, p. 216.

[47] Hervey, p. 381.

[48] L. Melville, *Lady Suffolk and Her Circle*, pp. 229–31. Hervey, pp. 382–3.

[49] L. Melville, pp. 232–8.

[50] Hervey, p. 383.

[51] Ibid., p. 472.

[52] Ibid., pp. 381–2.

[53] *H.M.C.*, Egmont, II, p. 138.

X

BORN TO ENCOURAGE

[1] Berlin, Rep. XI, 73 convolut 54, Reichenbach's dispatch. Windsor, Oct. 15/26, 1728.

[2] *H.M.C.*, Egmont, I, p. 476.

[3] Ibid., p. 7.

[4] Berlin, Rep. 81, no. 15, *Anécdotes Secrètes*, 5. London, March 15, 1734/5.

[5] Carpenter, *Sherlock*, pp. 26–7.

[6] Hervey, p. 498.

[7] *H.M.C.*, Egmont, I, pp. 101–2, 120, 395–7; II, p. 74.

[8] W. E. Schultz, *Gay's Beggar's Opera*.

[9] W. T. Laprade, *Public Opinion and Politics*, pp. 383–4.

[10] Hervey, pp. 487–8.

[11] Ibid., p. 733.

[12] Ibid., p. 720.

[13] Ibid., p. 732.

[14] Ibid., p. 292.

[15] W. H. Wilkins, II, pp. 151–4.

[16] *H.M.C.*, Egmont, II, p. 449.

[17] J. R. Magrath, *History of Queen's College*, II, pp. 91–4.

[18] Berlin, Rep. XI, 73 convolut 59 c, von Borcke's dispatch of 26 Oct./6 Nov. 1733.

[19] *H.M.C.*, Egmont, II, pp. 191, 428.

[20] Ibid., pp. 119–20.

[21] John Steegman, *The Rule of Taste*, chap. ii.

[22] Walpole Society, *Vertue Notebooks*, 3, 1933–4, p. 61.

[23] Ibid., p. 76.

[24] Hervey, pp. 501–2.

[25] Ibid., pp. 488–9.

[26] *Vertue Notebooks*, 3, p. 58.

[27] Ibid., p. 19.

[28] *Calendar of Treasury Books and Papers*, 1729–30, pp. 90, 402.

[29] Ralph Dutton, *The English Garden*, pp. 81–2.

[30] J. Whitley, *Artists and Their Friends in England*, I, pp. 41, 44.

[31] *Vertue Notebooks*, 3, pp. 61, 75. K. A. Esdaile, *The Art of Rysbrack in Terra-Cotta*, Spink and Son, July 1932.

[32] A. E. Popham, 'Drawings in the Royal Collections,' *Burlington Magazine*, May 1935, pp. 218–24.

[33] Vertue catalogued its contents in 1743.

[34] *H.M.C.*, Egmont, II, p. 138. R. Dutton, *The English Garden*, chap. iv.

[35] J. Rocque's Map of Richmond Gardens in 1748 gives an excellent view of them. Cf. *Rarities of Richmond*, E. Curl, London, 1736.

[36] P.R.O. Works 6/114, ff.30, 10–21. Charles Bridgeman's plans for the work as altered by Queen Caroline.

[37] Sophia van Roche, *Diary*, 1786, p. 135.

[38] P.R.O. Works 6/114, f. 16.

[39] Ibid., 6/8, ff. 37, 43, 49, 55, 57.

[40] *Memoirs of Viscountess Sundon*, edited by Mrs. Thomson, vol. I, p. 103.

[41] Hervey, p. 910.

XI

THE KING PLAYS TRUANT

[1] Berlin, Rep. 81, no. 5. *Anécdotes Secrètes*, 6, July 3, 1735.

[2] Michael, IV, pp. 431–2. Vaucher, pp. 126, 134–5, 451. Lodge, *T.R.H.S.*, XIV, pp. 165–70.

[3] Michael, IV, pp. 507–9.

[4] Cf. Hervey, pp. 458, 484–6, 496–7, 508.

[5] For the extreme anti-clerical view see Hervey, pp. 530–41. The bishops' case is stated by Carpenter, *Sherlock*, pp. 45–51, and Sykes, *Gibson*, pp. 161–3.

[6] *H.M.C.*, Egmont, II, p. 302.

[7] Grant Robertson, pp. 73–4. W. B. Pemberton, *Carteret*, pp. 133–8. For the Queen's attitude, see Hervey, pp. 573, 707, 709, 725–6.

[8] J. Morley, *Walpole*, p. 216.

[9] Hervey, p. 610.

[10] Ibid., pp. 598–607.

[11] Ibid., pp. 624–42.

[12] The Hague. Queen Caroline to Princess Anne, St. James's, Dec. 14/25, 1736.

[13] *H.M.C.*, Egmont, II, p. 330.

XII

THE PRINCE MARRIES

[1] Berlin, Rep. XI, 73 convolut 58A, Aug. 10, 1731 and Rep. XI, 73 convolut 13, July 9/20, 1734.

[2] Hervey, p. 814.

[3] Berlin, Rep. XI, 73 convolut 61B, von Borcke's dispatch of Jan. 30/Feb. 10, 1736.

[4] M. Thompson, *Secretaries of State*, p. 154.

[5] Berlin, Rep. XI, 73 convolut 61c, London, April 23/May 4, 1736.

[6] P.R.O., S.P. 108/551.

[7] *H.M.C.*, Egmont, II, pp. 263–5.

[8] Ibid. p. 264.

[9] Hague, Queen Caroline to Princess Anne. St. James's, April 19/30, 1736. Cf. *H.M.C.*, Egmont, II, p. 263. Hervey, pp. 552–3.

[10] Sir H. Imbert Terry, 'An Unwanted Prince,' *Trans. of the Royal Soc. of Literature*, New Series, vol. XV, pp. 135–6.

XIII

FAMILY HISTORY REPEATS ITSELF

[1] Coxe's *Walpole*, I, p. 525. *H.M.C.*, Egmont, II, p. 360. Leadam, pp. 356–7.

[2] Hervey, pp. 676–7.

[3] Ibid., p. 813.

[4] *The Diary of the late George Bubb Doddington*, Appendix, pp. 439–69, especially pp. 458–9.

[5] Hervey, pp. 680, 682.

[6] Ibid., pp. 701–5.

[7] Berlin, Rep. XI, n. 73 convolut 61F, von Borcke's letter of recall, April 6, 1737.

[8] Hervey, p. 755.

[9] Ibid., p. 749. *H.M.C.*, Carlisle, p. 181.

[10] Hervey, pp. 563, 614–15. Cf. Hanover, Cal. Br. 24, Dom. No. 37. King George I to Prince Frederick's Oberhofmeister von Grote, St. James's, May 11/22, 1722. The substance of the King's letter is that he has noted that: 'Der Prinz hat bei Eintritt des Neumondes *seinen gewöhnlichen Affect (Gliederschmerz)* wieder gehabt. Nach Aderlass hat sich eine Besserung eingestellt. Grote soll sich wegen seiner Krankheit nicht länger als nötig mit dem Prinzen aufhalten.' Knowing of her son's trouble gave Queen Caroline some justification for her doubts about his ability to have children, though they were soon proved wrong.

[11] Hervey, p. 757.

[12] Ibid., pp. 757–69.

[13] *Memoirs and Correspondence of George, Lord Lyttelton*, edited by Robert Phillimore (2 vols., London, 1845), vol. I, p. 82.

[14] The Hague. Queen Caroline to Princess Anne. Hampton Court, Aug. 13/2, 1737. Printed as appendix.

[15] Hervey, pp. 779–80, 782, 803, 806, 835–6.

[16] Ibid., p. 812.
[17] Ibid., p. 813.
[18] Ibid., pp. 795–802, 855–7.
[19] Dr. R. Drögereit, 'Das Testament Königs Georgs I . . .,' *Niedersächsisches Jahrbuch*, 1937, pp. 152–80.

XIV

'GOD GIVE HER LIFE'

[1] Hervey, p. 854.
[2] E. Beresford Chancellor, *The Private Palaces of London*, p. 349.
[3] The account of the Queen's fatal illness is based on Hervey, pp. 877–915.
[4] Coxe's *Walpole*, I, p. 550 states that Caroline sent a message of forgiveness to Frederick via Walpole, saying she would have seen him with pleasure but the interview might have embarrassed the King. Cf. *H.M.C.*, Egmont, II, p. 449.
[5] B.M. Add. MSS. 35349, f. 2. Caroline's will, bequeathing to the King and his heirs all her possessions and appointing him universal heir, executor, and legatee. Witnessed by E. Dorset, Grantham, (Sir) R. Eyre.
[6] Unsigned letter in the Windsor archives amongst George II's papers, dated Nov. 29, 1737, beginning 'I will not make any apology Dear Madam for not having wrote sooner'. From internal evidence the writer was one of the Queen's ladies.
[7] Ibid.
[8] Ibid.
[9] Coxe's *Walpole*, I, pp. 553–4.
[10] Ibid.
[11] *H.M.C.*, Egmont, II, p. 462.
[12] Walpole Society's vol. for 1927, p. 16.
[13] *H.M.C.*, Egmont, II, p. 459.
[14] Ibid., p. 461.

INDEX

Ahlden, 30.

Anne, Queen, 10, 34, 35, 37, 43, 46, 47, 48, 51, 52, 53, 55, 57, 59, 60, 61, 62, 65, 103, 194

Ansbach, 3, 4, 8, 13, 15, 16, 18, 19, 21, 22.

Anthony Ulric, Duke of Brunswick-Wolfenbüttel, 15.

Amelia, Princess (Emily), 47; inoculated against smallpox, 135; character and tastes 180–1; 187; 278; and Queen's illness, 289, 293, 294.

Argyll, Duke of, 67, 80, 83, 86, 92, 113, 149, 189, 259.

Artists and architects mentioned in Chap. XI: Amiconi, Giacomo, 240, 241; the Coopers, 244; Dolci, 246; Gainsborough, 245; Gibbs, James, 242; Gossett, Isaac, 242; Guelphi, 244; Hawksmoor, 242; Hogarth, 243–4; Holbein, 244; Hollar, Wenzel, 245; Jervas, Charles, 240–1, 243; Jones, Inigo, 242; Kneller, 242; Oliver, Peter, 246; Osterwyck, Maria van, 246; Reynolds, 245; Romney, 245; Rysbrack, 244; Talman, 242; Vanbrugh, 242, 247; Vanderbank, 242; Vandyck, 241; Vertue, 243, 244; da Vinci, 245; Wilson, Richard, 245; Wootton 240; Wren, 242; Zincke, Fred., 241–2.

Augustus II, Elector of Saxony and King of Poland, 6, 229.

Austria, 9, 10, 174, 217, 218, 220, 222, 254.

Bacon, Lord, 62, 76.

Berkeley, George, 231.

Bellenden, Mary, 71, 113, 128.

Berlin, 3, 5, 14, 18, 21, 42, 55, 159, 160.

Bernstorff, A. G., Baron de, 63, 71, 77 note, 85, 86, 87, 99, 101, 103, 114, 117–18, 123, 125.

Bolingbroke, Viscount, 50, 51, 52, 55, 59, 60, 61, 80, 145, 182, 201, 206, 225, 233, 237, 256, 272, 276.

Borcke, Count von, 267, 276.

Bothmer, Hans Caspar, Count von, 53, 59, 60, 62, 77 note, 87, 123.

Bridgeman, Charles, 247, 249.

Brunswick-Wolfenbüttel, Augustus William, Duke of, 152–3.

Bückeburg, Countess of, 44, 78, 95.

Butler, Joseph, 231, 293.

Cadogan, Lord, 42, 53, 83.

Caroline, Queen: birth, 4; leaves Ansbach, 5; self-taught, 6; wooed by Archduke Charles, 8–17; wooed by George Augustus, 18–24; marriage, 26; allowance, 27; 29, 30, 31, 32; gives birth to Frederick Louis, 33–4; has smallpox, 38–9; good

329

George I—*continued*
    to Hanover and death, 138; his
    will, 143, 152–3, 162, note
    2 p. 316; wife's love letters, 151;
    grandchildren's projected mar-
    riages, 133, 158; 194.
George II: woos Caroline, 18–25;
    love-letters to Caroline, 23–4;
    marriage, 26–7; 28, 29; enmity
    to father, 30, 55, 81; appearance,
    30; 31, 32, 33, 34; invested K.G.,
    36; Duke of Cambridge, 37;
    has smallpox, 40; bravery at
    Oudenarde, 42–3; letter to
    Caroline, 46; his writ of sum-
    mons, 48–56; character, 58–9,
    113, 125, 149–50, 249–50; in
    England, 65; 67, 71, 73, 76;
    visits to theatre, 78; takes his
    seat as Prince of Wales, 80;
    Governor of South Sea Com-
    pany, 81; attracted to Tories,
    82, 91; income as Heir Ap-
    parent, 82; appointed Regent,
    86–7; successful Regency, 88–
    97; love of soldiering, 31, 38,
    97, 170, 173; attempt on his
    life, 97; quarrel with King over
    son's christening, 100 seqq.;
    arrested and royal privileges re-
    voked, 102–4; buys Leicester
    House, 105; attends debates,
    106; declines to pay for child-
    ren's households, 109; acquires
    Richmond Lodge, 111–12; and
    Mary Bellenden, 113, 129;
    creature of routine, 113; refuses
    King's terms for peace, 114;
    reconciliation to King, 121–2;
    angry at not being left Regent,
    124–5; governor of a copper
    company, 126–7; liaison with
    Mrs. Howard, 129–30; in *Gulli-*

George II—*continued*
    ver's Travels, 136; accession,
    141–4; epithets for chief minis-
    ters, 142; Civil List, 146–8;
    egoism, 150; and his mother's
    love-letters, 150–1; suppresses
    George I's will, 143, 152–3;
    Coronation, 154–5; love of
    hunting, 91, 98, 156, 186; ad-
    vice from a masked lady, 157;
    affection for Hanover, 162,
    167; and bringing Prince of
    Wales to England, 162–3; and
    Prince of Wales's allowance,
    146, 147, 165, 214–15, 268–9;
    stinginess, 165–6; visits to
    Hanover, 167, 253, 257; returns
    to England, 172; opens Parlia-
    ment, 173; fondness for Princess
    Anne, 179; court routine, 184–
    192; kisses an actress, 191; sup-
    ports Excise Bill, 197–8; Wal-
    pole in favour, 198, 202; dis-
    solves Parliament, 205; wedding
    gifts to Princess Anne, 209, 210;
    rebukes Prince of Wales, 216;
    desires intervention in Polish
    Succession War, 221; never ad-
    mits to illness, 223; tributes to
    Queen Caroline, 150, 251, 282,
    292, 295; tired of Lady Suffolk,
    225–7; despises learning, 232;
    a philistine, 241, 244; capti-
    vated by Mme. Walmoden;
    254–5, 257, 261; returns from
    Hanover ill and bad-tempered,
    255; unpopularity, 260, 264;
    almost drowned at sea, 262–3;
    ill again, 264; enraged by Par-
    liamentary debates over Prince
    of Wales's allowance, 274; and
    Lady Deloraine, 276; deprives
    Prince of Wales of royal privi-

PRINTED BY WESTERN PRINTING SERVICES LTD., BRISTOL